The Exiles

The Exiles

Actors, Artists and Writers Who Fled the Nazis for London

Daria Santini

BLOOMSBURY ACADEMIC
LONDON · NEW YORK · OXFORD · NEW DELHI · SYDNEY

BLOOMSBURY ACADEMIC
Bloomsbury Publishing Plc
50 Bedford Square, London, WC1B 3DP, UK
1385 Broadway, New York, NY 10018, USA

BLOOMSBURY, BLOOMSBURY ACADEMIC and the Diana logo are
trademarks of Bloomsbury Publishing Plc

First published in Great Britain 2019

For legal purposes the Acknowledgements on p. xvii constitute an extension
of this copyright page.

Cover design by Alice Marwick
Cover image: Fog scenes in central London at night, 1934. Photograph
by James Jarche (Daily Herald Archive/SSPL/Getty Images).

A catalogue record for this book is available from the British Library.

A catalog record for this book is available from the Library of Congress.

ISBN: HB: 978-1-7883-1690-3
        ePDF: 978-1-7867-3628-4
        eBook: 978-1-7867-2622-3

Typeset by Integra Software Services Pvt. Ltd.
Printed and bound in Great Britain

To find out more about our authors and books visit www.bloomsbury.com
and sign up for our newsletters.

This book is dedicated to the memory of
Julia Casterton (1952–2007)

Contents

October–December

Figures

Preface

In the early 1930s London seemed to be changing faster than ever before. The din of traffic was becoming louder, the suburbs expanded, and imposing new buildings began to alter the old urban landscape. Although Londoners welcomed the latest car models and flocked to fashionable picture palaces, they also retained a strong attachment to tradition. The same could be said of Britain as a whole, yet London – as its cultural core – reflected these contradictions more clearly than anywhere else in the country.

While London appeared resistant to change, it was in constant ferment. It offered a peculiar combination of new and old. There was the bustle of the Lyons' Corner Houses, for example, the great 'food mansions' that catered to thousands of customers; the centre of town was teeming with people, cars and buses; and in 1932 the BBC's move to its brand new quarters at Broadcasting House inaugurated the era of mass-communication. On the outskirts, too, modernity was leaving its mark, as in the bold lines of Arnos Grove tube station, on the northern edges of the city.

At the same time, Londoners idealized the past. In 1934, an exhibition of English art at Burlington House elicited sentimental comments from a critic, who waxed lyrical about the beauty of one's own country, while later that year the disappearance of two long-established features of the Strand – a dummy called Freddy in the window of an old tailor's shop, and the royal coat-of-arms over a famous outfitter's shop next to Somerset House – caused them to be remembered by journalists as symbols of a lost time.

London was a cosmopolitan metropolis that resisted external influences and kept its visitors at a distance. Paul Cohen-Portheim, the Austrian author of a book entitled *The Spirit of London* (1935), wondered why the city, as opposed to Berlin or Vienna, for instance, lacked a municipal tourist bureau. More generally, writings of the period present the capital as a place whose inhabitants are still haunted by memories of the First World War and remain suspicious of foreigners, especially Germans. Yet many of those who sought refuge in London after Hitler came to power thrived there and – as a recent study about travellers in the Third Reich has shown – Germany was a favourite travel destination for British travellers. Similarly, the experience of being a German in London in the 1930s

Figure 1 Arnos Grove Underground Station (1932), designed by Charles Holden, London, 2017.

does not follow an established pattern and, just as the city's nature, is not always consistent.

Compared to the larger influx of refugees following Hitler's annexation of Austria and the horrors of Kristallnacht in 1938, many of those who fled during the first years of Nazi rule were either representatives of an artistic and intellectual elite or political enemies of the regime. Their presence in Britain is noteworthy not only because of their cultural impact, but also because it happened at a time when the country – and its capital in particular – was, on the whole, ready for the new art forms and ideas the émigrés had to offer.

In this book, I have chosen to focus my attention on the year 1934, because it marked an important moment in the history of continental immigration to Britain, and because I felt that a narrow temporal focus could produce a more vivid impression of a moment in time.

The idea to write about German-speaking refugees came to me from the streets of London and, indirectly, from my own personal circumstances. I was born and grew up in Italy, learnt German at school and university, and became a historian of German literature. I then lived in Munich and Berlin before coming to London, which has been my home for the past two-and-a-half decades. During my first few years in Britain, I would often visit the University of London's Institute of Germanic Studies, which was then in Russell Square, in a beautiful house with a well-stocked library and a cultured, distinctly Anglo-German atmosphere. At the time, I couldn't quite put my finger on what exactly was Anglo-German about it. The place felt very English to me, with its creaky stairs, its friendly yet reserved library staff, tea at 4 p.m. and the gardens of Russell Square outside the tall Georgian windows. But there was also something Germanic about it all, a special respect for high culture perhaps, and a strong commitment to keeping alive the memory of the Nazi émigrés, whose lives in exile I knew to be closely bound up with that particular area of London. Soon the institute – later incorporated into the Modern Languages Department in the university's main building – became the home of the Research Centre for German and Austrian Exile Studies, one of the leading institutions on the history of the emigration from Germany and the Nazi-occupied territories between 1933 and 1945. Over the years, academics associated with the centre have overseen the publication of several volumes and run programmes of events about the émigrés' experience and their contribution to British culture. And so it was with a mixture of personal fascination and scholarly interest that I began to look for traces of the presence of German-speaking exiles in London.

More recently, the Research Centre organized a guided tour past the Bloomsbury locations that held a special significance for the people who fled Nazi Germany all those years ago. Among these were Woburn House, seat of the Jewish Refugee Committee and site of long queues of refugees throughout the 1930s; the building at 3 Regent Square, once a meeting place of left-wing exiles and a lending library for books in German; and the quaint terraced house at 12 Great Ormond Street, where two German women, refugees and anti-Nazi activists, died mysteriously in April 1935. Seeing these landmarks, anonymous today yet full of history, reminded me that – as a foreigner in England with a passion for German culture – I had long regarded various corners of London as places connected with the Hitler émigrés. I also knew that this important part of the city's history was unknown to most Londoners.

To take just one example, an unprepossessing yet meaningful place connected to the presence of these exiles is the stage door of the Apollo Theatre in the West End. Hidden in a Soho back street, it is an old entrance like many others in the area, framed by two wooden shutters and surmounted by a rectangular window. Above it hangs a sign with the words 'STAGE DOOR' painted in black letters. This door is small and plain compared to the entrance to the theatre's main foyer on the other side of the building. Its modest appearance contradicts the glamour usually associated with the actors who pass through it. When I first noticed it, I was reading a biography of Sir John Gielgud in which he is described reminiscing about the days when the Austrian Jewish actress Elisabeth Bergner, playing at the Apollo in 1934, created such a sensation that crowds of fans regularly lined

Shaftesbury Avenue waiting for her to arrive. And it occurred to me that this woman – then an international star – had walked through that little door nearly every day for several months that year, defying her paralysing stage fright and the burdens of exile. I also thought that her role in the history of London culture deserved to be better known. The same goes for the other characters who feature in this book: the photographers who portrayed England and the English in a new light; the art historians who revolutionized the way we read artworks; the actors, directors and technicians who injected fresh energy into the British film industry; and the writers who tried to articulate their displacement. Many more could be added to the list, but I have limited my choice to these five case studies.

Figure 2 The stage door of the Apollo Theatre, Archer Street, London, 2017.

In the past few years, there has been a renewed interest in the German-speaking refugees who came to Britain that falls outside the vast field of specialized studies on the subject. In English, a fictional account of the Great Ormond Street deaths was published in 2011, followed by two books on the life of Stefan Zweig and a new biography of Bertolt Brecht. In 2013, a BBC radio series on the history of migration included an episode, entitled 'Ode to Finchleystrasse', about the exiles who settled in the area around the Finchley Road, in north-west London. In his recent play *The Moderate Soprano*, David Hare told the story of the establishment, also in 1934, of that unique example of Anglo-German collaboration, the Glyndebourne Festival. And in 2017 a performance installation by dancer and choreographer Siobhan Davies was inspired by Aby Warburg's research on the hidden meaning of human gestures. Nonetheless, the history of the German and Austrian immigration to Britain is still unfamiliar to many.

'Exile' and 'refugees' are sadly familiar words nowadays, and the surge in nationalism, which coincided with events such as Britain's recent decision to leave the European Union, is a worrying reminder of the dangers of the sorts of political extremism and intolerance that were rife in the 1930s. True, the people who fled Nazi Germany represented an intellectual and social elite very different from today's migrant communities. Yet the tensions produced by the encounter between different cultures and the human stories that accompany them are universally significant.

Another reason to revisit this particular exodus is the sheer brilliance and sophistication of the culture embodied by the Hitler émigrés. Having rejected the distortions and falsehood of Nazi ideology, they came to represent the spirit of a culture that combined the classical German and Austrian heritage with the humanistic ethos and admiration for learning of the Jewish tradition. In Britain, the émigrés had a particularly strong impact on academia, but also on architecture, art, design, music, dance, photography and film. Their aesthetic vision was classless, often political and almost always daringly innovative.

In writing this book, I have considered the links that existed among different groups of refugees, and between the refugees and the British. And I have thought of London as a backdrop to the exile experience. Continental foreigners were usually both intrigued and bemused by London's peculiarities – its architecture, its inhabitants' reserve, its social rituals, its cultural conservatism and the rigidity of its class structure. The émigrés were exposed to the London fog, to its cold winds and summer heatwaves; they endured the misery of its rented rooms and boarding houses; they found respite in its parks and squares; they met in its tea rooms, libraries, theatres and cinemas; and they noticed the gulf between the city's opulent neighbourhoods and its dreary working-class districts. This vibrant yet in many respects old-fashioned metropolis welcomed the new arrivals with a mixture of courtesy and suspicion. At a time when Britain had just begun to recover from an economic crisis, the political establishment was deeply ambivalent towards the refugees coming from Germany, and the Nazis had well-organized groups of party members and sympathizers operating all over London.

This book tells stories of exile, and at its centre, seen against the émigrés' intellectual and biographical background, are some of the works that originated from those experiences. My readings of them are informed by a respect for the past as a vital link to the present and by an admiration for the achievements of people who are chronologically distant from us but also, in many ways, excitingly near.

Acknowledgements

My first debt of gratitude goes to Philippa Brewster, whose support, encouragement and editorial advice during the final stages of my work on this book have been more valuable than I can express in a few words. Heartfelt thanks also to my editor at Bloomsbury, Jo Godfrey, and to Olivia Dellow; to my copy-editor, Robert Whitelock, to Damian Penfold and Deborah Maloney, who have overseen the production process, as well as to Jeffrey Richards for his editorial comments and to the anonymous reader who recommended the book's publication.

I am deeply grateful to the following people and institutions: Peter Suschitzky, Wolfgang Suschitzky (†), Claudia Wedepohl at the Warburg Institute as well as the staff of the Akademie der Künste, Berlin; the British Library; the London Library; The National Archives, Kew; and the British Film Institute National Archive.

To all the others who have assisted in different ways during the realization of this project I am immensely thankful. They are: Nicola von Albrecht, Nick Baker, Francesca Bottari, Sakino Deutschländer, Ralph Emanuel, Hilary Fairclough, Marco Fernandelli, Lesley Levene, David Moore, Mary Ottaway, Clare Savory, Franco Serpa, Daniela Sikora and Daniela Zimmermann.

To Stephen, Enrico and Emily Elson my love and thanks, always.

Introduction

A monster called Man

On 1 January 1934, British economic prospects were improving and unemployment figures encouraging. The country had a stable government. In *The Times*, the archbishop of Canterbury voiced positive sentiments through a meteorological metaphor that saw 'the light … breaking through the clouds of the last three years'. Yet on the same page, the cheery tone of an article about Germany created a sense of disquiet. Its content, at once exuberant and menacing, smacked of propaganda. Entitled 'A Happy and Free Germany: Herr Hitler's Aim for 1934', the piece announced: 'Official[:] Germany and the Press are welcoming the New Year with hearty optimism. The theme of the day is the moral revival of Germany, the unity of the people, the regaining of self-respect and honour, the annihilation of the enemy and the break with outworn Liberalism.'

Articles in the more liberal *Manchester Guardian*, on the other hand, while optimistic on the prospect of economic recovery and international peace, expressed concern over the threat posed by Germany, whose 'sinister side' was visible through the reassuring façade it displayed to the world. To many Britons, Hitler's Germany was a heap of contradictions: self-assured and confident of its new stability, but also marred by accounts of senseless institutional violence, racial discrimination and human rights abuse. Disturbing news from Germany fuelled the sense that living in the 1930s meant inhabiting a 'morbid age', as the historian Richard Overy called the interwar years. The term describes a 'gloomy view of civilization' caused by a feeling of general decline, by a lack of trust in the economy and by the fear of an impending new war. The rise of right-wing dictatorships in Europe and the threat of Fascism in Britain intensified such concerns. Publications about Nazi Germany and the imminence of war abounded, as did radio broadcasts and public debates on the subject: 'by the mid-1930s predicting world war at any moment was embedded in popular discussion'.

From this perspective, reports of bad weather in England on the first day of the year – the poor visibility that endangered the life of aviators and the all-engulfing London fog – could be read as a more general warning of impending danger, and popular obsession with the Loch Ness Monster as a metaphor for collective anxiety. Early in 1934, sightings of the mysterious animal, whose supposed presence in the Scottish loch had been revealed for the first time eight months earlier, were reported almost daily in British newspapers. The creature was the subject of public fascination. On 5 January, the *Manchester Guardian* accompanied the publication of an indistinct photograph of the monster with a journalist's ironic remarks:

> There is no convincing some people. Even now, after all the evidence that has been published, they persist in complaining of a lack of definiteness about the characteristics of the Loch Ness monster … In a second … he might appear as anything you like, perhaps – shall we say? – as a log of wood, and then, in an hour's time, there he would be again, thirty miles off, as monstrous as before.

The shape, size and nature of the beast changed; the monster wandered to other places, other countries (at the end of February it was found, dead, in Cherbourg on the Normandy coast; in April it was said to be back in England, near Hayling Island).

The ubiquitous news item was good for tourism, a lucrative business, but it was also an escape into fantasy at a time of insecurity. The inflated concern with a creature whose true nature and appearance were changeable and ultimately unknown reflected something more disturbing. If the unsettled winter weather mirrored a lingering uncertainty over the economic and political developments of the year ahead, the obsession with the Loch Ness Monster stood for a more pressing fear of alien invasion.

Were the British really concealing painful anxieties behind the foil of mythical imagery? Despite enduring memories of the First World War and the misery caused by the Great Depression, there were evident signs of recovery. New industries were developing and modernization progressed at a steady pace. As ever, people were fond of royal ceremonies, and events in the sporting calendar – such as the Oxford and Cambridge Boat Race and the Wimbledon Tennis Championships – were all-important national rituals. On the whole, the worrying developments on the Continent were, in the words of Stephen Spender, 'none of their business'.

In January 1934 British citizens enjoyed cruise- and sea-holidays and visited Austria, France, Germany, Italy and Spain. They spent the 'winter in the West Indies' and travelled up the Nile. Several London hotels were proud to offer 'running water, telephone and gas fire in all bedrooms'. Ladies bought 'the world's finest furs' and Persian rugs at Gooch's of Knightsbridge. The automobile trade was thriving, and a particularly popular model, the Hillman Minx, was being sold as 'an improved car with no lack of power and acceleration'. Now Britons lived longer – 'during 1933 the deaths of 475 persons of 90 years and over' were the highest recorded so far – and their passion for popular entertainment was about to reach new levels. In the words of a *Times* journalist: 'Promise of greater prosperity for 1934 was the keynote of New Year's Eve celebrations in the West End of London which was exceptionally crowded even for that occasion. One of the largest and most famous restaurants was transformed into a large circus in appearance and trappings; another into an Alaskan winter scene.'

Yet history is not clear-cut, and the euphoria that came with new energy coincided with darker presentiments of doom. Despite the novelties, the luxury and fun, a wild beast was lurking in the darkness. News reports about the Loch Ness Monster were escapist fantasies and a sign that something sinister was exciting people's imagination. But not everyone was fooled by the publicity surrounding the story.

On 6 January the prophetic voice of G. K. Chesterton rose from the pages of the *Illustrated London News* to announce that he was not interested in the monster, because he saw a far more menacing threat: 'I do not know, or care, whether there is a monster in the loch, or a sea serpent in the sea. But I am much more interested in another monster: a much more monstrous monster ... This monster is called Man.' There was no beast, and even if there had been one, it would not have mattered a great deal at such a delicate stage in the history of the Western world.

Was Chesterton thinking of Germany? He certainly understood the critical nature of the German problem and the fragility of peace. In the first year of the Hitler regime, Germany was still a demilitarized power, its army crippled by the limitations stipulated by the Versailles Treaty. But the Nazis were rearming, and their dream of creating a military force was a threat to European stability and international cooperation.

The extent of German rearmament was difficult to assess. The establishment of the Defence Requirements Committee in November 1933, soon after Hitler's withdrawal from the League of Nations, revealed Britain's need to deal with the question of Germany's plans. One of the committee's chiefs of staff was Sir Robert Vansittart, permanent undersecretary to the Foreign Office. Years later, his name became synonymous with a hatred of all things German. Vansittart loved France and disliked Germany. His long-standing antipathy against the country and the national character of its inhabitants developed into unrestrained contempt. In a series of broadcasts, published in 1941 under the title *Black Record: Germans Past and Present*, Vansittart expressed his unmitigated hostility towards Germany and an almost irrational belief in the wickedness of the German people as a whole. In 1933–4, however, at an early stage of British defence policy between the wars, Vansittart's opposition was mainly a concern about Hitler's expansion plans as a threat to the European balance of power. Around the same time, G. K. Chesterton admonished his readers in a similar vein. In pointing to the futility of a preoccupation with the Loch Ness Monster, he was hinting at the presence of a more tangible menace. Chesterton's book *The End of the Armistice*, written during the 1930s and published posthumously in 1940, confirmed this view, as it warned of the danger posed by the unresolved problem of German resentment after the First World War. Meanwhile, the rise of British Fascism was cemented, on 1 January 1934, by the founding of the January Club, a dining and discussion group conceived by Oswald Mosley with the aim of attracting prominent and financially influential sympathizers to the Fascist cause.

By then, eleven months after Hitler's rise to power, examples of a new system of German oppression had already been plentiful. A quick succession of traumatic events and the introduction of repressive measures between February and December 1933 drove many Jews and opponents of the regime out of Germany. At the end of February the Reichstag was set on fire. In March, the Enabling Act gave Hitler both executive and legislative power, marking the eradication of most civil liberties on German soil; Goebbels took over the 'Ministry of Popular Enlightenment and Propaganda' and Himmler announced the opening of the Dachau concentration camp. On 1 April 1933, the boycott of Jewish shops and businesses paved the way for the 'Law for the Restoration of the Professional Civil Service', which legalized racial discrimination and sanctioned the first exclusions of 'non-Aryans' from universities and other professional organizations. On 10 May spectacular bonfires of books deemed offensive to the German spirit were staged in every city. In September, the Dutch bricklayer Marinus van der Lubbe was found guilty of arson at the Reichstag fire trial and condemned to death. His alleged accomplices, the German Communist Ernst Torgler and the Bulgarians Georgi Dimitrov, Blagoi Popov and Vasil Tanev were acquitted but kept in prison.

In August 1933, the extent of Nazi brutality was revealed in *The Brown Book of the Hitler Terror and the Burning of the Reichstag*. Published in Basel and Paris (and soon afterwards in London) by Communist sympathiser, propaganda genius and founder of the World Committee for the Victims of Hitler Fascism Willi Münzenberg and his astute collaborator Otto Katz, the book became a worldwide sensation. With a preface by Lord Marley, deputy speaker of the House of Lords and convinced anti-Fascist, the volume disclosed a series of shocking documents and first-hand accounts from victims of the Hitler regime with the aim of keeping alive the memory of its criminal acts. Although later discredited as tendentious and inaccurate, *The Brown Book* – in the early 1930s the title must have sounded like a dark echo of the *Official Book of the German Atrocities Told by Victims and Eye Witnesses* of 1915 – exposed the dreadful cruelty of the Nazi regime. It is startling to think that a volume published in Europe in the civilized era of technological progress, when people danced on luxury cruise ships and delighted in sophisticated new car models, could bear an appendix entitled 'List of Murders'. Chesterton was right: the monster called Man was at work.

Another threat to Europe's stability was the sudden exodus of large numbers of German refugees. The thousands of Jews and political émigrés who escaped Germany to find a new home and opportunities abroad during the first year of Nazi rule were bound to pose a problem for their hosts. Throughout 1933, with a peak in the spring, masses of people fled to neighbouring European countries and to Palestine. In England a sense of ambivalence reigned. Despite the British government's accommodating stance towards the Nazi regime and feelings of resentment towards newcomers, philanthropic impulses were strong and aid was being organized on multiple fronts. Government regulations to control the influx of refugees were discussed in Parliament in early April 1933 and implemented within days. Entry into Britain was restricted to a period of between one and three months, and came with conditions that forbade refugees to seek or accept work, except in domestic service and other manual occupations. At the same time, humanitarian efforts, both international and British-led, were a source of help and respite to the immigrants.

In March 1933, the German Jewish banker and British citizen Otto Schiff set up the Jewish Refugees Committee under the auspices of another relief organization, the Central British Fund for German Jewry. It was located at Woburn House, in Bloomsbury's Tavistock Square. Eighty years later, a couple of hundred yards from that very same building, a bilingual German–English information booklet is still kept in the archives of the Wiener Library for the Study of the Holocaust and Genocide. The booklet promises 'to give useful information and friendly guidance to all Refugees' and contains details of 'Organisations Useful for our Visitors'. Most of these organizations were housed in the London streets and squares between the Euston Road and High Holborn. A popular area for boarding houses and affordable hotels, and home to some long established cultural and academic institutions, such as the British Museum and University College London, Bloomsbury became the first port of call for refugees from Germany and Austria. On 7 April 1933, also in Bloomsbury, the Quakers' Germany Emergency Committee was founded. Over the following years, it would provide emergency relief and educational support for refugee children. In May 1933, after a Cabinet discussion on the future of exiled German scholars, the director of the London School of Economics, William Beveridge, established the Academic Assistance Council, a non-political institution whose activities offered a solution to the crippling effect of Nazi racial policies on science and learning by providing employment and maintenance grants to German academics.

With the intensification of the refugee problem throughout the spring of that year, the British government turned to the League of Nations for a solution. On 12 October, after months of deliberations and lobbying, the League appointed the American diplomat James G. McDonald as High Commissioner for Refugees Coming from Germany. The post was fraught with limitations, because the commissioner could only deal with refugees who had already left Germany, and had neither support from the Nazi government nor financial help from the League. McDonald's diaries, and his letters to allies, donors and supporters of the cause he had wholeheartedly embraced, record countless transatlantic travels, private consultations and official meetings.

One of McDonald's correspondents in 1933, and a high-profile campaigner on behalf of German and Jewish refugees, was Albert Einstein, who had renounced German citizenship in March of that year. On 3 October 1933 Einstein addressed a crowd of over 10,000 at London's Royal Albert Hall during a charity event for displaced German scholars organized by the Refugee Assistance Fund, supported by various relief groups and hosted by the nuclear physicist and president of the Academic Assistance Council, Lord Rutherford. Although the pro-Fascist, German-friendly *Daily Mail* had urged people not to attend and, according to *The Times*, 'in spite of statements that trouble would be provoked by anti-Jewish elements', the event was peaceful and the neighbourhood around the Royal Albert Hall almost deserted.

Einstein's speech, entitled 'Science and Civilization', is often remembered for its author's endorsement of 'lighthouses and lightships' for scientists and thinkers as quiet havens for research 'in a time of danger and want'. Einstein delivered it in English, with a strong German accent, still clearly audible in the scratched recording available on YouTube. Yet his tone was measured and strangely soothing, as if infused with the force of a moral and humane purpose. Einstein spoke 'as a man, as a good European and as a Jew', and the main argument of his talk, the freedom of the creative individual, emphasized a belief in humanity. The spirit of the Enlightenment, and that peculiarly German faith in the power of education as a path to our self-development as human beings and citizens of the world, were at the core of Einstein's answer to the threat to civilization posed by the Nazis. In response to Chesterton's warning, Einstein's words seemed to say that if Man was a monster, he was also the only being on earth capable of defeating other monsters.

Three months after that gathering, a new year began amid hopes for prosperous times to come and fears of foreign intrusion. In London, the number of German-speaking émigrés grew. Not all of them would settle in Britain, as the immigration rules allowed only people with a solid professional reputation to establish themselves. Others, especially the young, did manage to forge a new career despite constant struggles with temporary residence and work permits. Some had already arrived in Britain as economic migrants (such as the actors Elisabeth Bergner and Conrad Veidt), or simply to escape the first symptoms of turmoil in their own country (Stefan Zweig, for example).

Figure 3 Albert Einstein delivering his 'Science and Civilization' speech at the Royal Albert Hall, 3 October 1933.

The combined presence of a successful intellectual elite and a group of well-educated, hard-working refugees explains the impressive achievements of German and Austrian émigrés in Great Britain after 1933. Some had a strong and lasting impact on British culture. Many just came briefly, or passed through on the way to somewhere else. Some are no longer remembered. Yet their stories are testimonies of a rich cultural exchange and of a plea for human values at a time when individuals ran the risk of becoming dehumanized through exile and persecution. In this respect, 1934 marked an important phase in the history of the German immigration to Britain.

That year, Elisabeth Bergner became a hugely popular star of British film and stage, and the Glyndebourne Opera Festival was founded with the help of German exiles. Several talented photographers settled in London from Germany and Austria, and Stefan Lorant, a Hungarian-born author, introduced the British public to a completely novel type of photojournalism. One of Germany's most prestigious schools of modern dance, the Ballet Jooss, relocated to Devon, and the German educator Kurt Hahn founded Gordonstoun School. A group of art historians moved a whole library from Hamburg to London, where they opened the Warburg Institute, a scholarly institution thriving in Bloomsbury to this day. English film studios brimmed with talented exiles from Central Europe.

Cinemagoers were enthralled by Conrad Veidt, a charismatic German actor, and lovers of operetta idolized Richard Tauber, the internationally acclaimed Austrian tenor. The German architect (and founder of the Bauhaus) Walter Gropius found refuge and work in England before moving on to the United States. Stefan Zweig felt safe in London for a time, while Bertolt Brecht spent two months there, and wrote some memorable poems about his experience.

Many more scientists, artists, writers, philosophers, academics, film technicians and ordinary people could be added to the list of German-speaking exiles who either travelled to England or were there at the time. This book is about some of them. Its five chapters are devoted to émigrés who worked, respectively, in the worlds of theatre, photography, art history, film and literature. The year is 1934 and the setting London, yet the boundaries of time and place are not fixed, as the narrative moves back and forth between continental Europe and Britain, between the characters' past in their own country and their present in exile. The following chapters introduce a cast of characters who rarely feature prominently in the history of London in the 1930s. Their names may be familiar to some, but the achievements from their time in England are still largely obscure. This book aims to change this perception; it presents a collective biography of sorts, reconstructing a piece of London history from a time to remember.

January–March

The Austrian actress Elisabeth Bergner becomes a star of the London stage and a close friend of J. M. Barrie

On 3 January 1934 John Christie, owner of a small opera house recently completed at Glyndebourne Manor, East Sussex, learns that producer Carl Ebert and conductor Fritz Busch, both German exiles, have agreed to help him to set up an opera festival on his estate.

Around the same time, Nikolaus Pevsner, a struggling German academic, is appointed external examiner in the History of Art at University College London.

In the first week of January, the newly published English translation of Heinz Liepmann's denunciation of Nazi terror, *Murder – Made in Germany*, is reviewed in all major British newspapers. In those same days, from his house in Wimbledon, the Nazi activist and journalist Hans Wilhelm Thost writes inflammatory articles for the official newspaper of the National Socialist Party, the *Völkischer Beobachter*, bemoaning any attempt to mobilize England against Germany's involvement in Austria.

On 15 January, the Jewish Board of Deputies is in session at Woburn House, where the president of the Anglo-Jewish Association, Leonard Montefiore, presents a report about Nazi eugenics and race theories.

On 21 January, Virginia Woolf writes in her diary that she longs to see Bruno Walter's rehearsals. Walter, who is living in exile in Vienna, is due to conduct the Royal Philarmonic Orchestra at the Queen's Hall. The concert is sold out. That morning the conductor arrives in London, where he is staying at Claridge's.

On the same day, two events draw the attention of the British public to the Nazis' abuse of power: a large demonstration, presided over by the Labour peer Lord Marley, takes place at Kingsway Hall to demand the release of the four acquitted prisoners at the Reichstag fire trial; and a letter appears in *The Times* from its former editor, Wickham Steed, alerting readers to the plight of the German pacifist and journalist Carl von Ossietzky. Ossietzky has been interned for months in a concentration camp and is now 'unlikely long to withstand the suffering … inflicted upon him'.

On 24 January, the Commissioner for Refugees Coming from Germany, James G. McDonald, arrives in London. Over the following six days he discusses the question of funds and placement for German refugees with, among others, Felix Warburg, Otto Schiff, William Beveridge, Lord Cecil and Anthony de Rothschild.

On 29 January, the leader and the secretary of the Nazi movement in England, Otto Bene and Edmund Himmelmann respectively, move to 102 Westbourne Terrace, London W2, after being evicted from the Park Gate Hotel, where their frequent political gatherings attracted the attention of the Metropolitan Police Special Branch.

The following day, the Ballet Jooss, founded by the German choreographer Kurt Jooss, open their London season at the Gaiety Theatre with a programme that includes Jooss's most famous piece, the expressionist anti-war ballet *The Green Table*.

On 8 February, it is announced that the first prize for the design of the new De La Warr Pavilion in Bexhill-on-Sea, East Sussex, has been awarded to the German émigré architect Erich Mendelsohn and to his Russian-born colleague, Serge Chermayeff. A week later, the author of an article published in the *Architects' Journal* and entitled *Alien Architects Invade Britain* warns of the dangers of foreign modernist tendencies.

On 23 February, Winston Churchill addresses more than 500 undergraduates at the Oxford University Student Union advocating the need for rearmament. During a debate with the German Rhodes Scholar Adolf Schlepegrell, Churchill has no hesitation in declaring the Germans responsible for the First World War.

That same day, three officers from Special Branch send a two-page memorandum headed 'Extremists' to the British Security Service, better known as MI5. The document concerns a young Viennese photographer and political activist, Edith Tudor-Hart, who is said to have 'a good interest in the furtherance of Communism both in this country and abroad'.

On 14 March, the Queen's Hall hosts the most outstanding musical event of the London season, the first English concert performance of Alban Berg's controversial opera *Wozzeck*. The twenty-year-old Benjamin Britten is in the audience.

Three days later Gerhart Seger, former Socialist deputy in the German Reichstag, arrives in England, 'fresh from a series of lectures in Denmark and Sweden'. He escaped from a German prison and is one of the first victims of Nazi persecution to give account of his experiences as a political detainee. In Germany, Seger's British-born wife and their twenty-month-old child are held hostage in a concentration camp.

On 17 March, Hans Wilhelm Thost and a colleague visiting from Berlin watch the Oxford and Cambridge University Boat Race from Putney Bridge. Thost roots for Cambridge, because he feels that it has 'a cleaner, healthier atmosphere than Oxford'.

At the end of the month Sigmund Freud's eldest son, the architect Ernst Freud – in London and working mainly for fellow émigrés – lands one of his first jobs since emigrating from Berlin a few months earlier. A refugee couple, Fritz and Ann Hess, have asked Freud 'to advise them on the interior of a rental apartment' in Highgate.

Chapter 1
Limelight and fading shadows
Elisabeth Bergner and J. M. Barrie

A portrait of J. M. Barrie

Sometime in January 1934, Peter Scott painted a portrait of his godfather, Sir James Barrie. The son of Captain Robert Scott and the sculptor Kathleen Bruce, Peter was twenty-four years old at the time (he was to become one of Britain's most celebrated ornithologists and wildlife conservationists). After Captain Scott's death in Antarctica in 1912, Barrie fostered his friendship with widow and son. Peter's childhood memories of his godfather conjure up the ambivalent image of Barrie as a silent and moody character, but endowed with great generosity and a remarkable talent for amusing children. Peter's earliest recollections of the author at home in the top-floor flat at Adelphi Terrace House, the Georgian building between the Strand and the River Thames where Barrie had lived since 1909, evoke a gloomy atmosphere enlivened by the old man's occasional bouts of good humour.

In 1931, Peter Scott had lived in Munich for several months to study painting. This was a time when the cultural richness of Weimar Germany was being threatened by the increasingly strident tones of National Socialist rhetoric, yet Scott remembers the Bavarian sojourn as a romantic period in his life. He also recalls being surprised by the anti-Semitism displayed by members of his otherwise friendly and cultured hosts, and going to a Bierkeller in the centre of town to hear Hitler deliver one of his inflammatory speeches. But he didn't take these disturbing signs seriously. He enjoyed walking in the Bavarian countryside and became passionate about German opera. Those were special times for him, and Germany, less than two years before Hitler came to power, appeared to be an enchanted place.

In January 1934 Scott had been back in England for two-and-a-half years. His life was now an intense mix of outdoor activities, social engagements and artistic pursuits. He had recently moved into East Lighthouse at Sutton Bridge in Lincolnshire, an idyllic retreat where he could paint undisturbed and observe wildlife in its natural habitat. Yet he would often drive down to London in his open Morris to see friends and go to the theatre. Three years earlier Peter Scott had received a letter from his famous godfather, who asked to meet him, and had begun to visit Barrie regularly in his flat. Then Barrie agreed to pose for him.

Scott's painting is an unconventional portrait. It shows a profile of Barrie seated on a high-backed wooden settle by his large inglenook fireplace (this was a beautiful but rather cave-like feature of his study room that had been designed by his friend, the architect Edwin Lutyens). The old man is shown in an informal pose, slightly stooped, with both hands on his knees. He seems to be gazing downwards. His head is round and minute, and his body appears dwarfed by the space and objects around him. His left eye, the only one visible to the viewer, is a small, dark smudge on the side of his pale face. This is a painting full of shadows. On the right, the first things we notice are a shady partition wall and the dark, tall side of the bench. A double-armed wooden chair and a small table are barely visible in the foreground. Above them, a shaft of light illuminates an empty section of wall above the settle and a nebulous, framed picture on the other side of the partition. On the left, a large kettle rests on an upturned log near the hearth. In the fireplace there is a mound of ash and no flame, except for a spark-like, lighter patch of paint at the back of the recess. On the wall next to the sitter, two large fireplace accessories, a bellows and fork, create three spiky shadows. Behind these, on the right of Barrie, his shadow is round and black. It does not resemble him at all, and is far too large compared with the diminutive size of his head. Scott portrayed a man who looks inwards, a silent, pensive little figure strangely detached from his surroundings.

The painting is a truthful depiction of Barrie's mood in the final years of his life. It portrays the melancholy side of his nature. The genial individual who was capable of great wit and sudden enthusiasms, the world-famous author who amused children with funny rhymes and adventurous games, was also a deeply troubled and almost sinister figure. He could be possessive, elusive and depressed, but also attentive, altruistic and high-spirited. The complexities of his personality and some thorny details of his private life (such as his relationship with women and the question of his possibly dubious behaviour towards his adopted sons) have been widely discussed by his biographers and it would be superfluous to reiterate them. But it is important to understand Scott's decision to portray his godfather as he did.

In January 1934 J. M. Barrie was seventy-three years old. He hadn't written a play or published a major original work for at least ten years. The sudden death

Figure 4 Peter Scott's portrait of J. M. Barrie, 1934.

(from probable suicide) of his favourite adopted child, Michael Llewelyn Davies, at the age of twenty in 1921 had been a shattering experience for him, and one from which he never recovered ('what happened was in a way the end of me', he confessed some time after Michael's death). The boy's eldest brother, George, had been killed in action in France in 1915. The two tragedies aggravated Barrie's sense of isolation and his bouts of melancholy. They must also have added a deeper sadness to the memory of other losses (his wife, Mary, had divorced him in 1909, and Sylvia, the boys' mother, whom Barrie adored, had died the following year). In 1933, another severe blow to his private world had been the news that the historic houses of Adelphi Terrace, where he lived, were to be pulled down to make room for a new building. As ever painfully aware of the passage of time and the impermanence of things, he was deeply distressed by the daily disruption and the roaring noise caused by the demolition work.

In the early 1930s Barrie was much loved by the public and had many friends in high places, but he was often dispirited and his health was failing. Deprived of the company of his three remaining adopted children, who were now grown up, and faced with the loss of his home, he was very much the old man in the portrait: pensive, alone and shrouded in silence. Other portraits and photographs from this period show Barrie reading or writing, or surrounded by books. In Scott's painting, there seems to be nothing left to do.

By the time he agreed to sit for Peter Scott's portrait, Barrie was an illustrious personality, but also a lonely, frail old man. This is how Cynthia Asquith, who was his secretary and confidante, described his predicament during this time:

> One severe bronchial attack followed another. His cough racked him. All the while that private hell of insomnia in which he had suffered so long grew steadily worse. 'I can't sleep!' he would complain more and more often, his sunken eyes now so darkly encircled as to look positively bruised … Worst of all … he was haunted by the fear that his mind would become clouded before he died.

On 28 January 1934 Barrie wrote to Peter Scott's mother, who had asked him how he liked the painting: 'How do I like the picture? Uncommonly well, thank you. I call it a noticeable success and I hope you do also. Peter and I are rather big about it … My shadow of course is not really mine but represents the intrusion of Miss Bergner.' These lines explain the reason why, in Scott's portrait, the shadow on the wall next to the sitter is at odds with his body: it is someone else's shadow. But who was 'Miss Bergner'? She was the thirty-six-year-old Austrian Jewish actress who revived and inspired J. M. Barrie in the final years of his life.

Enter Bergner

Elisabeth Bergner had moved from Berlin to London in 1932 and was now enjoying phenomenal success in the West End. She had the leading role in a play by Margaret Kennedy, then a very popular author. The piece was entitled *Escape Me Never* and was a rather unremarkable romantic drama about two brothers in love with two very different women, an heiress and an innocent waif. It had recently been adapted from Kennedy's novel *The Fool of the Family* and was being staged at the Apollo Theatre on Shaftesbury Avenue. Bergner played Gemma Jones, a mysterious girl with a gamine-like quality who has an illegitimate child and is in love with a struggling English composer. The mediocrity of the piece did not prevent Bergner from achieving one of the most memorable theatrical triumphs the West End has ever known.

The show, produced by the famous impresario Charles B. Cochran, had premiered at the Opera House in Manchester on 21 November 1933. Cochran had seen the actress for the first time as Saint Joan in a Berlin production of Shaw's play in 1924 and had never forgotten her: 'Here, I thought, was the real St. Joan, even if not Shaw's conception. From that time on, whenever I was in Europe, I inquired where I might find Bergner.' Years later, in January 1933, he heard that she was in London and decided to cast her in Margaret

Figure 5 Elisabeth Bergner as Gemma Jones in the screen version of *Escape Me Never*, 1935.

Kennedy's play (Bergner had been the protagonist of a successful adaptation of Kennedy's bestselling novel *The Constant Nymph* in Berlin in 1927). Cochran recalls that one of the most exciting moments in his life had been 'the fall of the curtain at the Opera House, Manchester, on Bergner's first performance on the English stage … the storm of applause broke like a great wave. It was no ordinary applause, but such as one only hears on some very great occasion, when people have been very deeply stirred.'

After Bergner's triumph in Manchester, the show transferred to the Apollo Theatre, where it opened on 8 December 1933. Although Cochran had preferred not to publicize her fame in advance of the London production, 'echoes of her success in Manchester had reached Shaftesbury Avenue'. The day after the premiere, the box office's telephone lines were permanently engaged, and all seats and standing places for every performance were sold out. Cochran never had so many requests for tickets from his friends: 'H. G. Wells wrote: "Can you tell somebody to do something about it, so I can get two seats or a loge either Friday or Saturday evening or matinée? Don't let it bother you; but if a wave of your hand can do it, please wave your hand."' John Gielgud, who was an admirer of Bergner and a friend, associated her debut in London with a golden age in British theatre. In 1976, commenting on the success of a play he was in, he wrote: 'people applaud in the streets when we come out of the matinées, something I've not seen since Bergner in *Escape Me Never* in the 30s'.

Throughout January 1934 the British press recorded Bergner's success with a torrent of news and gossip. She was called 'a German genius' and compared to Eleonora Duse and Sarah Bernhardt. Although she was very private, Bergner's appearance, dress sense and personal habits on and off stage, details of her personal and social life were scrutinized in newspapers and magazines on a daily basis. A legend had been created almost overnight.

Elisabeth Bergner was born in Drohobycz, in the Austro-Hungarian province of Eastern Galicia, in 1897. Her father, a Jewish merchant, moved the family to Vienna when Elisabeth was four years old. To many class-conscious assimilated Jews, life in the imperial capital was considered a social and economic necessity. The Bergners were not poor – they had a servant and a cook, and could afford a private tutor for their children – but neither were they affluent. Bergner remembers her early years in a tense household, where her parents often argued and money was a constant preoccupation, yet she rejected her parents' bourgeois aspirations. Instead, she was drawn to her eastern roots and to the theatre. As a child, she was first struck by the magic of the stage when she saw the artistes, acrobats and magicians in Vienna's popular funfair, the Wurschtl-Prater. It is easy to imagine that Bergner's Galician origins and her fascination with the emotionally freer world of the East were partly accountable for her soulful and somewhat exotic personality as an actress.

Impatient to enrol in drama school from an early age, Elisabeth attended the Vienna Conservatoire, and learnt her trade at a provincial theatre in Innsbruck, where she played disparate roles, from Greek heroines to operetta leads. Her chance to pursue a serious acting career came when she was called to join the cast of the Zürich Schauspielhaus at the age of nineteen. Here, this tiny, naive-looking girl with big brown eyes and a small, childlike face was cast mainly as a character actress in sentimental roles. Her debut as Ophelia to Alexander Moissi's Hamlet in 1916, however, is remembered as an extraordinary moment in the history of twentieth-century European theatre and set her on the path to fame.

Moissi, thirty-seven years old at the time, was an Italian-Austrian actor of Albanian descent known for his warm southern temperament and a gentle, melodious voice. He was a protégé of Max Reinhardt and considered by many to be the greatest classical performer of his generation. Interned in Switzerland during the First World War, he had been engaged to play Hamlet in Zürich in October and November 1916. He arrived in his uniform, and there was to be only one rehearsal. His Ophelia was Elisabeth Bergner, a young unknown from Vienna, a girl so small and slight that her costume had to be adjusted several times. All other members of the cast had already played with the famous actor during his yearly visits to the Zürich theatre. Only Elisabeth was meeting him for the first time. Although she found him to be kind and helpful, she was terrified of the challenge to come. Having rehearsed the play only once, on the night of the performance she stood anxiously behind the curtain, in awe of Moissi and enchanted by his clear, expressive voice. When her turn came, just before the madness episode, she absent-mindedly dropped the bunch of flowers which the manager had given her for that part. Unaware of how the monologue should be delivered, she mimed the scene, handing out an imaginary bouquet. She had created a new Ophelia. Her friend, the actor Alexander Granach, witnessed that moment:

> In the madness scene, a gentle, childlike Ophelia quietly enters the stage, smiling to herself, her wide eyes filled with tears. On her left arm, with great care, she holds a colourful bouquet and tentatively hands out the flowers with her right hand. But in truth she has no bouquet and no flowers – with empty hands, from an empty arm, she hands out non-existent flowers from a non-existent bunch. Yet the world has never seen more colourful, more scented flowers than these! Both the audience and the other actors hold their breath before the spectacle of this sweet madness, before this beautiful Shakespearean child, this beginner! Her name: Elisabeth Bergner.

Her breakthrough had come. Bergner, as she would be known from now on, was born. After a successful time in Vienna, where she played Rosalind in *As You Like It* – one of the androgynous roles that she would make her own – Elisabeth Bergner relocated to Berlin in 1922. During the ten years that followed, she worked with the foremost actors and directors of the Weimar era, from Emil Jannings, Fritz Kortner, Werner Krauß and Conrad Veidt to Viktor Barnowsky, Max Reinhardt and Leopold Jessner.

Although loved by the public, Bergner's idiosyncratic acting style appeared affected at times, and her look and personality unsuitable for certain roles. The dreamy quality of her delivery, her instinctive way of inhabiting a character and disregard for methodic work during rehearsals could be fatal to a production (as in Reinhardt's much anticipated *Romeo and Juliet* in Berlin in 1928, which was a failure). Yet Elisabeth Bergner's importance as a wholly original, inimitable actress cannot be overestimated. She is said to have produced a sort of magic in the theatre. Countless reviews and contemporary witness accounts acknowledge the startling quality of her presence on stage. She came to embody a place and an era. Her enigmatic nature mirrored the peculiar allure of Berlin and the vibrancy of its cultural life between the wars. With the city of her greatest successes, Bergner shared a duplicitous aura. She conveyed an ambiguity that blurred the distinctions between male and female traits, between purity and seduction, fragility and strength. Her colleague and compatriot Fritz Kortner (a famous Shylock to her Portia in 1927) wrote that at the time 'the whole of Berlin [had] a relationship with Bergner'. She had a strange and wonderful ability to electrify entire audiences. After her first performance as Saint Joan, a local newspaper reported that 'one could see from a change in Berlin's cityscape that there had been a Bergner-Premiere' the previous night. (Another example of the transformational power of theatre was Bertolt Brecht's *Threepenny Opera*. The play's first night in Berlin in August 1928 caused such a sensation that the word *Dreigroschenfieber* (Threepenny-fever) was coined to describe its effect on the city.) The Bergner phenomenon illustrates the central role of the stage in Germany at a time when the country, and its capital in particular, was full of gifted actors and progressive directors. Theatre in the Weimar Republic was not only a diversion – light entertainment enjoyed great popularity – but an artistic endeavour.

Thanks to Austrian-Hungarian film director Paul Czinner, her future husband, Bergner also became a successful film star, and Berlin's highest-paid actress. Film in Germany was a sophisticated art form, which had become increasingly popular in the years after the First World War. Cinema programmes were diverse, as was the choice of film genres, and it was not unusual for prominent stage actors to become popular screen stars. Bergner's greatest screen triumph came in 1929, when the first showing of Czinner's film version of Arthur Schnitzler's novella *Miss Else*, with Bergner in the title role, caused an unprecedented and frenzied rush for tickets. Even Joseph Goebbels went to see it, and described Bergner in his diary as a 'dear Jewish child'.

Today, the only way to evaluate Bergner's acting style is by observing her on film. Despite her popularity as a film actress, her cinematic performances fail to reveal the spellbinding quality of her presence on stage. And yet it is obvious that she acted like no one else.

Catherine the Great (1934) was her first feature in English and a lavish historical drama produced by Alexander Korda and directed at Elstree Studios by Bergner's husband, Paul Czinner. That year, Marlene Dietrich's portrayal of the same character in Josef von Sternberg's *The Scarlet Empress* created a more memorable Catherine in terms of visual impact and erotic intensity. But if one wants to understand what made Bergner's acting style completely unique among her contemporaries, her screen performance as Catherine does offer some interesting clues.

Figure 6 Elisabeth Bergner taking tea with her husband, Hungarian director Paul Czinner (centre), and Max Schach, on the set of *Dreaming Lips* at the Trafalgar studio (*c*. 1936).

In her first scene, the young princess, who has just arrived from Germany to marry Grand Duke Peter, makes her entrance accompanied by two courtiers. She is small, pale, wide-eyed and somewhat helpless. She seems to be out of place in the palace's lavish rooms, uncomfortable in her large crinoline. Bergner acts with her arms, which she opens and closes, slightly lifting her shoulders and clenching her hands into fists to signal worry and distress. Her voice is melodious, deep and high-pitched at the same time. She speaks slowly, as if to follow an inscrutable internal rhythm. When she says 'Russia takes my breath away … The country is so vast', the last 'a' is very long, and the word 'vast' impresses itself into our minds conveying the sense of Russia's enormity compared to the young woman's position and diminutive stature. In her first meeting with Peter, whom she does not recognize, she appears humble yet determined. Dismayed at the fact that the grand duke refuses to marry her, she tells the young man that she cares deeply for Peter, and explains: 'I was told about him ever since I was born.' As before, the vowel in her last word is elongated for emphasis. Here, it is also followed by a pause during which she pulls at some ribbons on her dress with a seemingly involuntary movement of her small hands, her fists contracted in apprehension and vague embarrassment. The next line is delivered in a sort of whisper: 'I thought about him. I dreamed about him', whereby the 'ea' of 'dreamed' is a long sound and 'him' a short explosion. Bergner's way of speaking was like nothing that had been heard before. Her diction possessed both the unguarded innocence of a child and the fierce determination of a woman who knows exactly what she wants.

Similarly, in the film version of *Escape Me Never* (1935), Bergner's character combines infantile traits and feminine charm. When Gemma Jones bursts into a Venetian palazzo and finds herself, uninvited, among the members of a wealthy English family, the viewer is just as startled as the other characters. She is asked to leave. A servant tries to drag her away, but she resists, runs off screaming and threatens to jump out of the window into the canal if they get closer. Here is a strange girl with a deep, yet piercing voice. She is slim, with soft, golden hair cut into a short bob and a long side-fringe. Her complexion is fair, she has dark eyes and simple facial features: a small, straight nose and a wide mouth with thin lips that pout when she speaks. She is exuberant and determined, like a spoilt child. Once again, Bergner has created an enigma, a character in whom vulnerability and force coincide, someone whose eccentricity and foreignness transcend national boundaries, age and gender.

The German critic Arthur Eloesser defined Bergner as a *femme-enfant* and described her aura on stage as a peculiar combination of childlike naivety and intoxicating eroticism. He also called her a witch because of the way she could captivate a contemporary metropolitan audience – men and women, young and old – like a fairy-girl, a sort of a modern-day Ariel. In this respect, Bergner differed from other actresses, both on stage and on screen. She was one of the first stars of the 1920s to sport a masculine look and liked to play cross-dressing roles. In life, Bergner dressed with simple yet sophisticated elegance, often wore trousers and, unlike most of her female colleagues, did not curl her hair. (One of the newspaper columnists writing after her London debut in December 1933 remarked: 'Elisabeth Bergner has not personal beauty in the accepted sense, and she is very tiny. She must be one of the few actresses on the London stage without waved or wavy hair.')

A foreign star in London

Bergner's decision to work abroad matured after her appearance in the premiere of Gerhart Hauptmann's play *Gabriel Schilling's Flight* at Berlin's Staatstheater on 15 November 1932 – two days before Chancellor von Papen's resignation. A celebration of the playwright's seventieth birthday, the evening was the first important cultural event at which members of the Nazi leadership displayed their official credentials to a select audience. The spectators included several members of Germany's intellectual elite. Albert Einstein sat in the first row, as did Heinrich

Mann. Behind them were the writer and diplomat Count Harry Kessler and other representatives of Germany's cultural, military and political establishment. The occasion embodied all the spectacle and complexities of a tense historical juncture. In her autobiography, Bergner recalls a feverish atmosphere:

> All the actors on stage were peering through a spyhole, pointing at some members of the audience: There is Hitler, there is Goering, there is Goebbels, Hauptmann is in Hitler's box – and things like that. Suddenly I heard: there is Kerr, there is Theodor Wolff [the two men were, respectively, Germany most feared drama critic and the owner of Berlin's liberal daily *Berliner Tageblatt*. Both were Jewish]. Such cries – it cannot possibly be all true. Hitler and Theodor Wolff, Hauptmann in Hitler's box, Kerr and Goebbels – ghosts!

This surreal moment in the history of German theatre was to have serious consequences for Bergner's own life. The premiere was a success, but that same night a friend came to see her in her changing room begging her to leave the country as soon as possible. She did not listen to him. When, a few days later, a colleague rushed to her house to announce that the Nazis would not extend her contract because she was Jewish, Bergner, forsaking her home and most of her possessions, joined Paul Czinner in London. She did not return to Germany until after the war. Even then, she visited the country for professional reasons and stayed only for a limited period. She died in London, in a beautiful apartment overlooking Eaton Square, at the age of eighty-eight.

Paul Czinner and Elisabeth Bergner became British subjects in 1938. A report by the special branch of the Metropolitan Police dated London, 27 May 1938, destined for the Home Office and now kept in The National Archives at Kew in south-west London, recounts the main details of Czinner's biography from his arrival until the time the document was drafted. From this account we learn that he arrived in England on 18 December 1932 and that on 9 January 1933, at the Register Office in London's Hanover Square, 'the applicant married Elisabeth Bergner, Austrian, correctly registered with Surrey County Constabulary, Weybridge Police Station, under serial No. E.Z. 221313. (Certificate of marriage seen)'.

It is difficult to reconcile thoughts of people's real life and feelings with the impersonal nature of an official report. In such papers, the rigidity of the immigration process turns individuals into faceless entities, so that one can imagine only glimpses of their lived experience. Of the countless police reports and Home Office files on the German and Austrian émigrés who travelled to or settled in England in the 1930s, Bergner's and Czinner's record is one of the least disheartening, for they were both successful, had influential acquaintances and quickly established themselves in their new country. Mental snapshots of their first months in London include luxury hotels and the elegance of Hanover

Square on a winter's day when, according to the weather reports, a fresh south-westerly wind blew over a cloudy sky. At 6°C on the evening of 9 January 1933, the weather in London was described as mild for the time of year. The couple resided at the Ritz at the time, and their friend Carl Mayer had just arrived from Prague to work on the script for the film they were preparing for Korda. He was a witness at their wedding.

Despite her fame and her lucrative employment opportunities from the moment she arrived in London, Bergner was anxious. The political upheaval in Germany and the flight from Berlin had been like losing the ground under her feet. As was the case for many German-speaking émigrés who relied on language for their livelihood – especially writers and actors – the loss of the mother tongue added a further traumatic dimension to the experience of exile. In Bergner's case, her success abroad also meant that she had to deal with ever more frequent requests for help and money from the friends who had stayed behind. And help she did, with great generosity and selflessness, sending what she could and arranging what could be arranged.

By her own admission, Bergner's rushed marriage to Paul Czinner was a way of easing the situation in which they both found themselves. Bound together by a long-standing friendship and a professional relationship that had just been bolstered by Korda's offer, the actress and her director embarked upon a partnership that lasted until Czinner's death almost forty years later. She is said to have called him 'my father, my brother, my nurse', and the true nature of their marital union remains something of a mystery.

Bergner was notoriously reserved and fiercely protective of her privacy, and details of her often turbulent personal life are scant. Only the biographies of some of those who knew her and private papers in the Elisabeth Bergner Archive in Berlin reveal some telling aspects of her relationships with friends and lovers. A picture of a somewhat restless psychology emerges. She was attracted and attractive to both men and women. Independent, capricious, insecure, but also strong-willed and infectiously cheerful, she carried in her the exoticism of her Eastern European roots together with the liberal spirit of Weimar Berlin. It appears that Czinner's devotion to Bergner and his reassuring presence in her life were a source of emotional security to her, rather than a passionate attachment. Bergner was a loyal and generous friend, but many of her friends were in love with her. This was true of Alexander Moissi, who loved her intensely and whom she eventually spurned. And it was true of the Austrian poet Albert Ehrenstein. Eleven years her senior, Ehrenstein met a young Bergner in 1915 and became her most ardent suitor, as well as an important friend, lover and mentor. They had a tempestuous and uneven relationship. He was one of the first older men to assume a fatherly role in her life. It is also likely that Bergner was romantically involved with her closest female friend, Viola Bosshardt, with whom she bought and shared a house in Berlin in the 1920s. Elisabeth Bergner appears to have been more flirtatious than interested in sex, and she often teased those close to her by being both emotionally demanding and imperiously distant. Her coquettish nature was somehow related to the same mesmerizing quality with which she dazzled her audiences. It inspired the relationships she forged in England as it had done in Vienna, Zürich and Berlin.

In exile, the challenge lay in having to create an identity for herself as an outsider in a foreign land. The sudden exposure to a new culture was for some an insurmountable obstacle. Bergner was one of the few émigrés who succeeded in assimilating into the English way of life while, at the same time, retaining her distinctive individuality as an actress and as a person. Some have argued that she failed in her career in England, that she only repeated old acting patterns and mannerisms from her glory days on the Continent and never really adapted to her identity as a British actress. This is partly true. From a professional perspective, her loyalty to Paul Czinner prevented her from working with more talented filmmakers. She also failed to explore more challenging theatrical roles later in her career (she admired Beckett, but never acted in one of his plays). Yet there is no doubt that she tried to conform to her new country. For example, she created her own peculiar brand of English and became more feminine and sentimental in her English roles, more attuned to a different sensibility. And she undoubtedly caught something of the British imagination at the time, as her meteoric rise as a foreigner in London in the 1930s is unparalleled in the history of British theatre.

It is not easy to define the reasons for an émigré's achievement in a foreign environment. Luck and other external circumstances can play a decisive role in the process of assimilation. Age is also an important factor, as it is often the young who manage to transfer their skills and forge a new identity. Many other elements determine a newcomer's acclimatization to their country of asylum, such as a facility with languages, good connections or an extroverted personality. But there is also something else, a trait less tangible and possibly more significant: the ability to discover within a different culture something that one carries within oneself. This entails a moment of recognition, one in which a foreigner perceives a meaningful connection with new places despite their unfamiliarity. Such a feeling may arise from a sudden intimacy with a foreign landscape or from the unexpected gift of a new friendship. It is something that allows an outsider to feel at ease in the most profound sense of the word, and one thanks to which the seeds for a new life away from home can be sown. In Elisabeth Bergner's case, the intensity of her relationship with a quintessentially British author such as J. M. Barrie must have derived from a similar experience. But the story of their encounter is still to come.

Bergner's first important task on arriving in London in December 1932 was to learn the language – and quickly. She had had some English lessons as a student of Vienna's Conservatoire, and in 1929 had attended a summer course in England while Czinner directed a film in Cornwall. Although a biographical note on the programme for *Escape Me Never* reported, falsely, that she had 'complete command of the English language, which she started to learn when she was six years of age, in the Vienna of her childhood', her knowledge of English was not good enough at first to play the main role in *Catherine the Great* next to acclaimed actors such as Gerald Du Maurier, Flora Robson and Douglas Fairbanks Jr.

And so a teacher was found for her, a certain Florence Freedman of Grosvenor House, 17 Dorset Square, London NW1 – or Flossie for short. Florence had taught an impressively long list of actors from all over the world. Her most famous pupil before Bergner had been Francis Lederer, the Austrian screen-and-stage star, who had been Romeo to Bergner's Juliet in the Max Reinhardt Berlin production of Shakespeare's play. In 1931, Lederer had come to London to take the lead role in *Volpone* at the Garrick Theatre and Flossie had given him English lessons every night, first in his dressing room and then at the nearest Lyons' Corner House until dawn (she later recalled: 'The manager knew us, and so there we sat, with his sheepdog and my peke and a German dictionary and the script. We must have been a funny sight'). In her autobiography, Bergner described Flossie Freedman as an angel who worked miracles. Apparently she gave up all her other students to devote herself only to Bergner. The fact that the actress played the role of Hedvig in a BBC radio production of Ibsen's *Wild Duck* in May 1933 (a mere six months after her arrival) testifies to Flossie's skills as a teacher. Bergner remembers her as 'a very petit bourgeois English spinster of about fifty, a famously good teacher, especially recommended for foreign artists. She lived in a studio flat with a little Pekinese dog.' Other contemporaries, such as the journalist Charles Patrick Graves, portray Flossie ('known as Freedy throughout the stage world') as 'a woman of immense vitality and still more immense patience'. In the Elisabeth Bergner Archive, three letters from the teacher to her pupil corroborate this impression rather than Bergner's own description of Miss Freedman as a typical middle-aged spinster. Written on bright, pea-green, headed paper in large, flowery handwriting, Flossie Freedman's messages are lively and intense. They also show that she was probably in love with Bergner.

One letter is dated 22 August, the actress's birthday (the year is missing, but it is likely to have been 1933 or 1934): 'May the Almighty bless you today & every minute of your life. May he grant us many many happy returns & give you health, strength & happiness …Every beat of my heart beats with love for you. Have a happy day beloved, your own Floss.' Another missive, simply headed 'Wednesday', reveals a whole world of intimacy, mutual knowledge and private endearments:

My most beloved. What a lovely memory I have of our evening last night …
You were only teasing me I know, as I was you, because I couldn't & wouldn't

be jealous of that dear old man. The fact that he gives you so much happiness makes me happy too. I am grateful for and fully cognizant of your love which is my most precious treasure. Enclosed is for you my wish on the Queen Mary. It is not difficult to see where my thoughts always are, with whom & of whom, & will please dear God always be: But what a child of nature you are, & what a roguish tease. Remain so, you are adorable. All my hearts blessings & love love love. Your Floss. PS. Nicolette & Chinkeypoo send their love too.

Flossie's remark about the 'dear old man' is probably an allusion to Bergner's closeness to J. M. Barrie, whereas her 'wish on the Queen Mary' may refer to the official launch of the eponymous ship on 26 September 1934. The letter's tone and content give a distinct impression of the effect that Bergner's presence had upon the lives of the individuals to whom she was close. When she decided to strike up a friendship, she did so wholeheartedly. On stage, she beguiled her audience by acting from within, by baring the most intimate recesses of her being through seemingly unconscious motions and peculiar mannerisms. In life, she had an air of passionate spontaneity, even in old age. When watching or listening to the handful of interviews from the last two decades of her life, one is struck by the quick flow of her ideas; by the bubbling quality of her thoughts; by the force of a strong temperament behind her young, modulated voice and graceful appearance. This is probably what Flossie meant by calling her 'a child of nature' and 'a roguish tease'.

There seems to have been a refreshing and irresistible impishness about Bergner. The poet Else Lasker-Schüler, who remembered her from her earliest Berlin days, noted that Elisabeth Bergner was always acting. Yet the German expression – 'Es spielt aus ihr überall' (she acts with her whole being) – denotes not only the artifice of enacting a role, but also a natural and all-encompassing playful mode of being alive. This explains the impression of the actress, shared by those who knew her, as someone who exuded happiness (a colleague from the Zürich theatre remembers that she was always in a good mood). But she could also be needy and fearful, and she could be wilfully determined. George Bernard Shaw, who knew her well and was often exasperated by her tenacity of mind behind the whimsical exterior, wrote that Bergner was 'as tough as a Brazil nut'.

Behind the Bergner myth

An account of the whirlwind of emotions that usually accompanied the entrance of Bergner into people's lives was penned by the American poet and novelist known as H. D. (Hilda Doolittle) and by her partner, Bryher. Nowhere in her memoirs, papers and correspondence does Elisabeth Bergner mention H. D.

or the English author – and daughter of shipping magnate Sir John Ellerman –
Annie Winifred Ellerman, alias Bryher. Yet both women have amply documented
their complex entanglement with the actress.

H. D.'s autobiographical novella *Nights* (published under the pseudonym
John Helforth in 1935) is a fictional record of Bergner's disruptive intrusion into
their lives. Whereas Bryher venerated Bergner and was in thrall to her, H. D.
resented her partner's enthusiasm for 'the diminutive mercurial waif with large
brown eyes and lilting Viennese speech', but was nonetheless fascinated by
Bergner's personality and by her effect on other people.

Figure 7 Bryher in 1938.

Throughout the 1920s and 1930s, H. D. and Bryher led an itinerant and cosmopolitan lifestyle that saw them move among London, Switzerland, Paris, Berlin and Vienna. In 1927, Bryher and her then husband (and H. D.'s lover) Kenneth Macpherson founded a production company, Pool Productions, as well as a film journal called *Close Up*. This was the first and only serious publication about avant-garde European cinema at the time. It focused mainly on Russian and German films, and H. D. contributed several articles on the relationship among cinema, psychoanalysis and modernist aesthetics. *Close Up* found an interested following among some of Germany's greatest film directors, such as Fritz Lang and G. W. Pabst, and the latter became Bryher's friend. Bryher had been a frequent visitor to Germany since the late 1920s and was interested in Weimar cinema. She first met Bergner in Berlin, where she saw her in the film of *Miss Else*. From then on, she became obsessed with her and was captivated by her androgyny ('I could smack the Bergner', she wrote in one of her letters. 'She is so cute in her boy's ski-ing things but was coy in a lace or ruffled dress and I could pinch her behind for it').

Years earlier, Bryher had written *The Girl-Page in Elizabethan Literature*, a scholarly piece on cross-dressing roles in Shakespearean theatre that partly explains her fascination with the boyish Bergner. But her attraction to the actress's ambivalent charms was not only intellectual. The romantic – if somewhat neurotic – nature of their relationship is documented in Bryher's and H. D.'s correspondence. By 1931, Bryher's attraction had turned into an active pursuit, both encouraged and frustrated by Bergner's flirtatious game of seduction and rejection. The actress was a regular guest of the couple in London as well as in Switzerland, where Bryher owned Kenwin, a Bauhaus villa overlooking Lake Geneva. H. D., who was Freud's patient in Vienna between 1933 and 1934, remembers that after her psychoanalytic sessions she would often visit 'a certain shop' where she chose photographs of actresses in the nude for Bryher's collection. Bergner was a particular favourite. In a letter to H. D. dated 17 March 1933 Bryher, acknowledging the photos, revealed her jealous annoyance at Bergner's new marital status: 'I am sure the photos were taken at Vevey: the little wretch is now giving out interviews as Mrs Paul Czinner. I wish I could take her by the neck and lock her up for Papa [i.e. Freud] to do his very worst on. I like the one of her standing the best I think.'

The letters exchanged by H. D. and Bryher over the following months contain numerous references to the actress during her first two years in London. Bergner was relieved at having fled the Nazis. But events in Germany and political unrest in Vienna unsettled her, and she was worried about the family she had left behind – her mother and sister in Prague, her father in Austria. We also learn that she loved London, which she preferred to Vienna and Berlin: 'I do feel with E. B.', wrote H. D. from Vienna on 22 May 1933. 'I think London does something terrific to the psyche of the étranger ... London gives one a sort of anonymous freedom.' Two days later, Bryher added that Bergner 'melted into London – it was physically kind to her'.

Why did Bergner feel so at ease in London? Was it because she could enjoy its luxuries without having to suffer the deprivations endured by other émigrés? Or because of that seemingly effortless magic touch with which she enchanted whole audiences wherever she went? Her success may explain part of her love of London. But it is more likely that – as H. D. thought – the city gave Bergner a sense of freedom, for its vastness allowed her to blend in and feel invisible. London's international climate and its budding modernity in the 1930s coexisted with the safe, cosy essence of a typically British love of tradition. And although Bergner's androgynous appeal, her look and her unusual acting style epitomised the audacity and licentiousness of Berlin, she craved protection and loved secrecy. An interesting image emerges from something Bryher wrote to H. D. at the end of May 1933: 'I went to see Elizabeth [sic] yesterday, taking a small woolly blanket rug instead of the red roses advised by Dog [Kenneth Macpherson]. I had an ENORMOUS success therewith, as Elizabeth spends her spare time in slumber wrapt in woollies.' Less than a year later, Bergner would share her passion for warmth and seclusion with her new friend J. M. Barrie, who often shunned the world and spent days brooding in the shady glow of his fireplace.

H. D. and Bryher, as well as Freud and Bryher's psychoanalyst Hanns Sachs, were convinced that Bergner would have benefited from being psychoanalysed. The actress's emotional fragility, her neuroses and her complicated relationship with her older husband are recurring motifs in their correspondence. Yet Bergner always refused categorically to consider the idea. As Bryher put it to H. D. on 21 March 1933: 'Elizabeth … is at point of committing suicide but might come chasing to small dog [Bryher] for rescue if I guarantee not to pronounce the syllables analysis. That is naturally ridiculous … German thing has made Elizabeth desperate. Dog thinks she'll go probably soon: she can't sit, move or do anything for phobes.'

Bergner's anxiety at this early stage of her London exile exhausted her. Between December 1932 and June of the following year, she and Czinner moved house three times. Their Home Office file reports them at the Ritz between 19 December 1932 and 8 January 1933, at 38 Devonshire Street in Marylebone between 9 January and 1 April 1933, and at the Mayfair Hotel until the end of the year. Admittedly, they could not have chosen more exclusive addresses, yet Bergner was under great physical and mental pressure. There were thoughts of her distant relatives, cries for help from less fortunate friends and colleagues, and her own insecurities about a new career in a new language. At the same time, her talent, ambition and what seems to have been an unbounded amount of energy kept her going. Her first English job in the BBC production of Ibsen's *Wild Duck* went well. Although Bryher called the production as a whole 'a dismal flop', she thought that Bergner was its only merit: 'Her voice was lovely and not much accent.' But five days earlier Bryher had also written to H. D. that Elisabeth had 'spent two days in tears as she hates broadcasting: she says it is like going to school for the first time'.

The passages about Bergner's restless personality and sexual ambiguity are fascinating. For example, in a letter to H. D. dated 25 July 1933 Bryher describes a quarrel with Bergner, who is shown in a new and very private light:

Such a scene with Elizabeth [*sic*]. She called me a 'crude taxi driver' and kicked me out. She said any question of zoo [sex] was piggish and never to be spoken of in her presence and that she had never been with anyone, male or female, or inanimate, except C[zinner] for a week which she would always remember but never repeat. She must be raving mad. She said her one emotion was jealousy. That she was jealous of my having spoken to Mrs. Williams [Bergner's secretary and travelling companion], to Alice, to anyone. That she spent half her time thinking of your great beauty as you moved across the Kenwin grass and the other half wondering how you could be poisoned!!!!!!!!

Several months after this episode, Bryher followed Bergner to Manchester to be near her during the actress's run at the Opera House, and was treated with the usual tantalizing combination of allure and aloofness. Bryher fictionalized this visit in a short novel entitled *November*, in which she portrays Bergner as the genial but emotionally fragile actress Cordelia, and herself as the English writer and businessman Ernest. A comparison with letters from Bryher's correspondence reveals the story as a fairly faithful version of Bryher's and Bergner's relationship in real life. Cordelia likes being reassured by Ernest; they meet on an emotional level despite the actress's refusal to be tied down or seduced into a physical relationship; Ernest is unsure about his own attractiveness to Cordelia, but he is near her whenever possible and lets 'her tighten into a hunch of gloom under her blue rug'.

The most interesting aspect about *November* is the light it throws on Bergner's character, especially on her insecurity as an exile and a performer. Her nervousness before the Manchester premiere as described in the story is entirely believable. Bryher turns Bergner's terrors into vivid images. She describes the actress's fear of rejection, her autocratic temperament, her desire to be alone or surrounded only by people who offer comfort and reassurance. The actress's worry over her first appearance on a foreign stage turned her life into a nightmare. In Bryher's words:

Ernest … could see Cordelia only as a tiny airplane in a storm, shaken by rage and tears, until to-morrow night were over … Cordelia 'was' her imagination, her ordinary life revolved to nightmare. Her bed folded into a prehistoric monster to torment her, the messenger who brought her roses, through a mere knock on the door, set her shivering from insecurity. Even the blowing curtains were a threat.

H. D.'s novella *Nights* is also a fictional portrayal of Bergner and an account of her behaviour towards Bryher. Although one should bear in mind its author's antipathy for the woman who tormented her own lover, the story offers precious insight into Bergner's character. It also includes a striking description of her appearance.

H. D. changed Bryher's and Bergner's names to Renne and Una respectively. Una is capricious and bewitching, always accompanied by a stern, masculine lesbian named Barton (modelled on Bergner's secretary and travelling companion, Mrs Williams). Renne is her victim. Written from the viewpoint of John Helforth, the story is a *roman à clef* in two parts, in which the narrator tries to untangle the mystery of a woman's suicide by reading entries from her diary. The book is also about multiple identities, as both Helforth and Natalie, whose diary we read, are different facets of H. D.'s own bisexual self.

Nights was written in 1931 and revised in 1934, when Bergner was filming *Escape Me Never* at Elstree Studios and H. D. and Bryher had leased an apartment at 49 Lowndes Square, in London's Belgravia. This elegant address concealed an unconventional household, where the world of English-speaking bohemian intellectuals and that of continental cinema, modernist culture and psychoanalysis converged. Bergner was probably the most glamorous member of H. D.'s and Bryher's complicated ménage. In her novella, H. D. fictionalizes the actress's presence in their lives by exposing her beguiling yet irritating capriciousness:

Chestnut-red-lion-hair, the wide eyes opening to show darker brown like chestnut burrs, revealing dark kernel of the fruit. Una's eyes stared wide, from the famous spikey lashes. All the things publicity allowed Una were tripled when one saw her. She was as simple (they were right there) as a child. Whether she had or had not slept with a semi-detached wealthy Jew who was her husband, was nobody's and everybody's business. She was not even demi-vierge, was tiresomely Peter Pan. She stared with wide eyes.

In these lines, the Bergner character is a *femme fatale*, but also someone who, like Peter Pan, is childlike, sexless and ultimately mysterious. In H. D.'s portrait, Bergner's elusive personality begins to take a more definite shape. The qualities that turned her into a great actress also made for a difficult, if fascinating, human being.

Perhaps a reason for the impact of her encounter with J. M. Barrie on both their lives lay in the characteristics that the Scottish playwright and the young Austrian émigré recognized in each other and in their respective creative geniuses. A few days after meeting Bergner for the first time in early 1934, Barrie began writing for the stage again. She revived his passion for the theatre and became an all-important friend. He was inspired by the unusual combination between Bergner's sophisticated allure and her impish, androgynous qualities. She certainly evoked the physical and psychological traits of some of his characters – Peter Pan above all others. For her part, Bergner must have been attracted by Barrie's protective fatherly role and by the vivacity of his imagination. In her novella, Bryher had alluded to Cordelia's social snobbery, to her preference for people who could further her career ('she liked [Ernest], yes, but as he was neither a best-seller nor a dramatist, in her circle he did not count'). But it would be wrong to argue that Bergner's openness towards Barrie stemmed from ambition and design. Perhaps she felt an affinity with the darker sides of his character, with his moodiness and manipulative temperament. What is certain is that they were both extremely successful individuals whose fame rested on a guileless appeal and whose private self was a closely guarded secret.

This is how they met.

One night in January

Sometime in January 1934, Barrie's godson Peter Scott also fell for Bergner's charms. In his memoirs, he admits to having lost his heart the moment he saw her in *Escape Me Never*. He went to see the play three more times that month and another thirteen times before the end of its run. He dated his first visit to the Apollo Theatre soon after he had begun painting Barrie's portrait, but it is impossible to establish precisely when Scott first met Bergner. He certainly knew her quite well when he introduced her to Barrie towards the end of the month.

In her memoirs, Bergner describes Scott as a particularly loyal young 'fan'. They became good friends. His biographer speculates that Scott and Bergner were lovers, but it is difficult to say. She enjoyed his company and saw him often in the winter and spring of 1934. They certainly flirted with each other. As we know, Bergner breezed into people's lives with an energy that dazzled them and filled their days with longing for her. If one were to believe Bryher's account of her quarrel with Bergner in July 1933, the actress's seduction strategy lay more in flirting than in her physical appetite. As for Peter Scott, his infatuation may also have been enhanced by the memory of his Munich days. It is likely that Bergner's fervent vitality reminded him of those times and places. In his recollections, he portrays the actress – as Flossie Freedman had done – as a child of nature, an almost roguish, impulsive and irresistible presence. He recalls that she liked being driven around in his Morris touring car with the hood down, and that he used to accompany her to the cinema, where she wore 'dark glasses so as not to be mobbed'. He used to take the longest route possible when he drove her from Hampstead to see Barrie, so as to spend more time in her company. (Between April and June 1934, Bergner and her husband rented Admiral's House, a Georgian building close to Hampstead Heath, from an aristocratic friend of Scott's mother.) One day Bergner visited Peter at his house and, having arrived an hour early, went to sleep in the drawing room, where he 'found her curled up in a chair like a kitten, fast asleep'. Another time, she scolded him for having sat too close to the stage during one of her performances at the Apollo ('How could you! ... How could you do it!'). Then she forgave him, running gaily across the room and kissing him in a playful display of reconciliation.

The light-hearted liaison with the twenty-four-year-old Scott contrasts greatly with the emotional force of Bergner's friendship with Barrie. The relationship between J. M. Barrie and Elisabeth Bergner had a different intensity from the moment they shook hands for the first time. They met in her dressing room after one of the evening performances of *Escape Me Never* sometime before 28 January 1934, when Barrie mentioned Bergner's shadow in his letter to Scott's mother. A few days beforehand, Scott had suggested a visit to the Apollo Theatre to his godfather, and bought the tickets. 'Barrie was full of excuses. He said that he did not go to the theatre these days and did not think that he would enjoy it very much anyway.' As ever in his later years, the playwright was reluctant to leave the seclusion of his own home, the shelter of his cavernous room with the great fireplace. His chronic bronchitis and the winter weather were plausible excuses for avoiding the outside world. Moreover, Barrie's dislike of noise and crowds must have made the thought of a night in the West End especially unpalatable. The atmosphere of a theatre, with its bright lights and glamorous guests, may have alarmed him, and brought back memories of his youth. But his godson insisted. In collusion with Barrie's butler, he managed to drag the old man out of the flat and drove him to the theatre. According to Scott, Barrie let the first interval pass without a single comment. Perhaps he sat in the dark auditorium, falling under Bergner's spell, surrendering himself once more to the magic of theatre, suddenly and unexpectedly. After the show he hardly said a word.

When Scott took Barrie to meet Bergner backstage, they found her still in character. Like a method actor *ante litteram*, she was still crying Gemma Jones's tears well past curtain call. Her two guests did not stay for long, and very little was said. Yet surprisingly, Barrie asked Bergner to tea the following Friday. Even more surprisingly, that most elusive of stars accepted. Barrie was quiet on the way home. What might he have been thinking as he sat in his godson's car, moving through the London night? Perhaps images of the evening were still going through his mind as he looked out of the car window, trying to recall that beguiling creature on the stage – Elisabeth Bergner's voice; her tiny hand; her tears through those fine, long lashes.

Not until the following morning, when he returned to Adelphi Terrace to work on the portrait, did Peter realize the full impact of the previous evening upon his godfather, whom he remembers saying: 'I told you that I had given up writing. Since last night I've decided to take it up again.' Then, after a pause: 'I haven't felt like this about an actress since the first time I saw Pauline Chase.'

Pauline Chase was an American actress who had become a famous Peter Pan on the London stage, a part she played for many years to much acclaim. Like Bergner, she was small and vivacious, and embodied an attractive combination of sophisticated feminine beauty and boyish charm. Chase was Barrie's goddaughter and one of his favourite actresses. The playwright, who had married an actress, had made a habit of falling in love with his performers.

It has been said that Barrie's passion for Bergner was the last in his long string of crushes on attractive and successful women, and that his attitude towards Bergner displayed all the signs of the sycophantic, self-deprecating mood that he had often used in such flirtations. This may well be the case. But the nature of his infatuation with the Austrian star seems to have been more constant and more profound. This is surprising, especially considering that Bergner barely knew who Barrie was when they first met. She had only heard of him as the author of *Peter Pan*. Barrie's liking for her may have been due to the fact that an exceptional young woman had come to inspire him when failing creativity and memories of happier days had become an almost unbearable burden. Or perhaps they were united by certain affinities of character. They both hid an inscrutable personality behind an infantile exterior. And they had both created their own respective legends. Yet the most fascinating aspect of their encounter lies in their very different backgrounds, as the national, cultural and linguistic barriers that separated them did not seem to matter. In fact, these barriers probably brought them closer together.

Cynthia Asquith recalls that the morning after Barrie first saw *Escape Me Never* she found him 'neither immersed in *The Times* nor able to pay any attention to his correspondence. He was much too eager to tell me of the impression made on him by Elizabeth [*sic*] Bergner.' That same night, Barrie went back to the Apollo Theatre with Cynthia to show her the actress who had so galvanized him. A few days later, Bergner joined Barrie for tea at Adelphi Terrace. He was very secretive about this meeting, and neither Cynthia Asquith nor Peter Scott was allowed to join them. In this respect, it is interesting that Bergner's shadow should have found its way into Barrie's portrait. The dark shape to the right of the sitter in Scott's painting suggests the scale of Bergner's role in Barrie's life and is, at the same time, a nod to his delight in mystery and concealment.

What did Sir James Barrie and Elisabeth Bergner say to each other on that first afternoon in the shadowy privacy of his study, while Peter Scott waited downstairs in his car? All versions of the story suggest that they spoke about the play that Barrie had offered to write for his new friend. Bergner remembers that they drank tea and talked in front of the enormous fireplace. Barrie, puffing on his pipe, asked her about her favourite roles. She mentioned some, by Shakespeare, Schiller, Hauptmann, O'Neill. Barrie was interested in Gerhart Hauptmann, of whom he knew very little ('he knew as little about Hauptmann as Germans know about Barrie'). He particularly liked the idea of the character of Hannele in Hauptmann's mystical play *Hannele's Journey to Heaven* (1893), and was surprised when Bergner told him that she thought she had outgrown child roles. He kept enquiring about a character or a story that had affected her, until she mentioned Rembrandt's painting of David playing the harp to Saul. This is the biblical image in which the king appears grief-stricken and wipes his tears on the curtains while the young David is playing for him. Bergner thought that Rembrandt's David was, in contrast to the tragic figure of Saul, innocent and radiant. She remembers:

> Barrie stood up. His pipe had gone off again. He put it away and said: 'That's my play.' I didn't understand what he meant. Anyway, Peter had just come up to collect me, as it was half past six. When we had already said goodbye and Peter and I were in the lift, Barrie pulled me out again and whispered in my ear: 'Goodbye, David'.

This is how Barrie came to write his last work for the stage and his only biblical story, *The Boy David*. The play depicts the pivotal moments in David's youth: his anointing by the prophet Samuel; his meeting with King Saul; the slaying of Goliath; and, in the third and final act, his six visions of the future and his friendship with Jonathan, Saul's son. In the play, Barrie included three references to Rembrandt's painting of David playing the harp before Saul, as well as his own version of the episode in the second act, when Saul is 'devilish of one eye and with a tear for David in the other'.

Barrie set to work on his new project almost as soon as Bergner left his flat that January afternoon. Cynthia Asquith remembers that the following morning she found him 'in terrific eruption' and that he sent her out 'to search bookshops for various works on Jewish history and customs'. Four weeks later, he had already completed a rough draft of the first act. He seemed rejuvenated and was full of energy, as if 'driven by a special sense of urgency'. Barrie was secretive about the play. For months, only Elisabeth Bergner and Cynthia Asquith knew anything about it. Finally, on 18 June 1934, a brief announcement appeared in *The Times*:

> Sir James Barrie is writing a three act play for Miss Elisabeth Bergner for production early next year. Miss Bergner has discussed the matter with Sir James Barrie and has even offered to overcome the language difficulty if it

should be found necessary for her to speak Scots. The draft of the play, however, provides her with an English-speaking part.

We don't know whether the rumour of Bergner being prepared to speak Scots was invented news gossip or whether it was Barrie's idea in order to enhance the mystery around his new project. On the one hand, his need for secrecy was dictated by his anxiety about working on a new play after many years and about approaching a historical subject of which he knew little. On the other, concealment was part of Barrie's way of creating his own alternative version of reality, of controlling the truth. Moreover, his infatuation with Elisabeth Bergner had revived his tendency to weave a half-playful, half-serious web of deception around the people he loved. A feature of his close friendship with Bergner was his control over a possible jealousy between the actress and Cynthia Asquith. It is interesting to note that, in an interview recorded with Barrie's biographer, Andrew Birkin, in 1977, Bergner maintained that Barrie was in love with Cynthia. As with so many aspects in the playwright's life, the full story of his entanglement with Lady Asquith has yet to be told.

'Goodbye, David'

Despite Barrie's enthusiasm after meeting Bergner, his health was failing. He was restless and slept badly. *The Boy David* was draining him of energy, and the production became fraught with insurmountable complications. Now almost forgotten, the play was in many respects a failure. Barrie never blamed Bergner for this. In his will, he left £2,000 'to my loved Elizabeth Czinner professionally known as Elizabeth Bergner for the best performance ever given in a play of mine'. Although Bergner had been responsible for the play's repeated postponements, many of the subsequent problems that beset its staging and rehearsals were beyond her control. The premiere of *The Boy David* in Edinburgh at the end of November 1936 was a success, but the play failed to conquer London when it opened at His Majesty's Theatre on 13 December. The audience was distracted by King Edward VIII's abdication crisis, the theatre was too big for the production and Barrie, who was ill, did not attend. Charles Cochran withdrew the play after a run of only seven weeks.

From a literary perspective, *The Boy David* is too long, its dramatic impact burdened by too many stage directions and its language a somewhat jarring combination of plain speech and archaic expressions. This is partly due to the fact that Barrie chose to portray David as a young boy whose biblical stature is at odds with his innocence and childish demeanour. In Barrie's hands, the legendary tale became the exploration of a boy's need to overcome danger and fear. According to the theatre critic Harold Child, in *The Boy David* the theme of childhood that had occupied Barrie throughout his career had finally obtained universal significance. But to today's reader, the play appears as an odd-sounding hybrid creation of different styles and modes of expression.

During his first conversation with Bergner, Barrie had been struck by her mention of Gerhart Hauptmann's dramatic fairy tale about Hannele, the exalted little girl who wants to join her mother in heaven. The story must have appealed to Barrie for its romantic portrayal of childhood and its mystical, visionary elements, which he introduced in the third act of his own play, when David dreams of the future of Israel. Yet Barrie ignored Bergner's remark about not wanting to keep playing childish roles. Disregarding her wishes not to be typecast again, the playwright cast the thirty-six-year-old actress as a boy of thirteen. The temptation was too strong. Bergner's boyish charm, her impulsive behaviour and youthful appearance appealed enormously to Barrie. She was an incarnation of eternal, genderless youth, and he must have recognized her as the type of character he had been creating throughout his career. The comparison with Peter Pan is unavoidable. Ivor Brown, the drama critic of the *Manchester Guardian*, noticed the connection in his review of the Edinburgh premiere: 'The David in the play is very young indeed – a mere child, who looks no older than Peter Pan, and seems to have Peter's objection to growing up. Miss Bergner displays all the waywardness of a capricious child in a fairy tale, and one feels rather far away from the stark philosophy of the Bible story.' George Bernard Shaw had predicted this outcome long before the opening night. When Bergner chose to act in Barrie's play instead of bringing Shaw's *Saint Joan* to the British stage back in February 1934, Shaw had asked drily: 'Are you going to play another Peter Pan?'

A fascinating aspect of the collaboration between J. M. Barrie and Elisabeth Bergner is the extent to which the topic suggested by the actress for his new play concerned the most significant theme of the playwright's life and work. In his early years as a journalist, Barrie had already considered writing a biblical tale about David in a comic vein. The David theme runs like a painful thread throughout his life. The greatest irony of Bergner's suggestion lies in the fact that she had unwittingly touched upon the deepest chord in Barrie's soul.

David was the name of Barrie's father, of his maternal uncle and, most importantly, of his older brother. David Barrie was their mother's favourite son, a strong, clever and high-achieving boy who died in a skating accident at the age of thirteen. The impact of David's death upon his adoring mother was immense, and the emotional consequences of Margaret Barrie's withdrawal from her family and children were just as momentous for the six-year-old Jamie. Much has been written about the heartbreaking particulars of the mother's rejection of her youngest son. After David's death, the younger boy tried to become invisible in his attempt to assuage his mother's pain. Then he began to console her by pretending to be the dead child to the point of wearing David's clothes and imitating his behaviour. The psychological roots of Barrie's overwhelming love for the Llewelyn Davies brothers and his artistic obsession with the motif of boyhood probably lie in the early trauma of his brother's death.

The first and most powerful literary permutation of the biographical David complex is *The Little White Bird* (1902), Barrie's first book about Peter Pan. The novel is framed by the narrative voice of Captain W. (a retired bachelor and a thinly veiled fictional disguise for Barrie himself), who speaks to a little boy called David. The story is centred in and around Hyde Park and Kensington Gardens, with the Round Pond, 'which is the wheel that keeps all the Gardens going', and the Serpentine Lake, its 'drowned forest' and the island 'on which all the birds are born that become baby boys and girls'. Modelled on George, the oldest of the Llewelyn Davies brothers, David is much loved and pursued by the narrator, who used to take him to the gardens nearly every day. One of the most striking themes of the Captain's tales regards the bird-like nature of children before they grow up. David, too, had once spoken the language of birds, but now that he is older he is no longer able to understand it.

Several chapters are devoted to the story of Peter Pan, the boy 'who escaped being a human when he was seven days old'. The narrator recounts that 'when David heard this story first he was quite certain that he had never tried to escape, but I told him to think back hard, pressing his hands to his temples, and when he had done this hard, and even harder, he distinctly remembered a youthful desire to return to the tree tops'. In Barrie's world, the theme of infants as birds, of their latent desire to escape this earth in order to soar high above it, is part of the mythology of the dead child. And boyhood, the growing up of the child that was once a bird, symbolizes the tragedy of loss: a loss of innocence and, most strikingly in Barrie's case, the loss of the natural love bond between mother and child. Boyhood is also the moment in which the ideal freedom of timelessness becomes the real prison of time.

A friendship in trying times

It is a touching coincidence that Elisabeth Bergner should have given Barrie the idea of a dramatization of the tale of David. To Barrie, David was the eternal boy. To the Jewish émigré Bergner, the biblical story may also have evoked significant associations with her own cultural background and personal plight. Despite her success in England, she was coming to terms with the shocking developments in Germany, with its sudden transformation into a dictatorship and with the state's persecution of Jews.

Once again, it may seem inappropriate to emphasize the afflictions of someone as famous and privileged as Bergner was in London. And yet, as Bryher had noted, the émigré's worry about the predicament of family and friends, and her deep insecurities about her own talent were all consuming. A letter dated 28 January 1934 from an old friend in exile in Switzerland, Albert Ehrenstein, gives an impression of the emotional strain that the thought of distant friends caused Bergner at the time. In desperate need of help, Ehrenstein had left a house he could no longer afford and moved temporarily into a friend's sanatorium. He was now asking for financial support, both for himself and for the anti-Fascist cause ('If only you could help until the end of May, please do so'). A few days later, he sent Bergner another letter, asking why he had not heard back from her and admitting to being 'gnawed by pretty little red worry bugs'.

Bergner herself was under stress. Around the same time, in a letter about a possible American contract for the film of *Escape Me Never*, Charles Cochran hoped that she was not too tired. On 13 February, following the brutal oppression of the workers' uprising against the right-wing coalition headed by Engelbert Dollfuss in Austria, Cochran wrote to her again: 'I am so worried about you. All last night … my mind kept straying to you. I do hope all that you are fond of are out of harm's way.'

In March, having received Ehrenstein's letter with a delay of several weeks, Bergner replied:

> I am sorry that your letter was without reply for so long. I wrote to my brother-in-law immediately and enclose his response. Let me know if you still need the monthly bank transfer from Prague, or if you prefer that I stop it as long as my mother lives there. But I could only help you in monthly rates … I'm still under a contract signed before my great success, and I wouldn't be able to send you a larger sum in one go.

Less than a month later, the situation for Jewish actors in Germany went from bad to worse following Goebbels's ban that forbade them to work on stage and screen. The injunction would soon also include Jews appearing in foreign films. At the beginning of March 1934, *Catherine the Great* was banned in Germany because it starred 'the Jewess' Elisabeth Bergner. On 7 March, a brief yet eloquent article entitled 'Nazi Campaign against Non-Aryan Actors' appeared in *The Times*:

> The production in Berlin next Thursday of the second British film recently to achieve international success, 'Catherine the Great', has an especial interest in that the chief part is taken by a German Jewish actress who may no longer play in Germany, Miss Elisabeth Bergner. The production comes at a moment when a new campaign against Jewish and alien players is being launched …
> Audiences at Berlin picture theatres have warmly applauded the preliminary announcements of 'Catherine the Great', for the first performance of which all seats have been sold. Fräulein Bergner in her German days was a great

favourite and has not been forgotten. *Der Deutsche*, however, says: 'No matter how good actors may be; they are not ours and can never be ours. Away with them.'

The first performance of a Bergner film had sold out as in the old Weimar days. Berliners still had a relationship with Elisabeth Bergner, as the saying went. But their interest would not last for much longer. The organized ferocity of the racial boycotts was beginning to take hold. Not even her English triumphs could console the actress for the cruelty and stupidity of Germany's betrayal.

Soon after these events, Bergner took several breaks from the stage. In a letter dated 24 March 1934, Cochran advised her to 'make good use of your week's rest'. Less than a month later, she collapsed backstage after playing the first scene of *Escape Me Never*. *The Times* reported on 13 April that 'Miss Bergner and other members of her household were suffering from a slight attack of fish poisoning'. That same month, Bergner had a longer rest by the sea, as her admirer Maurice Baring – a poet and biographer of Eleonora Duse and Sarah Bernhardt – lent her his house in Rottingdean near Brighton. She was back at the Apollo on 7 May. The following day, she had resumed her role with her usual trance-like absorption ('it is part of her mastery that the cheers seemed inaudible to her, and she betrayed no sign that she was aware of the presence of an audience until she came to take her curtain-calls at the end'). In June, however, she was still unwell. On 19 June, she wrote to Ehrenstein:

> I was very ill and the theatre had to close for four weeks, during which time I had to lie in bed and even now I lie in bed all day and only get up before the show. Nonetheless, I have a ludicrous amount of commitments, for I am the island of the emigrants and must also make decisions about my own future, & that's not at all easy. I would so much like to help you but at the moment I can't.

In July, Shaw asked Cochran to undertake the negotiations with Bergner for a filmed version of *Saint Joan*. He then worked on the play's scenario throughout October and November. Yet the project never materialized, and Shaw eventually withdrew the film rights from the Czinners. This was partly a result of the playwright's indignation at Czinner's decision to work on the project with another author, the Scottish writer James Bridie, behind his back. Another reason for dismissing the plan was that Shaw disliked Bergner's interpretation of the role. Years later, Czinner asked him to review his decision about the film rights, but after seeing Bergner as Saint Joan at the Malvern Festival in the summer of 1938, Shaw stood by his word. His frustration with Bergner and her idiosyncratic acting style had already been apparent during rehearsal. In April 1938, for example, he had complained to the director H. K. Ayliff: 'What the little devil has done is to cut out all the unfeminine and unladylike speeches so that she can give a pathetic repetition of her *Escape Me Never* stunt.'

Whereas Bergner's relationship with Shaw was fraught with tensions, her friendship with Barrie seemed to withstand every obstacle. In 1935, he agreed to postpone the production of *The Boy David* because of her health. He was concerned about her, patient and affectionate, even when she caused him problems. His feelings were reciprocated. Bergner recalled in her memoirs that at the time of her collaboration with Barrie on *The Boy David* she used to pay regular visits to Shaw, who was Barrie's neighbour in Adelphi Terrace, and she stated quite plainly that she was much fonder of Barrie.

If Elisabeth Bergner was 'the island of the emigrants', she and Barrie appear to have been islands of comfort to each other. A series of photographs of the pair together at Cortina d'Ampezzo is revealing in this respect. Three images show Barrie and Bergner outdoors, with the Dolomites in the distance. In two of them, they face each other and are in conversation. In one photograph Bergner is talking animatedly; she is leaning towards Barrie, smiling, while he is gazing at her, also with a smile. In another shot, they are sitting next to each other. Barrie is looking ahead and Bergner is hugging his arm, her head on his shoulder, her eyes closed, her face softened by a serene expression.

Barrie's and Bergner's relationship was a quite unique occurrence in both their lives. There was warmth and familiarity between them, and an intensity that is likely to have stemmed from the knowledge of deeper affinities. The exiled Bergner appealed to Barrie's parental instincts. She let him reassure and protect her. At the same time, she flattered and amused him. Wary of romantic attachments, they both enjoyed affectionate friendships as a safer kind of human contact against their fear of rejection and as a defence against their darker moods. In his obituary of Barrie, tellingly entitled 'Barrie: The Man with Hell in His Soul', Shaw wrote that he was 'a most affectionate creature, and his work … full of affection. Yet his plays are terrifying. Behind all the tenderness and the playfulness there is the sense of inexorable destiny.' In a way, something similar could be said of Bergner. Her playful nature and whimsical charm went hand in hand with her fearfulness, her nervous energy and her almost demonic ability, as an actress, to reach into the deepest recesses of her soul. Just as Barrie's stories and plays hide an undercurrent of tragedy and sadness behind the veneer of a sentimental fantasy world, Bergner's tantalizing playfulness could be disturbing.

James Barrie and Elisabeth Bergner were also bound on an artistic plane. Barrie's Scottish origins and his fascination with myths and fairies were closer to Bergner's almost otherworldly wistfulness and to her early passion for circus and magic than to the background of any other actress he had met in the past. She was not just the right actress to play his surreal, childlike characters. She was such a character herself.

The roots of Bergner's visionary acting and her waif-like persona are partly reminiscent of the simple forms of entertainment of the Viennese funfair of her childhood. Her style and diction were subjective and in stark contrast with the codes of classical theatre. When her friends referred to Bergner as a 'child of nature', they alluded to her particular ability to be spontaneous and emotionally truthful. Yet her emotions ran deep, and she exposed them through her characters. This is what drew the English in their thousands to Shaftesbury Avenue in the winter of 1934. At a time when British theatre offered mainly entertainment and the opportunity for social interaction rather than emotional depth, this Jewish girl from Vienna stirred people's feelings as few had done before. Despite her openness towards a new culture and her ability to act in a language that was not her own, Bergner did not change the face of British theatre. Nowadays, very few people remember her name. Her foreignness must have been too palpable and her choice of roles did not always work in her favour. But her extraordinary triumph in London marked a unique moment in the history of Anglo-German encounters. Elisabeth Bergner, a creature imbued with the artistic vitality of Jewish Vienna and the transgressive spirit of Weimar Berlin, awakened dormant feelings within the British psyche. On a personal level, her friendship with J. M. Barrie is a reflection of this. On a wider scale, she bewitched men with her childish ways and made English ladies cry. At the London premiere of *Escape Me Never* in December 1933, Queen Mary asked to meet her and is reported to have said: 'You make me cry, Miss Bergner.' One wonders if Bergner detected the Queen's slight German accent.

April

Stefan Lorant settles in London. Wolf Suschitzky, Edith Tudor-Hart and Bill Brandt take photographs of the city and its inhabitants

On 2 April 1934, the Austrian tenor Richard Tauber arrives at Dover. The object of his visit, according to his landing card, is to 'make films'. His address for the following three months will be 'Elstree Studios'.

On the afternoon of 5 April James G. McDonald lands at Southampton.

On 12 April, Stefan Zweig writes to his friend Romain Rolland that he recently heard an impressive speech by Wickham Steed, in which the journalist described the horrors of a forthcoming war with Germany with chilling clarity. Zweig believes Steed to be one of the few Englishmen aware of imminent danger, as most British people seem completely immune to fear.

On 16 April, an exhibition entitled *Austria in London: Austrian National Exhibition of Industry, Art, Travel and Sport* opens at Dorland Hall, on Lower Regent Street. It is a nationalistic affair supported by Chancellor Dollfuss. At the opening ceremony, the president of the Anglo-Austrian Association laments the end of the Austrian monarchy and introduces the show as a testimony to the country's former glory. A concert by Richard Tauber at the Austrian Embassy completes the celebrations.

On 19 April the Liberal politician Robert Bernays, a committed anti-Nazi, writes in his diary that 'news from Germany is very grave, since the country is claiming complete sovereignty in regard to her armaments, just as she did before the war'.

The following day, the German poet Max Herrmann-Neiße moves with his wife and their Jewish benefactor, the precious-stone dealer Alphonse Sondheimer, into a four-bedroom flat on the sixth floor of a new apartment block on Great

Cumberland Street, near Marble Arch. Herrmann-Neiße does not feel at home in London, speaks very little English and misses Berlin.

On 21 April, *The Times* reports that 'Herr Hitler spent his birthday quietly at Munich'.

On 23 and 24 April, Richard Tauber performs the part of Goethe during a BBC recording of the romantic operetta *Frederica* by Franz Lehár, to be transmitted on both evenings on national radio. Tauber's English dialogue is spoken by an understudy.

On 25 April, Inspector Hubert Morse of Scotland Yard's Special Branch reports on Nazi plans to establish a German House in London in order to promote German business and to boost Anglo-German relations. He notes that 'the old-established club here, the Deutsche Verein, and also the Anglo-German Academic Bureau' are reluctant to 'relinquish their individuality and go entirely into the Nazi Party camp'.

On the afternoon of 26 April, James G. McDonald has tea with several notable supporters of the refugee cause. 'In the discussion period', he writes, 'Wickham Steed emphasized the increasing militarization of Germany and the greater degree of antisemitism there'.

That night, the thirty-year-old Theodor Adorno is staying at a small hotel in Bayswater. He is preparing for an interview with the Academic Assistance Council and hopes that he will be offered a position at a British university.

On the following evening, the Vienna Philharmonic arrives at Victoria Station 'accompanied by its conductor, Herr Bruno Walter, and [is] given an enthusiastic reception by a number of its compatriots and English admirers'. Over the weekend, Bruno Walter conducts a programme of German and Austrian music at the Queen's Hall and at the Royal Albert Hall.

On Monday 30 April, Covent Garden opera season opens with a new production of Wagner's *Ring* conducted by Sir Thomas Beecham.

Chapter 2
A living art

The work and world of refugee photographers

Figure 8 Wolfgang Suschitzky, *Near Monument Station, London*, 1938.

A talented family

A photograph of a London street corner near Monument underground station is dominated by a huge advertising poster showing a baby's face. The child looks up, holding its hand to its mouth with a serious expression, but he or she may also be hiding a smile behind those chubby fingers. Beneath the poster, in 1930s London, life goes on as normal. On the left, a policeman in a custodian helmet and a long black coat with white cuffs over the sleeves turns his head towards the oncoming traffic. Behind him, a car is approaching and a man on a delivery bicycle is cycling by, a large metal box mounted on the front wheel. At the centre of the scene, a horse-drawn cart is veering behind a van, while two larger lorries move into the street on the other side. On the right, a young man, dressed in a dark suit with a white handkerchief peeking out from his breast pocket, strolls through the photograph's foreground with his head turned towards the cart. The railings and the round sign above the station's entrance are visible on the edge of the picture, where another man is walking up the stairs. Each one of these people is looking in a different direction and no one seems to be aware of the child's face that towers above them. Yet our own gaze is inevitably drawn towards it. In this picture within a picture there are two worlds: the older, familiar world of daily routine, order, commerce and tradition, and the unusual, modern world of that arresting image, whose caption boasts the arrival of a new illustrated magazine: 'The world's largest photograph announces *Illustrated*. 64 pages 2d. every Wednesday.' The child is startling because it looks very real. The portrait is not the result of a static studio photograph, but a natural close-up, animated by a lively, spontaneous gesture.

The author of both images – the street scene as well as the poster – is Wolfgang Suschitzky, an Austrian émigré who had been in London for about four years by the time this picture was taken. He lived in London until his death, at the age of 104, in September 2016. He arrived from Vienna in March 1934 at the age of twenty-two. 'I left because of Fascism there', he recalled. Worsening anti-Semitism and the intolerant climate after the armed suppression of the Socialist revolution by the Dollfuss government in February of that year would have made life in Austria impossible for him.

Wolf Suschitzky was born in 1912. He grew up in a cultured, loving family with his older sister, Edith, and their parents, Wilhelm Suschitzky and Adele Bauer. Theirs was a liberal, secular Jewish background. Though middle-class, the family lived in the Viennese working-class suburb of Favoriten, in a street aptly named Petzvalgasse after the nineteenth-century inventor of the first lens for photographic portraiture. Wolf's parents were left-wing. His father and uncle, Wilhelm and Philipp Suschitzky, founded Vienna's first socialist bookshop and publishing house, which they managed for many years until the Nazis invaded Austria in 1938. This is how Wolf described his father's beginnings as a pioneering bookseller in one of city's more disadvantaged areas:

> My father was known to be a socialist and had a bookshop in the working-class district of Favoriten. You had to have a permit to start any job in Vienna. And they said you don't need a bookshop in this district, it's all working-

class people. They can go into the centre of town where there are plenty of bookshops. Until somebody in parliament brought it up and then they had to give him and his brother permission to start the bookshop.

This was in 1901. Despite being subjected to frequent opposition from the authorities over the years, the shop thrived. It became a successful business and an influential centre for progressive culture. The brothers began to run a lending library, so that the poorest could have access to books, and founded their own publishing house. At a time of rapid population expansion and social unrest, their guiding principles were belief in the enlightening value of books and a firm commitment to the education of the disadvantaged. After the war, their ideas and business practices reflected the pioneering achievements of the Austrian social democrats during the period known as 'Red Vienna'. In 1919, the Social Democrats had won the elections and the old empire had collapsed. Despite bleak postwar conditions, the Vienna city council had embarked on an impressive plan of social welfare and administrative reforms. A housing programme was initiated through public funding (Favoriten was one of the districts affected by the new housing strategy). Other services, such as public baths, social kitchens, laundries and nursery schools, were set up to improve the living standards of a city with a large working-class population.

The Suschitzky brothers printed works by social democratic authors, such as the founder of the Austrian Social Democratic Workers' Party, Victor Adler. They published studies on pacifism, psychoanalysis, psychiatry and women's rights, as well as educational material on – among other things – alcoholism, family planning and sexual health. In Wolf Suschitzky's words: 'They published books about women's health, about the right to abortion, about birth control – and against the clergy, which they didn't like at all. But the shop did last until 1938.'

Although the bookshop survived until then, its productive life had ended four years earlier:

Just after I left in 1934, my father shot himself. He didn't want to live any more. He suffered from depressions, which in those days couldn't be treated at all. His brother and his wife, my aunt, went to Paris, because they had a daughter there, running exercise classes mainly for women. She was well established for many years, but then the French police handed them over to the Germans and they ended up in a concentration camp and disappeared.

Wolf's mother, together with his uncle's sons, Joseph and Willi, managed to escape from Austria and settled in England in 1939. His two cousins also became booksellers. Joseph Suschitzky was for a time director of Foyles, before he and his brother set up a well-known antiquarian bookshop in Hampstead called Libris.

Wolf would have liked to study zoology, but thought that photography offered better employment opportunities. By 1934, he had spent three years at the Institute for Graphical Research in Vienna, where his teacher was Rudolf Koppitz, a leading fine-art photographer. 'I mainly learnt how to touch up a negative, to get the wrinkles out, that sort of thing, which I never used later', he remembered. Clearly, the course had taught him little about the kind of photography that he would go on to develop in exile.

His sister Edith, also a photographer, had already settled in London. She had married an English doctor and was now Mrs Tudor-Hart. She lived in a flat in a semi-detached, neoclassical building at 158a Haverstock Hill in Belsize Park, on the southern edge of Hampstead. By the 1930s the area, a comfortable upper-middle-class enclave in Victorian times, had been in decline for over a decade. Since the end of the First World War, many of its large houses had been converted into flats, and the appearance of rows of shops and new apartment blocks signalled the area's social transformation. Yet it always retained an aura of elegance and a reputation as one of London's foremost artistic and literary quarters. In 1934, Edith Tudor-Hart could count as her neighbours the artists associated with the newly established art group Unit One (among them Barbara Hepworth, Ben Nicholson and Henry Moore), as well as her own friend Jack Pritchard, one of the British pioneers of modernist design and architecture.

Sometime in March of that year, Wolf and his Dutch girlfriend arrived in London, where they married and stayed with Edith at 158a Haverstock Hill. They only remained in England for a short time, probably a month, which was the usual limit for a visitor's permit. Wolf Suschitzky:

I couldn't get a working permit so I couldn't earn any money here. I was with a Dutch girl whom I met in the photographic school I went to in Vienna and we could earn a little money taking portraits of children in Holland, but luckily she left me after a year, because had I stayed in Amsterdam I wouldn't be alive any more.

In an interview, Suschitzky answered the question about whether he took photographs during those weeks in London with a simple: 'Yes, I always took photographs.' Indeed, he did. In fact, some of his best-known pictures were taken in London before his departure for Holland in the spring of 1934.

One is entitled *Lyons Corner House*. It shows a couple having tea at the Lyons' restaurant on Tottenham Court Road and it testifies to the photographer's ability to convey a distinctive sense of place, of social climate, of life being lived. Here is how Suschitzky commented on this photograph:

The Corner Houses were pleasant places to eat in, or simply to have afternoon tea. A quartet played music in the afternoons. The waitresses wore white headbands and were called Nippies, because they nipped around very quickly … I had tea there and noticed these neighbours. It looked to me as if she was giving him a bad time.

In Suschitzky's work, social observation and human interest coincide. Sometimes, as in the case of his remarks on this picture, his sense of humour affectionately interpreted a detail in his subjects' behaviour. He was a discreet yet accurate observer of the rules of social interaction. This is particularly evident in his early photographs of London, where, as a newly arrived foreigner, he noticed aspects of British life that might have escaped the attention of someone local.

After returning to London from Amsterdam in 1935, Wolf began to work as a professional photographer and then as a filmmaker. At first, he worked as a freelancer. In 1937–8 he took a series of photographs of London's Charing Cross Road, a street for which – as someone who grew up surrounded by books – he had a particular fondness. Today, these pictures are among the most evocative images of London in the 1930s.

In the years that followed, Suschitzky became a successful photographer of children and animals and, as the assistant of one of the initiators of the documentary film movement, Paul Rotha, he made educational pictures for the Ministry of Information during the war. Suschitzky's training as a documentary

Figure 9 Wolfgang Suschitzky, *Lyons Corner House. Tottenham Court Road*, 1934.

filmmaker shaped his future career as a cinematographer. In one of his best-known collaborations, with Mike Hodges on *Get Carter* in 1971, the long shots that reveal the oppressive bleakness of Tyneside's industrial landscape are a testament to Suschitzky's career in realist filmmaking. In other films, such as the Oscar-winning short film *The Bespoke Overcoat* (1956), the photographer's lyrical use of light and darkness is so striking as to appear almost expressionistic. Yet his reply to the question of whether he was influenced by Weimar cinema is disarmingly modest: 'Not really, no. The idea was to get on to the screen what the director wanted. I didn't want to create a work of art, but I always encouraged directors to look through the camera to see what they're filming.'

In 1942, Wolf Suschitzky collaborated with Rotha on *World of Plenty*, a documentary that addressed the question of food production and distribution before, during and after the end of the war. One of the scriptwriters on the film was Carl Mayer, the legendary playwright of Weimar cinema and author of *The Cabinet of Dr Caligari* (and good friend of Elisabeth Bergner). Asked if he remembered him, Suschitzky recalled the sad end of a man for whom emigration had meant ruin: 'I met him once or twice. Poor man, he had no money and had no way of earning any. Rotha gave him some script corrections, but he really died of hunger. He was an important man.'

Figure 10 Wolfgang Suschitzky at his home in London in 2010.

Wolf Suschitzky, on the other hand, was able or – as he would have it – 'lucky' enough to launch a successful career in Britain. His particular fortune lay in the fact that he often encountered people whose interests coincided with his own. His passion for zoology, for example, found expression when Rotha introduced him to a team of filmmakers who were working with the biologist Julian Huxley, secretary of the Zoological Society at the time. Suschitzky's professional association with Huxley lasted for many years and sealed his fame as the first great animal photographer: 'I was the first photographer to take animals seriously, not just as four legs and a tail.'

Suschitzky's empathy towards animals extended to all his models. The engaging way with which he looked at the world through his camera lens – be it in still or moving images – is a legacy of his tolerant and democratic upbringing. But there is also something else: a communicative impulse, and the visual ability to capture a meaningful section of what he is seeing. In this respect, the most profound influence on the development of Wolf Suschitzky's style is likely to have been his older sister, Edith Tudor-Hart.

Figure 11 Edith Tudor-Hart, *Child Staring into Bakery Window*, London, *c.* 1935.

Edith transmitted her passion to her brother, who decided to study photography thanks to her encouragement. She gave him his first camera, and he deeply admired her work: 'There are some people like my sister was, for instance, who have a great talent for choosing the right thing to separate from the surroundings. I have a little bit of that probably. But that is necessary to have in order to take an aesthetically pleasing picture.'

'The Eye of Conscience'

Almost exactly eighty years after the spring of 1934, one of Edith Tudor-Hart's most famous photographs hung in her brother's sitting room, high above the trees and canal of his west London street. It was probably taken in 1935 and is entitled *Child Staring into Bakery Window*. The setting is the East End of London. It is a powerful and troubling image, perfectly executed. It is also a classic example of political photography. Originally published in a pamphlet by the National Unemployed Workers' Movement, it was part of a campaign to raise awareness about social inequality during the lavish celebrations for George V's silver jubilee. The photograph's caption in the pamphlet read: 'On her way to collect garbage after the market has closed'. It was one of Tudor-Hart's most popular pictures in the 1930s.

The child of the title is a girl, perhaps ten years old. Her face is smudged and she has unkempt, dark curly hair. She is wearing an old jumper full of holes. On her left wrist hangs a crumpled paper bag and her hand grips a small parcel. She is standing by a bakery window, staring at its contents. Behind the clear glass, four shelves are stacked high with cakes and buns, some resting on clean paper doilies. The whiteness of the paper contrasts with the child's scruffy appearance and with the black contour of the window frame. Anything beyond the frame is irrelevant and thus invisible. The image is realistic yet carefully lit and composed. As Wolf explained, his sister was very good at separating an aesthetically powerful image from a larger picture. Tudor-Hart used art as a political weapon. Here, she is showing only what she wants us to see, namely the stark contrast between poverty and wealth and its effect on innocent lives. The camera's point of view is so close that we can read the shop's labels. The list of mouth-watering names amplifies the food's almost indecent abundance. The little girl fixes the cakes with a serious expression, her lips pressed together. There is great dignity in her stillness. The scene is touching, but the clarity with which it is recorded prevents it from becoming sentimental.

Child welfare was one of Tudor-Hart's most heartfelt causes. She was an expert in matters of children's education. In Vienna, she had studied with Lili Roubiczek, the founder of the first Austrian Montessori nursery school, which was in the same working-class district where the Suschitzkys lived. Edith was a fast learner and a gifted teacher. In 1925, at the age of seventeen, she was sent to London to attend a three-month seminar with Maria Montessori herself. In England she met her future husband, Alexander Tudor-Hart, a Communist doctor who had studied economics with John Maynard Keynes in Cambridge and orthopaedics with a renowned Viennese surgeon. Back in Austria, Edith Suschitzky became close to social democratic circles, partly encouraged by her family's humanitarian ethos, but also inspired by a more radical impulse towards revolutionary change. By 1927, she had joined the Austrian Communist Party, where she appeared under the English-sounding code name of 'Betty Gray'. Her personal and political ties with England were intensifying. She returned to London several times, and in 1930 settled down with Tudor-Hart in a house in Paddington that they shared with other Austrian Communists. Around this time, the British Security Service became aware of Edith's political connections. At the end of October 1930 she was spotted at a demonstration in Trafalgar Square. Believed 'to be on friendly terms with many of the Communist leaders', she was expelled and returned to Austria.

In Vienna, Edith continued to combine artistic practices and political activities. She published a photographic essay on Montessori education in an illustrated magazine and documented her city's social conditions through a series of pictures on poverty and on the life of ordinary people. She had done similar work in London, as in a powerful sequence of photographs taken at the Caledonian Market, published in 1931 and entitled *The Market of Naked Misery*. Her gift for capturing the humanity of ordinary people and their dismal living conditions was becoming increasingly related to her need to instigate change. In her own words, photography 'ceased to be an instrument for recording events and became a means of influencing and stimulating events. It became a living art, embracing the people.'

Despite the secrecy required by the underground activities in which she was involved, Tudor-Hart emerges as a person of great determination, generosity and warmth. Both her life and her art were guided by an ideal and her creativity was inseparable from her social commitment and revolutionary beliefs. This was a result of her upbringing and of her father's strong social principles. But the avant-garde ferment of 1920s Vienna and the studies she chose to pursue were also important elements in her personal and political development.

Edith studied photography at the Bauhaus in Dessau between 1928 and 1930. The Bauhaus was the German art school that advocated a union of art, crafts and technology guided by rationalism and functionality. It had been founded by Walter Gropius in Weimar in 1919 and had moved to the industrial city of Dessau six years later. In 1928, the Swiss architect Hannes Meyer replaced Gropius as the school's director. Meyer was ideologically left-wing and reformed the Bauhaus along radical socialist lines. He emphasized the educational elements of design and restructured the school's workshops in order to promote its connections with industry for a more practical – rather than aesthetically motivated – realization of egalitarian ideals. He stressed the needs of the people above all others. His motto was: 'The people's needs instead of the need for luxury.' Under his leadership, the Communist influence increased and the students became more politicized. Art was seen as a means of changing society and empowering the individual. To this end, Meyer adapted the school's production to the needs of the market and incorporated new workshops, such as printing, advertising and photography. The director of the photography department was Walter Peterhans, by then a successful industrial and portrait photographer in Berlin.

It seems likely that Edith Tudor-Hart pursued photography consistently only after leaving the Bauhaus, as no records remain of her work there. Although her name does not appear among Peterhans's students, she may have studied with him as a 'guest student' in 1929. The realist Bauhaus ethos during Meyer's directorship certainly made an impact on her development as a political photographer.

Another possible influence on Tudor-Hart's artistic development was the so-called 'Neues Sehen' (New Vision) movement. Though shaped by diverse artists and ideas, the movement – like the Bauhaus – evolved in Germany in the 1920s from a modernist drive towards objectivity and clarity in the decades after the devastating trauma of the First World War. To the followers of New Vision, a fresh engagement with reality entailed a great deal of experimentation with various visual and technological media, such as typography, collage, photomontage and new camera angles. These avant-garde elements were very distant from Edith's realist documentary style, yet she probably shared the movement's belief in photography as a window onto reality rather than as an abstract artistic pursuit.

Above all, Edith remained a political photographer. Her focus (as that of her brother) was on human beings and urban spaces, and her main preoccupation was the use of photography as a means to instigate social change. Her eye, which Wolfgang Suschitzky perceptively referred to as 'The Eye of Conscience', showed reality from a perspective intended to make the viewer think and react.

Conspirators

In late May 1933, after the interdiction of the Austrian Communist Party earlier that month, Edith Tudor-Hart was stopped by the police outside a bookshop in Vienna, arrested for carrying illegal material and detained for several weeks. In August she was free. Meanwhile, Alexander Tudor-Hart had arrived from London and the couple married at the British Consulate in Vienna. Before leaving for England, they were both recruited for Soviet intelligence work by Arnold Deutsch, a graduate student from the University of Vienna who had known Edith since 1926. Her new marital status allowed her to settle in England.

Once in London, she moved into a flat at 68 Acre Lane, Brixton, with her husband. It is unclear how long she remained in south London. The couple's security file from Special Branch does not provide her whereabouts after her return to England ('efforts will be made to ascertain her address'), but it seems likely that sometime after her arrival she moved to Belsize Park. A minute sheet in Edith Tudor-Hart's security file with details on another Austrian Communist refugee throws light on Edith's whereabouts after December 1933: 'Margarete Charlotte Moos, a student of economics … came to the UK in December 1933 … there is good reason to believe that for at least part of the time she resided at 158a, Haverstock Hill, N.W. 3, the address of Mrs Edith Tudor-Hart née Suschitzky … well known … as rendevous of persons interested in Communist matters.'

Figure 12 158 Haverstock Hill, London, 2017.

This shows that in late 1933 Edith Tudor-Hart had moved from Brixton to Hampstead, where her brother stayed after leaving Austria in March of the following year. By this time she, described in another security document as 'a freelance photographer and an extremist', was running a photography business from her flat. In Hampstead, she was close to her sister-in-law, Beatrix Tudor-Hart, whom she had befriended in Vienna, where Beatrix had studied psychology after graduating from Newnham College, Cambridge, in 1925. The Special Branch document about Edith and her husband mentions Beatrix as well: 'Dr. Hart's sister, known as Miss Helena Beatrice [sic] Tudor-Hart, who conducts a nursery school at 83, Fitzjohn Avenue, N.W. 3, is a well known extremist, and a known sympathizer with the Friends of the Soviet Union ... She lets her school premises to various gatherings of extremists.' The official tone of security documents and the sense of conspiracy they convey by reiterating words such as 'alien' and 'extremist' both simplify and demonize the life and activities of this particular community. Yet the Tudor-Harts and their circle of family and friends were gifted and cultured individuals, whose occupations and interests – in medicine, psychology, education and the arts – were driven by a powerful idealism and, above all, by the desire to combat Fascism and social injustice.

Both Alexander and Beatrix Tudor-Hart were well connected, intellectually sophisticated and highly regarded in their respective fields. After his marriage to Edith, Alexander worked as a public-health doctor in the Rhondda Valley in Wales and led the British Medical Aid Unit to Spain during the Civil War in 1936. Beatrix's first teaching post after her training in Vienna was at Beacon Hill, the progressive boarding school founded by Bertrand Russell and his wife, Dora. It was an unorthodox, free-thinking and sexually liberated environment, and Beatrix was a committed, inspirational teacher. In 1929, Beatrix had had a daughter with her lover, Jack Pritchard, whom she had introduced to Edith. Wolf Suschitzky remembers that Pritchard was very helpful to him on his first visit to London in 1929, when Suschitzky was only seventeen. Pritchard was also instrumental in furthering Edith's career after she settled back in England in 1933.

Jack Pritchard was a designer who, in 1931, founded the modernist construction-and-design firm Isokon with Wells Coates, a pioneer of modern British architecture. In their architectural practice, design was guided by the ideas of sobriety, rationality and contemporary industrial style. That summer, they travelled to Germany to visit the famous modernist Weissenhof housing estate in Stuttgart, an exhibition of family dwelling units for the working classes and an influential showcase for contemporary design. Each unit was a prefabricated model house built to a high standard in a minimal, practical utility style. The exhibition had been organized by the Deutscher Werkbund, the German Association of Craftsmen, founded in 1907 and inspired by the British Arts and Crafts movement. As in the case of the Bauhaus, the socialist ideal of good design for the masses coincided with the aesthetic imperative of combining art and craft, beauty and good quality. In 1931, Pritchard and Wells Coates also visited Berlin and the Bauhaus at Dessau. Two years later, Wells Coates began to work on his designs for the Isokon building, an experimental estate of thirty-two functional concrete units to be built on a site in Lawn Road in Hampstead and completed in the summer of 1934.

Edith Tudor-Hart, who had provided a photographic record of the construction work, was the official photographer at the opening ceremony of the Lawn Road flats on 9 July 1934. One of her photographs was taken from below and shows a section of the building's front, with part of a long white balcony and a cantilevered staircase. Groups of guests look down on the viewer from the balcony and from the flat roof. It is a sunny day. The unusual worm's-eye perspective and the geometrical architecture emphasize a modernist look. The sun gives a utopian feel to the scene, and it is interesting to think that a young Austrian Communist and former Bauhaus student should have recorded the launch of the first modernist building at the heart of one of England's oldest artistic neighbourhoods. Hampstead was already well on its way to becoming the centre of London's refugee community. Even at this early stage in the history of the German-speaking exiles in London, many foreign artists and intellectuals were living there. And as Edith's story demonstrates, the connections between the refugee community and the English progressive bourgeoisie were manifold.

Sometime in 1933, Pritchard had introduced Edith Tudor-Hart to the editor of the BBC magazine *The Listener*, R. S. Lambert, with whom she collaborated for several months. The front cover of the issue of 16 May 1934, for example, is illustrated by one of Edith's photographs, taken when she was still living in Austria. It is entitled *View from the Great Wheel on to the Prater, Vienna*, and it shows a section of the dark, spider-like metal structure of the wheel (which at the time was the tallest in the world) and a minuscule, indistinct universe below. This is an unusual image for Tudor-Hart, because there are no people in it and because, as in the picture of the launch of the Lawn Road flats, it accentuates a dynamic modernist perspective and the technological advances of industrial design. The photograph is hardly political, but the magazine's main features – entitled 'This Woman's Side of Unemployment' and 'Austria in Transition' – confirm her consistent involvement with social problems and current affairs.

While living on Haverstock Hill, a stone's throw from the Lawn Road flats, Edith Tudor-Hart was under constant surveillance by Special Branch. Her involvement with the Communist Party, with members of the bohemian intelligentsia and the refugee community in London posed a threat to the authorities. Margarete Charlotte Moos, who had already attracted the attention of the police the previous December through her connection with Edith, stated years later:

A casual acquaintance of my husband from Berlin ... thought Mrs T[udor]-H[art] might give me some work in her darkroom. This was in the summer of 1934. I went there hoping to find some work. However, there was hardly any work to be done, and later ... we went there mainly to take a bath ... and I to wash and iron my things, and to print photos, also sometimes to have a good meal, for Mrs T. H. had a very good cook. Many refugees did that, as a matter of fact. There were always two plain-clothes men standing at the corner, far away visible.

What the authorities did not know that summer was that Edith had already been enlisted as a Soviet agent at the beginning of the year. In February 1934 her old friend from Vienna, Arnold Deutsch, recruited her with the rather unsubtle code name EDITH. At the end of May, she introduced Deutsch to a new recruit, whose wife, Litzi Kohlmann, was another Austrian friend. His code name was 'Otto', his real name Kim Philby.

Tudor-Hart's reputation is partially tainted by the more obscure side of her political activities. Her close association with the names of famous spies such as Philby, and her involvement with Soviet intelligence over several years, often distract from her art. They can also cast an ambivalent light on her character. But the testimonies of those who knew her tell a different tale. As we gather from Moos's story, Edith was very supportive of her fellow refugees. Her brother also benefited from her encouragement and hospitality, and she assisted their mother and two uncles in exile at a time when her own life was becoming increasingly difficult. Edith had separated from her husband in 1936 and was raising a young child (who suffered from autism) without financial help or the security of a steady income. Her nephew, Peter Stephan Jungk, describes her as 'attractive, tall and charismatic' and records the impression of her friend, the sculptress Anna Mahler, according to whom 'Edith wanted to help anyone who was in material or emotional distress', always making other people's problems her own.

The secret police followed Edith's every move, and the unrelenting attention from the authorities weighed heavily on her. Eventually, it halted her career. In the early 1950s, the security services instructed Tudor-Hart to cease her activities as a photographer, and she destroyed many of her negatives for fear of exposing herself or her comrades. However, an MI5 report on Edith's political activities at the time of Kim Philby's interrogation in 1951 could only conclude that she had been 'possibly a talent spotter and a convinced communist in touch with top-ranking communists'.

Edith Tudor-Hart's personal story is that of a courageous and independent woman. Seen in the context of the struggle against Fascism, first in Vienna and then in England, her tireless political activity and her loyalty to her cause assume an admirable dimension. Yet her idealism was blighted by the stifling climate of intrigue and suspicion during the cold war and until her death, in a Brighton

Figure 13 Edith Tudor-Hart with her son, Tommy, photographed by Wolfgang Suschitzky.

nursing home, in 1973. As for her work, Edith Tudor-Hart's achievements – like those of other notable women photographers who came to London from central Europe – such as Dorothy Bohm, Lotte Meitner-Graf and Lucia Moholy – will always rank high in the history of modern British photography.

Even though the visual sophistication of her images was not particularly suited to the simpler, more overtly narrative style of mainstream photojournalism, in April 1939 two of Edith's pictures appeared on the pages of the popular *Lilliput* magazine, a pocket-sized publication whose aim was to inform and to entertain. The images are juxtaposed and the layout is part of the feature's message. The first photograph is of two ladies in white doctor's coats as they brush and blow-dry a bulldog that sits contentedly between them in a beauty parlour for dogs. On the next page is a photograph of an East End slum. Taken from above, it shows a small back yard enclosed by grimy walls on which hang the few, damaged possessions of a poverty-stricken household. The members of a numerous family are seen almost huddled together in the tiny space below. The high perspective of this image is in stark contrast to the clean decor and comfortable proportions of the dog parlour. The orderly whiteness of the first picture exposes the dim misery of the second. The feature is darkly satirical, but the two accompanying captions – which ask 'Should we have this?' and 'Must we have this?' – convey the urgency of a political message.

Tudor-Hart's discerning gaze highlighted the contradictions of capitalist society. She provoked her audience into engaging with reality in a direct and questioning fashion. Like her brother's photograph of the street scene at London's Monument station – albeit, in her case, with the added force of a subversive political streak – Tudor-Hart's images make us stop, look and think.

A new medium

The editor of *Lilliput* magazine who accepted Edith Tudor-Hart's photographs for publication in 1939 was called Stefan Lorant. The previous year, Wolf Suschitzky had showed Lorant some of his pictures: 'When I went to see him with my photographs of Charing Cross Road, he said to me: You're a very good photographer, but not a photojournalist.' Suschitzky's images, albeit realistic, did not possess the narrative drive that was necessary to tell a story through pictures. The practice of photojournalism was closely related to the idea of photographs as vehicles for information and relied on the skill of linking several images together in order to illustrate contemporary events. Photojournalism had made Lorant's name and fortune.

It had all begun exactly five years earlier. In April 1934, when Suschitzky was walking the streets of London with his camera, and his sister was working, helping friends in need and being watched by special agents on Haverstock Hill, two future protagonists of British photography and journalism arrived in London. One was Stefan Lorant, the other Bill Brandt.

Whereas Edith Tudor-Hart and Wolf Suschitzky had settled in London by chance, favoured by fortunate encounters from Edith's student days, both Bill Brandt and Stefan Lorant had a deep-seated affinity for England. Bill Brandt was born Hermann Wilhelm Brandt in Hamburg, yet claimed to have been born in south London, tried all his life to mask his German accent and was attracted to all things English. Lorant did not go as far as Brandt, and eventually became an American citizen, but he had nurtured a particular liking for England since his youth.

In June 1931, as editor-in-chief of the illustrated magazine *Münchner illustrierte Presse*, Stefan Lorant had accompanied the German chancellor, Heinrich Brüning, to meet the British prime minister, Ramsay MacDonald, in London. Lorant was dazzled by the English and their style: 'The prime minister was well dressed, good-looking, very impressive … At that time I was very much an Anglophile. I read the English writers: Shakespeare, Dickens, H. G. Wells. London was beautiful. I was impressed by Speakers' Corner, went to Wimbledon, the Derby, and the House of Lords.' The foreign observer employed all the conventional stereotypes of anglophilia: the liberal gentleman, the beauty of London and its traditions, British sporting rituals. Less than two years later Lorant, languishing in a Nazi prison for no apparent reason, dreamt again of England with even greater enthusiasm for those same old tropes:

> I love England. My happiest days were those I was able to spend in London. I love the City, Oxford Street, Pall Mall, and the Strand. I love the little restaurants in Soho and the endless streets of the East End. I love the docks and the wide space of the parks. I love the chimes of Big Ben and the bustle of Victoria Station. I love the street musicians and the political gossip in the Saloon bars. I love the high taxis and the motor-boats on the Thames. I love the flowers at Hampton Court and the speakers in Hyde Park.
>
> I always wanted to live in England. Whenever I had any free time I went to London. I would plunge into the crowd at the Derby; I would sit on the stands at Wimbledon and in the scorching heat at Lord's … The solidarity of the English people, the distinctive quality of their thought, their superiority, their conception of the gentleman, make them the guardians of civilisation in Europe.

Such extreme praise makes one wonder if this entry was edited for the benefit of the British market, where Lorant's prison diary was eventually published, with the title *I Was Hitler's Prisoner*, in 1935.

Lorant had been detained without warning in Munich in March 1933 and given no explanation for his arrest. The official organ of the Nazi Party, the *Völkischer Beobachter*, reported only that 'the arrested man is a Hungarian Jew and does not possess German citizenship'. A few weeks later, Lorant was informed of his dismissal from his newspaper firm 'by reason of official decree and emergency legislation'. He remained in prison for six months and was released at the beginning of October thanks to powerful contacts of his family in Hungary. He returned to Budapest without any money, bereft of the comforts of his old life and professional position. But he was a master of self-reinvention if ever there was one, and within two days he had been offered the editorship of a Sunday magazine, *Pesti Napló*. He also began to work on his prison diary, which he wrote at night. Six months later, his manuscript under his arm, he left Hungary with his wife, Niura, and their young son. They travelled to Paris, where Lorant tried unsuccessfully to sell his book. He then attempted his luck in England. On

Figure 14 Stefan Lorant in 1938.

the morning of 17 April 1934, he and his family registered their names as guests of the Strand Palace Hotel.

The tall, curly-haired and slightly unkempt-looking foreigner must have cut an unusual figure in London. But he had a plan, and refused to see himself as a victim of exile. Resilient, astute, business-minded and very resourceful, he had a flair for making the most of his many acquaintances. He was manipulative and flirtatious. An inveterate womanizer, he also knew how to charm male collaborators and business partners. There was something hypnotic about him. At the same time he could appear coarse, a little vulgar in his boldness. All his life, he liked to be seen with the right kind of people and had a particular talent for creating his own myth. His autobiographical tales are quite extraordinary, some probably untrue. For example, it is unlikely that he met Franz Kafka when looking for a job with a local newspaper in Czechoslovakia, but it is likely that the editor of the first magazine he worked for was a young Alexander Korda, that he shared a flat with the actor Conrad Veidt in the 1920s, and that he had a relationship with Leni Riefenstahl. It may also be true that he shot Marlene Dietrich's first screen test and that he used to meet Hitler regularly in Munich coffee houses.

István Reich was born into a Jewish bourgeois family in Budapest in 1901. He changed his name to Stefan Lorant in his early twenties, when he started to work in film. His first passion had been photography. The availability of portable cameras and the growth in the market for illustrated magazines was more advanced in continental Europe than in England. Moreover, Hungary had a vibrant and sophisticated photographic tradition. The court photographer of the Habsburg monarchy, Mai Manó, had been Hungarian. André Kertész, László Moholy-Nagy, Brassaï and Robert Capa were all originally from Hungary. The country also boasted an advanced film industry. Both the German cinema of the Weimar era and the British film industry of the 1930s and 1940s benefited greatly from the talent and experience of Hungarian producers, directors, playwrights and technicians (Alexander Korda and Emeric Pressburger spring to mind).

Lorant's enterprising spirit and early familiarity with photography and cinema allowed him to establish himself quite rapidly in both these fields. He worked as a stills photographer in Vienna and then as a cameraman at Berlin's Ufa studios. Although he did not stand out as a filmmaker, his experience in the world of silent cinema helped him to develop a keen sense of visual narrative through still images, which he later employed with enormous success in his role as a photojournalist.

His genius as a picture editor was apparent, for he knew the right formula for narrative photography. He put together picture sequences with a strong visual impact, and used short captions and chose themes that were likely to attract the attention of a wide section of the public. Sport, politics, celebrities, gossip, fashion, everyday stories – illustrated magazines reflected a dynamic, commercialized, socially and politically restless contemporary world. Thanks to the technological advances of modern photography and to the abundance of creative talent in this field, German photojournalism had emerged as a new and attractive form of communication.

A most productive week

Tuesday 17 April 1934 was a warm day for the time of year, and the sky over London promised rain. When Lorant and his family entered the noisy art deco foyer of the Strand Palace Hotel that morning, they must have been looking forward to a rest after the previous night's journey from France. Lorant's memories of this moment in his life as an immigrant do not dwell on the details usually remembered by foreigners about their arrival. He does not mention long queues at Harwich, the suspicious demeanour of immigration officers or the inevitably limited residence permit. Stefan Lorant had urgent plans, and did not know how long he was going to stay in England. His attempts to sell the manuscript of his prison diary had failed so far, and now he was going to call upon all his acquaintances in London to make things happen. In Paris, he had met John Lane and his nephew, the future founder of Penguin Books, Allen Lane, through a mutual friend. He had left his manuscript with them and had come to London a week later to elicit a response.

Lorant's choice of hotel denotes determination and ambition: determination not to be classed as an impoverished émigré and ambition to succeed. The

Strand Palace Hotel boasted one of the grandest entrance halls in London. It was an impressive, if somewhat garish, showcase of fashionable architecture. It had been designed by architect Oliver Percy Bernard in 1929 in lavish Hollywood style. Bernard knew how to mix traditional and contemporary designs, often creating an eclectic combination of Victorian abundance and linear art deco symmetry. The foyer of the Strand Palace Hotel was both decorative and geometric. It had light pink marble walls and a limestone floor. Illuminated glass features surrounded the central staircase producing a dazzling effect of bright angular patterns. In the 1930s, the hotel was favoured by guests from the Continent and by affluent refugees. Such opulence was perhaps a little too showy for English tastes, but it suited Lorant, who, although penniless at the time, had a penchant for luxury and high-priced establishments. Checking into the Strand Palace was probably meant as a statement to impress potential business partners. Lorant valued appearances ('Always, even when I had to go without food the rest of the week, I took people to the best places', he once told a girlfriend). The hotel's display of wealth, and its proximity to the Savoy – one of Lorant's favourite haunts in the years to come – suited this flamboyant Hungarian, who oozed confidence and self-belief.

That evening Stefan met Allen Lane at the Café Royal on Regent Street. But his hopes were dashed, as Lane told him that his prison diary had been rejected because a German reader thought that it would only interest the 'half a dozen people who knew the author'. The next morning Lorant went to Lane's offices at Vigo Street to collect the manuscript. Not discouraged by the setback, that same day he gave the diary to a German literary agent with offices on Oxford Street. The man was spellbound by the story, which he read through the night and sold to the Hutchinson Group for 100 guineas (£105). On the morning of Thursday 19 April, after only two days in London, Stefan Lorant had a book deal and, after paying the agent's fee, £70 in his pocket. Resolute in his desire to succeed, he turned to a Hungarian contact and headed to Fleet Street. The address was Keystone House, Red Lion Court. Here were the offices of the famous Keystone Press Agency, founded in the early 1900s by the Hungarian Bert Garai, who was now its editor and managing director. Lorant met him that afternoon. Garai offered him the chance to write articles for Keystone and promptly advanced him £7 10s. This sum, together with the money from Hutchinson, enabled the Lorants to remain in England for a while.

That same evening the family left the stylish interiors of the Strand Palace Hotel and moved into a more modest establishment, a 'private hotel' that occupied four adjacent houses on Seymour Street, near Marble Arch. Lorant continued to maintain his active calendar with undaunted energy. His poor knowledge of English did not seem to bother him, as he socialized with some of his most influential compatriots. On Friday 20 April, he dined at the home of yet another enterprising Hungarian, Nándor Fodor, who had been a journalist in New York before becoming the secretary and political advisor to the pro-Fascist press baron Lord Rothermere. Three weeks before Lorant's visit, Fodor's name was mentioned in a large advertisement in *The Times* as a member of the executive committee of the International Institute for Psychical Research. The purpose of this newly founded institution, whose vice-president was Julian Huxley, was to investigate psychic phenomena scientifically and to encourage 'every thinking person to consider the claims of life after death'. Lorant's affiliation with this curious world of wealth, spiritualism and right-wing political associations shows that he used every possible resource at his disposal to pursue his goals.

The following evening, Saturday 21 April, the German dancer and film actress Maria Matray and her husband, Hungarian theatre director Ernst Matray, visited the Lorants at their hotel. Maria's sister, the actress Johanna Hofer, was married to a star of the German stage, Fritz Kortner, who had also fled to London and was living a short walk away from the Hotel Seymour. On Sunday, Lorant visited London Zoo with his family and a friend of his wife, Dr Edward Hindle, a biologist and future regius professor of zoology at the University of Glasgow. Stefan's busy schedule also included the company of distinguished émigré writers. That night, the day at the zoo was followed by a trip to the cinema with the novelist Robert Neumann and the journalist Peter Smolka. The three men went to see the Hollywood version of H. G. Wells's *The Invisible Man*, which was being screened at the New Victoria Cinema at 5 p.m. Together with Stefan Zweig, who also lived nearby, Neumann and Smolka were among the few Austrian intellectuals who had left their country in the early 1930s, as most of their compatriots emigrated after the German annexation of Austria in March 1938. (Incidentally, Smolka's name leads us back to Edith Tudor-Hart, who knew him, as he was well acquainted with Kim Philby and his wife, Litzi, Tudor-Hart's old friend from Vienna.) Twenty-four hours later, on Monday 23 April, Lorant met with another German writer, the socialist novelist Leonhard Frank. They went to the Empire Cinema, Leicester Square, to see a glamorous Norma Shearer in *Riptide*, a romantic drama of adultery.

These were still early days in the history of the German and Austrian immigration. In April 1934 émigrés were not as conspicuous as they would be some years later when refugee cafés had 'sprung up all over London, under famous names from Berlin and Vienna'. In her fictional account of their turbulent affair, Alison Blair, one of Lorant's English girlfriends and cofounder of *Lilliput* magazine, gives a vivid description of Lorant's appearance:

> The hair, grey, yet without giving the appearance of age, curled energetically from the sloping forehead of a small, somewhat domeshaped head … [His] eyes were bold, darting, inquisitive, in a face alert and watchful as a lizard's and as a lizard does he seemed to listen as well as see with them. The nose, flattened but powerful, overshadowed a mobile, rather thin-lipped

mouth whose lower lip protruted stubbornly … He wore a dark blue suit … an obvious reach-me-down that was a little baggy here and there, as though he sometimes slept in it. His body, large and shaggy, looked softer than exercise-hardened English ones.

The sketch conveys a sense of Lorant's singularity and reveals something of how eccentric continental refugees must have appeared to the English in the 1930s. Yet Lorant was a particular type of refugee and eventually became 'the centre of a creative environment' that changed the face of British journalism. His self-belief, energy and drive knew no bounds and, despite the scepticism he elicited in some circles, he usually succeeded. On Wednesday 25 April 1934, just over a week after his arrival in London, he signed a contract with Hutchinson for the publication of *I Was Hitler's Prisoner*. In the end, the book was published by Victor Gollancz, as Lorant withdrew the rights from the Hutchinson Group because he did not approve of their English translation. With typically infallible timing, his prison diary was published almost exactly a year later. On 28 April 1935, the *Manchester Guardian* featured a detailed and enthusiastic review by Wickam Steed. '*I Was Hitler's Prisoner*', he predicted, 'will live longer than Hitler's Germany'.

At the end of what must have been one of the most productive weeks in Lorant's life, there was still an important meeting to come. That Wednesday evening, the Lorants celebrated Stefan's book deal at the home of yet another Hungarian with good Fleet Street connections. It was the thirty-one-year-old journalist Tibor Korda, whom Lorant had met during his first visit to England in 1931. According to Bernard Falk, former editor of the right-wing *Sunday Dispatch*, Korda was also a protégé of Lord Rothermere. Like Bert Garai – and, very soon, like Lorant himself – Tibor Korda was a Hungarian journalist responsible for introducing the English press to a new type of publication. He had founded the Cosmopolitan Press Agency in London in 1929. Seven years later, he would go on to create a weekly publication about current affairs, *News Review*, which prided itself on being 'Britain's first weekly news magazine'.

A meeting at Korda's home that Wednesday night sealed Lorant's fate as one of the most influential newspaper editors in the English-speaking world. Lorant was introduced to Philip Emanuel, advertising director at Odhams Press. Founded as a printing firm in 1847, Odhams had expanded considerably towards the end of the century, when it had absorbed another large printing company and added several titles to its list of publications. In the 1920s, these included the popular penny weekly *John Bull* and magazines related to the ever-expanding world of cinema, such as *The Picturegoer* and *The Passing Show*. Another weekly paper published by Odhams at the time was *Clarion*, a socialist publication created in 1891 by the author and campaigner Robert Blatchford. The magazine's leftist orientation and its association with the Clarion Cycling Club reflected Blatchford's humanitarian zeal and the effort towards the socialization of sport and moral development of the working classes in Edwardian England. By the early 1930s, with the rise of Fascism and the empowerment of the workers' movement, such ideals had become less relevant and *Clarion* was rapidly losing readers.

Lorant's personality and his journalistic knowledge made an impression on his new acquaintances, and a week later he spent a day at the Royal Automobile Club at Epsom playing golf with Philip Emanuel. Over dinner that Saturday, he also met Emanuel's son John, who was Odhams's advertising manager. On Monday, a note addressed to a 'Mr. Laurent' was delivered to the Hotel Seymour. It was from John Emanuel, who invited Lorant for lunch at the fashionable Casani's club on Regent Street on Wednesday 2 May. This time Lorant was introduced to Robert Fraser, the Australian editor of the ailing *Clarion* magazine. After further encounters with Philip Emanuel over the following week, on Tuesday 8 May Fraser, concerned about *Clarion*'s demise, asked Lorant whether he would be interested in redesigning the magazine. Eight days later, Stefan Lorant was introduced to John Dunbar, editorial director of Odhams Press:

> John Dunbar was in his shirtsleeves standing behind a desk, and he asked what I would do with Clarion. He asked me to provide an outline … I asked how long he would give me, and he suggested two weeks with a salary of £15 a week. So, shortly after arriving in England I had £30. I went back to Niura with the news that we could afford to stay for a few weeks.

On 17 May 1934, a month to the day after his arrival in London, Stefan Lorant had been entrusted with the responsibility of creating a new magazine for the British market. The following Tuesday, Dunbar introduced him to Maurice Cowan, editor of *The Picturegoer* and future editor of the publication that Lorant was about to produce. On this occasion, Lorant also met Tom Hopkinson, a young Oxford graduate who had joined *Clarion* as assistant editor in January of that year and was aware of the magazine's imminent collapse: 'As the extent of our failure became known, depression settled on us like an icy fog … at this precise moment … something altogether new arrived in the form of Stefan Lorant.'

On 1 June 1934 Stefan delivered the dummy of the new publication. It did not resemble *Clarion* at all. It was an illustrated magazine, consisting mainly of large, eye-catching photographs accompanied by short sections of text. Even its logo, white geometric characters in bold on a black square, emphasized its break with the decorative look of the past. On 7 July, the first issue of the simply titled *Weekly Illustrated* appeared without much publicity on the news stands. That same day, Dunbar applied for a resident permit for Lorant on the grounds of 'the expert knowledge of this person who had worked on a similar publication abroad'. A twelve-month permit was granted. Six weeks later, *Weekly Illustrated* could boast 200,000 readers, and the figures continued to rise.

Loo Hardy and the boarding house on Cleveland Square

After news of his initial commission for Odhams Press, Lorant and his family had moved from the Hotel Seymour to a boarding house a few hundred yards further west, near Paddington Station. It was a large Victorian building on Cleveland Square, probably at number 13. According to one source, the house did not survive the war.[1] But unless the buildings were renumbered, 13 Cleveland Square is still there today: a tall, white Victorian terraced house on five floors, with rows of unadorned identical windows and a neoclassical entrance. The area was insalubrious in those days, full of cheap hotels and single rooms to let. By the 1930s, it was inhabited mostly by workers, railway travellers, employees of the nearby St Mary's Hospital and foreigners. The streets closer to the station were known as the seedy destinations of prostitutes and their clients. With the progressive migration of the middle-classes to the suburbs, central London neighbourhoods such as Paddington, Hammersmith and St Pancras had become home to the lower strata of society and to outsiders. Today, Cleveland Square is an elegant address, a quiet, generously proportioned urban space, lined with rows of tall, early Victorian stucco terraces, with exclusive apartments and a central private garden shaded by mature plane trees. In 1934, many of those houses would have been shabby, overcrowded temporary residences for less fortunate Londoners and impecunious exiles – a world apart from the fashionable splendour of the Strand Palace Hotel.

The boarding house was one of the startling novelties in the émigré's English experience. Paddington and Bloomsbury were the most common addresses for many Central Europeans on their arrival in London. The rooms they occupied were usually simple dwellings, bleak and unwelcoming. Recurrent sources of frustration to continental foreigners were the fireplace, which was found to heat only a small space around it while leaving the rest of the room stone cold, and the blandness of English food. But there were also deeper reasons for the misery felt by many in the strange no-man's-land of boarding-house life. This kind of living caused a particular form of alienation, precipitated by financial hardship in an unfamiliar environment, characterized by the impersonal nature of communal accommodation and by a feeling of loneliness ironically combined with a loss of privacy. Boarding houses were places where estrangement from one's surroundings extended to everyday objects, smells, colours and sounds. Robert Neumann, Lorant's friend and a fellow resident at 13 Cleveland Square, put it this way:

---

[1] See Association of Jewish Refugees in Great Britain, *Britain's New Citizens: The Story of the Refugees from Germany and Austria, 1941–1951* (London, 1951), 55.

O second room in that London boarding house … the first of a long and gloomy series of boarding houses that changed as people's faces changed and yet remained diabolically equal. You can't look the room in the face any longer. You hate the mirror, the string of coloured-glass beads on the reading-lamp, the creaking door and the mouldy smell of the cupboard … Has anyone yet written the great martyrdom of wall-paper? … The wall-paper duller and yet more glaring, the mirror blind, plugs blocked, the souls of past tenants lurking in all the corners, two people squabbling next door and someone playing the piano.

This could have been an illustration of life at the Paddington boarding house. And yet this address appears to have possessed a spirit of hospitality and warmth that other similar establishments lacked. The merit went to its landlady, a cheerful and motherly character in her late thirties called Loo Hardy. She charged 'thirty shillings a week, including breakfast', and her rooms were well heated.

Born in Berlin to a Jewish family in 1898, Charlotte Levi had chosen Loo Hardy as her screen name. Having lost her husband during the war, she had become a music-hall and film actress in the early days of silent cinema. For a time in the 1920s, at the height of her career, she played lead roles in romantic melodramas and even had her own show, a series of comic and adventure sketches known as *Hardy-Streifen* (Hardy-strips). Her older brother was Manfred Noa, a film and art director who specialized in historical films. In 1922, he had directed a very successful screen version of Lessing's drama *Nathan the Wise*, with Werner Krauß as the protagonist. The film, like the original play, was a plea for humanity and religious tolerance, and had attracted a great deal of negative attention from a recently founded Nazi Party, whose members tried to ban the film's screening in 1923. Noa had also directed both Maria Matray and her husband, Ernst, on several occasions. It is easy to imagine that, years later, the conversations between the Matrays and their friend Stefan Lorant in London revolved around old memories of the Weimar film world and took place in the home of Manfred's sister in Cleveland Square. A photograph of Loo Hardy and her brother in 1921 shows them together as they perform a dance step called 'the Capuchin'. They are facing each other with knees bent akimbo, elbows resting on the hips, the tips of their index fingers touching. They are both smiling. Loo's smile is broad and open under her blonde bob and a floral cloche hat.

Manfred Noa died in Berlin in December 1930 and Loo emigrated to London sometime after the Nazis came to power in 1933. Her house was large enough to offer refuge to several émigrés and it became an institution of sorts, a German Jewish island known to many in the London exile community. In the summer of 1934, a twenty-year-old Lilli Palmer – future Hollywood star and Mrs Rex Harrison – arrived from Berlin and, having spent too much money on a taxi from Victoria, knocked timidly at Loo Hardy's door:

Loo Hardy

Figure 15 Loo Hardy as a young actress in Berlin.

The city seemed endless, jet black, hostile. At long last we stopped in front of an ugly old house, one in a long row of similar houses ... suddenly the door opened. I saw a light and tiny woman with platinum blonde hair, and a voice said in German: 'For goodness' sake, you poor child! We'd almost given you up.' Lo Hardy [*sic*] ... After a hot bath and a long night's sleep, I woke up in a warm room.

Palmer remembered the homely atmosphere of the house at Cleveland Square, which she recalled in less disheartening terms than her co-tenant Robert Neumann. Conversation among the lodgers, mostly from Germany and Austria, usually revolved around the tragic situation at home and the burning topic of English residence and labour permits, which were almost impossible to obtain. Many of the guests worked in film, and in the evenings their landlady liked to hear accounts of how they had fared in their search for a job in the London studios: 'Lo Hardy … in particular, reliving former glories, wanted to know all the details.' One can imagine how Loo, motherly, friendly, lonely at heart, busy shopping and looking after her lodgers, would warm her soul by reliving the memories of her glory days in film and by encouraging her young tenants as they pursued a career that she no longer had. In 1937, Hardy's lodgers revolted in protest, as the Nazi film director Franz Wenzler was planning to stay at the house. By that stage in her life as an exile, Loo was under heavy financial strain and struggling to pay her bills. She committed suicide at the age of forty. On 27 April 1938, a short announcement entitled 'German Film Actress's Suicide: Attempt to Run a Boarding House', appeared in *The Times*:

> At the inquest at Paddington yesterday on the body of Mrs Charlotte Levi, 40, formerly a German film actress known as Loo Hardy, who died in hospital during the weekend, it was found that death was due to narcotic poisoning, and a verdict of 'suicide while of unsound mind' was recorded.
>
> Police-constable Tarbat said that in a flat at her address at Cleveland Square he found bills for rent, renovations, and other things and a chemist's account for various pills and drugs. A tumbler in the bathroom contained the residue of certain tablets … The Coroner … said that Mrs Levi had been trying to run a boarding house, but was hampered by want of capital. She was behind on her rent and income-tax, for which she had received a final notice, and she was overdrawn at the bank. She had also been getting cheques returned by tradesmen and others who refused to supply goods any longer except for cash.

Glimpses of Loo Hardy's congeniality as she surrounded herself with people from a distant past and reminisced about her old life begin to fade. She is one of exile's victims, and the house in Cleveland Square is a touching testament to her attempt to forge a new existence out of the fragments of a world that no longer existed.

Thinking in pictures

Stefan Lorant and his family lived in Cleveland Square for eight months between May and December 1934. Loo Hardy's establishment was as much a piece of Germany in London as *Weekly Illustrated*, the magazine created by Lorant and launched on 7 July of that year. Yet whereas the former vanished with its landlady's death, the latter marked a new beginning.

By the time of Hardy's suicide in the spring of 1938, her former tenant Stefan Lorant was the chief editor of one of the greatest successes in the history of British journalism, *Picture Post*. Launched on 1 October 1938 and published by Edward Hulton, *Picture Post* was the first British weekly to reach a readership of over 1 million within two months. It had large photo spreads, with cutting-edge photography and a strong democratic message. Its ideology and format resembled those of the other pictorials created by Stefan Lorant: *Lilliput*, the diminutive magazine that entertained its readers through a clever mix of photography, humour and short fiction, and *Weekly Illustrated*, which ran from July 1934 until 1939.

Lorant only edited the first twenty-two issues of *Weekly Illustrated* before he left England in December 1934. He had quit his job in frustration at the difficult working conditions at the magazine. The publication had been entirely his brainchild. He chose the topics, images, captions and the general visual layout of every issue. Yet his official capacity was only that of picture editor. It was Maurice Cowan who featured as the chief editor, since it was considered safer not to have a foreign name at the head of a new British publication. Lorant resented this state of affairs, as he resented the intrusion and control from others in a crammed London office. He was not a team player; he had his own distinct editorial vision and pursued it with unshakeable determination. He did not feel valued by his superior at Odhams, and his only collaborator – photographers aside – was Tom Hopkinson (who would go on to become the editor of *Picture Post* after Lorant's departure for America in 1940). The magazine thrived under Lorant's supervision. Despite the almost complete lack of publicity, the publication caught on. It didn't reach the dizzying figures that followed the launch of *Picture Post*, but it achieved a considerable success. Most importantly, *Weekly Illustrated* introduced the British public to a new style of journalism.

Victorian England had been at the vanguard of pictorial journalism. Lorant's *Weekly Illustrated* revolutionized the genre and catapulted British newspaper readership into the twentieth century. In 1842, the *Illustrated London News* had introduced images into journalism. Much copied, and a staple of Victorian life for decades, the magazine was the precursor of the tabloid papers and Sunday supplements of today. Each issue had an average of twenty wood-engraved pictures to accompany articles that reported on a wide range of social and cultural events. The coverage of international news items next to images of places from distant corners of the globe began to narrow man's sense of time and space.

Lorant's *Weekly Illustrated* was by no means the first English-language publication to exploit the magical power of pictures. Documentary photo-reportages had already been published in America, for example at the time of the civil war in the 1860s and, decades later, during the Great Depression. In Britain during the First World War, Lord Rothermere's *Sunday Pictorial* boasted a reputation as the best picture paper. And in the 1920s magazines such as *Pictorial Weekly* had begun to employ the innovations of modern photography by juxtaposing texts and images, mostly as a visual commentary to sensationalist stories. Stefan Lorant, however, gave an entirely different twist to this kind of publication.

Now that we are used to seeing large photographs on the front pages of every newspaper, it is difficult to imagine the impact of *Weekly Illustrated*. Yet in 1934, utterly eye-catching, Lorant's creation was modern in a way unknown to the British press at the time. Its most revolutionary features were its left-leaning political stance, as well as the style, size and role of the pictures. One innovation in particular elevated this magazine above all others: *Weekly Illustrated* was the first British publication to subvert the relationship between words and pictures. Whereas all other pictorial magazines had used images to illustrate a story, here the images were the story; the photographs spoke for themselves.

The origins of this type of newspaper were distinctly German. *Weekly Illustrated* was modelled on the great picture weeklies of the Weimar era, especially the *Berliner illustrierte Zeitung* and the *Münchner illustrierte Presse*. It also resembled the Hungarian Sunday weekly edited by Lorant in Budapest after his release from prison. All these publications had benefited from the cultural ferment of postwar continental Europe. Their originality was both political and technological. On the one hand, they supported a socialist outlook by focusing on the common man. On the other, their editors were assisted by the advances in German photography, especially the introduction of small cameras. In 1924 and 1925, two new models from Ermanox and Leica allowed photographers to use natural light, wide-aperture lenses and fast exposure times. This enabled them to overcome the static nature of old-fashioned photography, to catch the fleeting moment. As a result, images became spontaneous and informal. Photography had become journalism. Images could show a whole social universe by documenting different sides of a single event, from a sporting match to a political demonstration. They fixed significant moments and revealed a person's psychology by catching a momentary glance or an involuntary gesture.

As picture editor of *Weekly Illustrated*, Lorant reused some of the most striking photo-essays from some of the magazines he had edited in the past. A notable example is 'A Day in the Life of Mussolini' by the German photographer Felix H. Man. Lorant had printed the feature in the *Münchner illustrierte Presse* in 1931, published it in *Pesti Napló* in 1933 and reissued it in *Weekly Illustrated* on 4 August 1934. These photographs provide a rare behind-the-scenes look at history as it happened. They show Benito Mussolini in a new light. Never before had a head of state – and an absolute ruler at that – been depicted in such a candid manner. The juxtaposition of images as printed in the *Weekly Illustrated* six-photo spread reveals Lorant's skill in devising the most arresting layout and graphic presentation. He chose a handful of particularly telling photographs and captured the reader's attention through a subtle use of contrasts: between close-ups and long shots, people and empty spaces, light and shade. People's curiosity for the real person behind the Duce's official image was satisfied through a series of pictures that show an ordinary human being as he conducts his daily affairs. There is Mussolini in his study talking to his subordinates. The objects around him – an ornate desk lamp, some papers, a wall relief – appear more prominent than the man himself. Then we see Mussolini reading the newspaper, his eyes lowered on to the page in an unguarded pose of simple concentration – a shot that illustrates the photographer's idea of showing the Duce's 'real face, unposed'.

The originality of Felix H. Man's pictures was partly due to the technical advances that enabled him to recreate natural lighting conditions indoors and work with small, unobtrusive cameras. There was no posing, no pretence. As Man himself put it: 'an entirely new way was approached by returning to simplicity, rejecting all artificial means and by giving psychological factors precedence'.

The collaboration between Man and Lorant reflects the cultural vitality but also the vagaries of life in twentieth-century Europe between the wars. These were years of upheaval, of travels and escapes, of chance encounters in exile and groundbreaking work in the face of personal hardship and external aggression. Man's real name was Hans Baumann. He was a German gentile

Figure 16 From the photo-essay by Felix H. Man, 'A Day in the Life of Mussolini', 1931.

and a committed anti-Nazi. He had fought in the First World War and taken photographs in the trenches. In the 1920s he moved to Berlin, became an experienced photojournalist and travelled the world with his camera. He left Germany with a small suitcase to avoid suspicion in May 1934 and travelled to London. He had no employment prospects and a residence permit that lasted three months. After two years of casual work and temporary labour permits, he joined the staff of the *Daily Mirror* in 1935 and eventually changed his name to his more English-sounding pseudonym.

Hans Baumann and Stefan Lorant had met in Berlin in 1929, when Lorant edited the *Münchner Illustrierte Presse*. Two years later, they travelled to Rome together for the Mussolini photo-shoot. Eventually, they parted ways – until they bumped into each other in Southampton Row in London sometime after Baumann's arrival in May 1934. 'You are exactly the man I would most have liked to meet', said Lorant. That was the beginning of their cooperation and of Man's English career.

Other famous photographers worked with Lorant that year, when some of the most remarkable photo-essays of the 1930s appeared on the pages of *Weekly Illustrated*. In the issue of 1 December 1934 – the last one edited by Lorant himself – Brassaï's two-page spread entitled 'Paris after Dark' featured a collection of images that combine the documentary style of continental photojournalism with an eerie quality, reminiscent of the Surrealist concern for the equivocal aspects of civilized society. The layout of his Parisian pictures is a brilliant example of Lorant's intelligent page design, characterized by a carefully calibrated contrast between mysterious urban landscapes and striking human portraits.

Visually compelling features appeared in *Weekly Illustrated* week after week during Lorant's editorship, as he and his collaborators fused new aesthetics and sophisticated photographic techniques with eye-catching page displays. In July 1934, the major report in the first issue of *Weekly Illustrated* concerned the Wimbledon tennis championship. The magazine's cover showed a large photograph of Helen Jacobs, the American runner-up at the ladies' singles that year. The decision to put a sportswoman of Jewish descent on the cover of the new publication signalled its editor's forward-thinking stance. Lorant wanted to appeal to a broad section of the public and champion an egalitarian perspective. Most British papers covered the Wimbledon championship every year, but Lorant did it differently. He chose to put Helen Jacobs on the cover not only because she was Jewish and had just caused a stir by becoming the first woman to play in shorts, but also because she had worn them in the presence of the queen. Another interesting fact about the Wimbledon photo-essay is that most photographs inside the magazine depicted the spectators rather than the athletes themselves. Lorant included several photographs of the visitors, of single individuals among the crowd. He knew how to bring his readers closer to important events and make them into protagonists. Even the feature's title –

'Wimbledon: A Mirror of the World's Greatest Tennis Tournament' – emphasized the idea of the event as seen from the people's viewpoint.

Lorant portrayed the common man (as in the Wimbledon pictures) and showed famous people as ordinary individuals (as in the photo-essay on Mussolini). This proved very popular with the public. The photographs published in *Weekly Illustrated* were not as overtly political as Edith Tudor-Hart's rousing images of social inequality, but they were poignant, often spectacular, and always intensely real. Not only was Lorant teaching his British readers to think in pictures. The picture-stories he printed also encouraged people to think.

A different gaze

Wolf Suschitzky, Stefan Lorant and Bill Brandt were very different personalities. Simplistically, Suschitzky could be described as young and idealistic, Lorant as ambitious and enterprising, Brandt as secretive and introspective. The first two clearly represented their respective backgrounds: Suschitzky the Socialism of Red Vienna and Lorant the modern cultural fervour of Austria-Hungary and Weimar Berlin. Brandt's personality was more complex, for he encompassed disparate influences and tried to suppress his German identity. Yet he was deeply imbued with German culture: his images possess the stark visual contrasts and the symbolic intensity of Expressionist aesthetics, and his subjects are often evocative of the critique of bourgeois values as portrayed in German and Austrian modernist literature. French Surrealism also played a significant role in his artistic development. Brandt's photography is strangely compelling because it is both foreign and very English.

On 2 April 1934 the twenty-nine-year-old Bill Brandt and his Hungarian wife, Eva Boros, left Paris for London. They arrived just after the Easter weekend, during a week 'made delightful by sunshine', and settled in Belsize Park, where they moved into separate flats. Brandt's address was 43 Belsize Avenue. His wife lived three streets up the hill, at 24 Lyndhurst Road. This unusual living arrangement reflects a non-conformist lifestyle as well as Brandt's need for isolation and seclusion. Bill and Eva Brandt were a strikingly good-looking and somewhat bohemian couple. For a time, after meeting in Vienna in 1928, they had lived in a seemingly harmonious *ménage à trois* with Brandt's previous girlfriend, the Russian Lyena Barjansky. Now Bill and Eva were settling in London after years of travels on the Continent, where they had both worked as photographers. They were unemployed and with no work prospects on their arrival in London, but received a monthly allowance of about £30 from Brandt's father. Despite their artistic existence in Hampstead, they were able to partake of the life of the privileged through Brandt's paternal uncles, who were merchant bankers and lived in luxury in South Kensington and in their Surrey country estates.

It is unlikely that at this early stage of their life in London Bill and Eva Brandt knew the young Wolf Suschitzky, who was visiting his sister nearby. Suschitzky remembered knowing Bill Brandt, but not very well. He probably first met him after returning to London from Amsterdam in 1935, and was better acquainted with Brandt's younger brother Rolf, whom he remembered as 'a very good artist' (Rolf Brandt, who had preceded his brother to London in 1933, was a distinguished painter and illustrator). Yet Brandt must have been aware of the artistic community around Edith Tudor-Hart, Jack Pritchard and their progressive Hampstead circle. He may have known Edith in Vienna, and it is even possible that he came to England in 1934 to photograph Welsh miners at her suggestion. But as a fellow Belsize Park resident, he appears to have kept his distance. On the one hand, Brandt shared the social concerns about poverty and inequality that animated Tudor-Hart's work. On the other, his images are never wholly political. Brandt remembered reading J. B. Priestley's and George Orwell's writings about the condition of the working class when he first arrived in London. Orwell's *Down and Out in Paris and London* had come out in 1933. Priestley's *English Journey*, the popular travelogue that charts the social divisions of early 1930s England, had been published amid great publicity just days before Brandt's arrival, at the end of March 1934. But although Brandt's documentary pictures of working-class Londoners and Welsh miners show an awareness of social injustice, and although he had a particularly keen eye for the peculiarities of the British class system, he remained a detached observer and his aim was primarily artistic. Brandt used to compose, develop and retouch his photographs very meticulously, often using friends and family members as actors. He created images that were arranged as scenes are on a stage. Reality was subtly altered to reveal a deeper, more ambiguous version of situations and objects. There is something unsettling in most of Brandt's pictures, a cryptic quality behind the naturalistic exterior.

Some of the photographs from his first year in England are telling in this respect. Like Suschitzky, in the spring of 1934 Brandt wandered the streets of London with his camera. During the weeks and months following his arrival, we imagine him leaving his flat with his Rolleiflex slung around his neck and descending into the centre of town from the suburban seclusion of Belsize Park. The photographs he took at the time reveal Brandt as a documentary photographer with a remarkable ability to hide secret meanings behind the surface. It is difficult to say what those meanings are. As in the works of Franz Kafka, the only German-speaking writer whom he openly admired, the people and objects in Brandt's pictures are both realistically vivid and disturbingly elusive.

Among the photographs probably taken in 1934 there is one entitled *Bond Street Hatter's Showcase*. It shows simply what it says in the title: rows of gentlemen's hats in the shop window of one of London's finest commercial districts. We don't see the street in the photograph, but the mention of its name is enough to evoke an upper-class setting. Six rows of neatly ordered hats are introduced by a rectangular label on the top shelf with the name of a long-established brand: 'Opera hats by Hillhouse & Co. Est. 1799'. There are black silk top hats, high cylinders of shiny material on which the reflection from the photographer's flash stands out like a flickering flame. Then follow two rows of grey top hats and one row of dark felt bowlers, under which a final line of black top hats completes the static display. A small label placed at the centre of each item indicates the hat's size. The photograph is objective and bizarre at the same time: it documents a privileged social practice, but it is also a ghostly representation of human absence, a record pertaining to the British upper classes and a universal affirmation of the visual power of objects.

Figure 17 Bill Brandt, *Bond Street Hatter's Showcase, c.* 1934.

Also dating to this period is a series of photographs taken at London's Billingsgate Fish Market. Compared with the previous picture, these images illustrate the other side of British life, a working-class order of things. Like the Bond Street hatter's window, Brandt's view of Billingsgate Market suggests a world of ritual and tradition. This time he is recording rituals of the everyday, performed by working men whose poses and features are as human and dignified as those of the opera-hat wearers were ghostly and removed from reality. But here, too, things take on a life of their own.

In two portraits of market porters, young men are photographed as they stand still while balancing a large fish on their heads. One porter is wearing dirty white overalls, his arms hanging at his sides as he stares somewhere into the distance and away from the viewer. The dark colour of his stained clothes affects the lower half of the photograph in its entirety, so as to emphasize the pale, luminous face of the man. He possesses a statuesque quality, and the enormous fish balanced on his traditional flat-topped bobbin hat adds a slightly alarming element to the impression of quiet gracefulness conveyed by the man's look and posture.

Figure 18 Bill Brandt, *Billingsgate Porter,* c. 1934.

A similar effect is achieved in another photograph, in which a market porter is wearing his normal clothes – a tattered, faded old suit and a dark waistcoat over a wrinkled white shirt with no tie. He is also looking into the distance, but his pose is more dynamic than that of his colleague in the previous picture. His left hand is in his trouser pocket and his right arm is raised so as to steady the fish on his head. This gesture creates an image of classical proportions, as if he were the model for an ancient statue, or a young David. Here, too, the man's calm and distant stare conveys the sense of a dignity that goes far beyond the mundane nature of his occupation. Yet the fish adds an element of disquiet. The animal is both attractive and repulsive. Its startling whiteness and physical enormity do not seem to refer to anything beyond itself. The fish is not a symbol, it doesn't necessarily allude to something else. After all, the photographs are social documents of contemporary working life in London. But the creature – its prominent place within the photograph, the shiny quality of its dead body, its strange beauty and the vague horror it evokes – adds depth to these pictures. Brandt created a dimension in which social commentary and artistic expression are fused together.

Bill Brandt was keen to dissociate himself from the other members of the German-speaking émigré community. His connections with his adopted country were admittedly stronger than those of other exiles. He was born in Hamburg into an affluent family of merchants and bankers in 1904. His grandfather had traded in timber and fur, and the family had substantial commercial links with England and Russia. Brandt claimed to be half English and half Russian. This tale is rooted in his family history. The grandfather, Augustus, had forged a successful career as a merchant banker in the London branch of the family firm, William Brandt and Son, and lived with his family in Denmark Hill, a well-established German enclave in Victorian London. All his seven children were born there and had British passports. In 1888, the family returned to Germany, and only three of Augustus's sons eventually moved back to London to work as bankers. Yet Bill Brandt's father remained in Hamburg, where he married the daughter of a wealthy lawyer and where his children were born. During the First World War, when Bill was ten years old, his father was interned as an enemy alien, being a British national, and the family's loyalty lay with England rather than with Germany. In Bill's case, the psychological impact of this unusual background was complicated by the influence of a controlling father, by the effects of an authoritarian boarding-school education and by his delicate health. In many ways, Brandt's childhood mirrors the experience of the young protagonists of the novels by authors such as Thomas Mann, Hermann Hesse and Robert Musil. In their fictional worlds, the natural development and inclinations of bourgeois youths are thwarted by the rules and expectations of a rigid society and by an emotionally repressed family environment. To complete this stereotypical picture of privileged but unhappy early years, Brandt was diagnosed with tuberculosis and asthma at a young age and, like Hans Castorp in Thomas Mann's novel *The Magic Mountain* (1924), was sent to a Swiss sanatorium. After over two years of such confinement, Brandt moved to Vienna in 1927. In the Austrian capital he was a patient of the psychoanalyst Wilhelm Stekel, who advocated the merits of psychoanalysis as a cure for tuberculosis. Even though Brandt left Stekel's care after only three months, psychoanalysis remained a significant aspect of his art, as most of his photographs seem to rely on the oblique depiction of reality as a mirror for unconscious meanings.

In Vienna, he also met his first girlfriend, Lyena Barjansky, the daughter of a Russian-Jewish businessman. At the time, Lyena was a pupil of the enormously influential educationalist and intellectual hostess Eugenie Schwarzwald. Both Bill Brandt (who was still known as Willy at the time) and his brother Rolf were part of Schwarzwald's circle. They were visitors at her villa on Grundlsee, an alpine lake in the Styrian countryside surrounded by luxurious homes and spectacular views. Here, Schwarzwald had founded a summer colony, where young people lived together in natural surroundings, inspired by culture, sport and a love of learning. Guided by enlightened principles and humanitarian ideals, she was a motherly friend and a mentor to many. Schwarzwald had a rich web of connections within the highest circles of the Viennese intelligentsia. This meant that her students would be taught music by Arnold Schoenberg, architecture by Adolf Loos and art by Oskar Kokoschka. (Edith Tudor-Hart also spent some time at Grundlsee as a teenager and, according to her brother, studied music with Schoenberg there.) In Brandt's case, Schwarzwald was instrumental in changing his name from Willy to Bill, a prescient idea given his future as an Englishman. Most importantly, she influenced Brandt's decision to become a photographer. As the great facilitator she was, Schwarzwald also introduced him to her former student Grete Kolliner, who ran a well-established photographic studio in Vienna. At the Kolliner studio Brandt learnt his craft and the darkroom skills that a young Wolf Suschitzky would be taught in the same city a couple of years later. But whereas Suschitzky found little use for the artifice of studio photography and would go on to develop an informal style based on immediacy and spontaneity, Brandt drew upon his technical knowledge throughout his career in order to produce carefully composed and often substantially altered images.

In 1930, some of Brandt's photographs were exhibited at the *Film und Foto* show that had travelled from Stuttgart and Zürich to Vienna in March of that year. Yet the exhibition, a milestone in the history of German modernist photography, was not wholly representative of Brandt's style and taste, and he may have been more impressed by an exhibition of nineteenth-century photography that had been shown at Vienna's Belvedere Palace the previous year. Considering Brandt's background, personality and artistic disposition, he must have found British photography particularly appealing, not only because of his affinity with England, but also because of the atmospheric and narrative quality of Victorian pictorial photography. This was not the dynamic and objective art in the German style, but a more traditional craft based on artistic composition and on the construction of scenes and settings.

Brandt became a professional photographer in Vienna, but he refined his visual style and artistic tastes in Paris between 1930 and 1934. His time in France and a productive trip to Spain in 1932 exposed him to an important influence on his aesthetic sensibility: Surrealism. In 1928, one of Grete Kolliner's assistants was the twenty-one-year-old Hungarian Eva Boros. Like Brandt, she was consumptive and all too familiar with the remote, artificial world of illness and sanatoria. She was a fair, slim, fragile-looking girl, with fine, regular features and an angelic face. She came from a cultivated family, was an avid reader, an aspiring photographer and a writer. Her ethereal beauty and cultured background made a profound impression on Brandt, whose family association with Russia may explain his life-long fascination with Eastern European women.

In Hungary, Eva had been a pupil of André Kertész, who was, like Brassaï, a honorary Parisian and one of the pioneers of creative photojournalism. Kertész shot contemporary reality from unusual perspectives and was a great experimenter in photographic still-lifes, nudes and portraits. In Paris, he probably introduced Bill and Eva to Man Ray, in whose studio the couple worked for several months. The encounter between Brandt and Man Ray was not a success. The retiring personality and secretive disposition of the young German were at odds with Man Ray's energetic creativity and social ambitions. Brandt, by now attuned to the urban photography of Kertész and Brassaï, was growing impatient with Man Ray's studio-based artistic methods. Years later, he declared that he had learnt very little during his time as Man Ray's assistant, though he also confessed to learning 'a great deal' by surreptitiously going through the artist's files in his absence. Moreover, Man Ray's extensive circle of eminent friends among the Dadaists and Surrealists had an impact on the evolution of Brandt's own practice. His work is informed by the Surrealist view of the world, in which external reality becomes a window into man's inner self. Most of his pictures convey the mysterious essence of everyday objects, the dream-like quality of cityscapes and the grotesque potential of class-bound customs.

An important figure in Parisian photography was Brandt's lifelong model: Eugène Atget. One of the precursors of modern documentary photography, Atget had died three years before Brandt arrived in Paris. He had lived on the same street as Man Ray, who hailed him as a Surrealist *ante litteram*. Atget's photographic collection entitled *Old Paris*, in particular, had the power to reveal the character of a city on the verge of modernity yet still imbued with the aura of past times. Among his most typical subjects were mannequins, shop windows, alleyways and staircases, the city's poor and the homeless. The blurred look of his images of everyday life was achieved through wide views and long exposure times and produced an almost ghost-like effect.

Atget's photographs are characterized by a nostalgic attitude towards the past and by an unsettling sense that they hide more than they reveal. Through Atget, Brandt became aware of the artistic potential of documentary urban photography. He learnt to depict the city realistically yet focusing on places and objects that hint at something uncanny and obscure, such as flea markets and rubbish heaps.

The other major influence on the young Brandt was Brassaï, whom he later recognized as his favourite photographer. The two men may have been acquainted through Kertész in Paris, and they certainly met in England in 1934, when Brassaï came to London to receive the P. H. Emerson medal for his feature 'Paris after Dark'. Brassaï went down in the history of photography for his French subjects as Brandt is remembered as a photographer of Englishness. They shared a taste for pictures of urban characters and landscapes, which were simultaneously naturalistic and meticulously composed.

In May 1934 one of Brandt's photographs was published in the French art magazine *Minotaure*, at the centre of an article by the Surrealist writer René Crevel. The picture is entitled *Shop Window, Mannequin* and encompasses all the visual lessons of Brandt's Parisian years. Two life-sized mannequins dressed in old-fashioned women's clothes stand, bizarrely prim-looking and erect, on a pavement in front of what looks like a market stall. The photograph is vaguely disturbing. On the one hand, it is rooted in a recognizable setting. On the other, it is unclear. Who or what are those figures and what do they evoke? Are they obscure feminine archetypes, nightmarish visions, relics of a haunting past, embodiments of childish fantasies and fears?

By the time the image was published, Bill Brandt and Eva Boros were living in London. In his new country, Brandt explored similar imagery, but he also found his own distinctive artistic personality. He did not emphasize the surreal elements of city life as he had done in Paris. But he showed an awareness of the eccentricity of certain aspects of British life and social conventions. It is this sense of strange rituals coupled with impassioned social observation that gives Brandt's English photographs their originality. His Bond Street opera hats are less surreal than the Parisian mannequins, but they are nonetheless a bizarre sight. The singularity of Brandt's British pictures lies in the puzzled yet steady gaze with which the continental photographer looks at his new surroundings. In England, Brandt noticed the sharp contrast between the strictly regimented universe of a bourgeois lifestyle and the misery and moral stature of the working class. He gazed at this world with wonder, detecting every peculiarity of English life, and perhaps delving back into the recesses of his own family's anglophilia. He photographed newspapers and milk bottles on the neoclassical porch of a Belsize Avenue terraced house; he noticed the garish wallpaper in an English sitting room; he portrayed two maids in their pristine uniforms in front of a luxurious, immaculately laid dinner table; he captured a quiet moment in a workmen's restaurant with its wooden partitions and a few silent customers sitting apart, with their felt caps and downcast eyes.

London was an immense metropolis, but it was not as modern as Berlin and Paris. In fact, it was rather old-fashioned in many ways, for the overall look and pace of London life were those of a city that revered tradition. Modernist avant-garde movements only affected a small elite in 1930s England, artistic photography was considered foreign, and British life went on according to old and – to outsiders – rather eccentric rules and conventions. 'There is a force in this country ... that turns one towards the past, and invests it with a continuous and almost mystic importance', observed Odette Keun, a French-Dutch journalist and traveller, whose book *I Discover the English* was published in the autumn of 1934. A few months later, Paul Cohen-Portheim wrote something similar: 'The secret of London is, in fact, that the Londoner, like all Englishmen, is not a creature of cities.' Most foreigners were spellbound by the peculiar power of British identity and customs, and they often noticed things that a native person would have taken for granted. This was certainly the case of the German-speaking refugee photographers. In Brandt's case, his fascination with the otherness of England was reinforced by the island's privileged place in his own family mythology.

Despite his desire to pass as a true Englishman, Bill Brandt was an artist whose value derived from his cosmopolitan upbringing and from his early experiences on the Continent. Brandt's first major contributions to the history of British photography, the collections *The English at Home* and *A Night in London*, were published in 1936 and 1938 respectively. In 1936, he worked occasionally for *Weekly Illustrated*, and two years later he joined the staff of *Picture Post*. By then, he had become a professional photojournalist.

Back in 1934, during his first year in London, the city that he would photograph so imaginatively in the years to come became a retreat at first, a place in which he began to reinvent himself as a British artist. Like Suschitzky and Lorant, Brandt had been to London before. His first visit was a long weekend with Lyena Barjansky in the spring of 1928. Brandt's younger brother had come to London to study English, and lived at the Hampstead boarding house of a Mrs Sybil Knight. In Brandt's artistic universe, the Knights came to embody the quintessentially English construct of the secure, cosy middle-class home and family, whose life was organized according to inscrutable laws that aroused the curiosity of the foreign observer. *Family Fireside*, a photograph of Mrs Knight knitting by the fire in her Hampstead sitting-room with her little boy reading at her side, reveals Brandt's fascination with English domestic interiors and with bourgeois existence. This is a life that keeps check on disorder and on the passing of time through a well-rehearsed daily routine.

Barely a month before Brandt settled in England Stefan Zweig, in a letter to a friend, compared the 'nervous tension of Vienna and Paris' with the friendly

Figure 19 Bill Brandt by Ida Kar, August 1968.

reserve of the English. He also added that life in London was 'as good as being in a sanatorium'. It is an interesting perception, and one that might partly explain Brandt's attraction to the city. Life in a sanatorium was highly structured and divorced from the real world. It was also an existence devoted to the banishment of death and, at the same time, one in which mortality was ever present. In the eyes of continental refugees, London often appeared as a strange oasis of calm in a restless and dangerous world. The Londoners' pride in their traditions and their cheerful detachment during an unstable historical juncture must have been reassuring to someone like Brandt, whose calm exterior concealed precarious health and a highly sensitive nature. From this perspective, the grid-like structure of the Bond Street opera hats and the inscrutable quality of the great fish on the heads of the Billingsgate porters belong to a dimension in which order and mystery are intertwined.

In old age, Brandt remembered his first impressions of England as an object of desire. His recollections of the crossing from Dieppe to Newhaven in April

1934 reveal that the journey was bringing him closer to an ideal: 'About an hour before Newhaven the Seven Sisters appear like a Fata Morgana on the horizon, brilliantly white in the afternoon sun – the sun always shines. England then looks like a small fairy tale island. It is an unforgettable experience and again and again a surprise for me.' How different this sounds from the usual descriptions of refugees crossing the English Channel! Brandt's England is sunny, exotic in its brightness and quaintly diminutive size. It bears no traces of the damp, grey mist that lingers in the memory of many German-speaking immigrants on their first arrival. Brandt's praise is an expression of love for the country that he chose as his own. His words are more sincere than Lorant's extravagant praise of England in his prison diary. To Lorant, London offered mainly business opportunities, whereas Brandt felt truly at home there. Lorant was an entrepreneur, an ebullient character with a strong practical streak. He believed in himself and charmed his prospective business partners with the overpowering personality of a showman who, albeit irrational and eccentric, managed to overcome the most formidable obstacles. Brandt, on the other hand, was quiet and enigmatic. His love of England stemmed from a sentimental imagination, rather than from actual knowledge of a country that he had visited only occasionally before he moved there at the age of thirty. To him, England was an aesthetic construct, a source of inspiration. His photographs of the landscapes and people of Britain in the 1930s and 1940s still inform our visual memory of those times.

Bill Brandt shrouded himself in secrecy all his life. Scenes from a BBC documentary about him filmed in 1983 show a tall, lean man, soft-spoken, with a noble, aquiline profile, white hair swept back to reveal a high forehead, and an imperceptible smile on his thin lips. Everything he says, every answer to the interviewer's questions, seems to veil rather than reveal his personality. He was a very different artist from Wolf Suschitzky, who was jovial and communicative, and whose pictures almost always portray living creatures. And he was unlike the fiercely committed Edith Tudor-Hart, who empathized with her subjects and saw her camera as a political tool. Brandt was a master at photographing not only human beings but also empty spaces and objects, as though he were trying to understand his surroundings through the impersonal quality of places and things.

All these refugees altered the face of British photography for decades to come. This was due to their status as outsiders and to their Germanic heritage. Despite their different backgrounds, these individuals had something important in common: they were familiar with modern aesthetics and technologies, and determined to place humanity and contemporary reality at the centre of their artistic vision.

May–June

The Warburg Institute opens its doors

On May Day, traditionally a date for Communist celebrations, German National Socialists in London organize a screening of the propaganda film *Hans Westmar* (1933) – the story of a young SA leader modelled on the Nazi hero Horst Wessel – at Victoria Hall, Bloomsbury Square.

On 8 May, in an attempt to secure the release of his wife and young daughter from the Roßlau concentration camp, Gerhart Seger has tea at the House of Commons with Nancy Astor and other women MPs, who are going to publicize the Segers' case through a letter in *The Times* and intercede with the German government.

On 15 May, Walter Gropius, on his first visit to England, attends the opening of an exhibition of his work at the Royal Institute of British Architecture (RIBA). The next day he gives a paper, in halting English, at the Design and Industries Association on the subjects of modern architecture and planning. 'It was the first time that one of the leaders of the Modern Movement had come personally to advocate the general proposition that architecture has a sociologically and economically significant role to play in a system of national planning for the future.'

On 26 May Gerhart Seger is reunited with his wife and daughter at Croydon Aerodorme 'in the full glare of publicity. This even included the British Gaumont News cameramen, which meant that the story would appear on the newsreels in every Gaumont cinema in the country.'

On 28 May, the Glyndebourne Opera Festival opens with a performance of Mozart's *The Marriage of Figaro*. The event is a success, described in *The Times* as a 'rare entertainment offered by the enterprise of Mr John Christie and the combined artistry of Herr Fritz Busch and Herr Carl Ebert'.

On 4 June, a conference organized by the Relief Committee for the Victims of German Fascism at London's Conway Hall to discuss the imprisonment by the Nazis of the Communist leader Ernst Thälmann cannot proceed, because the delegate who visited Thälmann in prison and was going to report to the committee has been refused permission to enter Britain.

Meanwhile, several Nazi Party members active in London are being intercepted by the British Security Services. Protagonists of an active exchange of letters are the journalist Hans Wilhelm Thost and the German diplomats Otto Bene, Walter R. Engelberg and Richard von Stradiot. The English transcript of their correspondence shows that on Monday 25 June 1934 a mysterious 'R' (probably Richard von Stradiot) was enlightening Engelberg – who was in Rome – about the activities of the London Party Group of the National Socialist German Workers' Party (NSDAP). Two days later, a letter from Stradiot to Engelberg reveals that the London Nazis were in regular contact with the British Union of Fascists and keen to address the Jewish question. Of his conversations with 'the head of the Foreign Department and the head of the London branch Stradiot notes that even if the struggle with the Jews does not take the same form as in Germany, they both have the same tendency to assert that Judaism is to be settled with'.

On Wednesday 27 June, the Wimbledon tennis tournament is in full swing (although 'a drizzle turned into heavy rain in the late afternoon'), and the German champion Gottfried von Cramm defeats his opponent, the New Zealand tennis champion Eskell D. Andrews.

On 28 June an article in *The Times* mentions intelligence about 'German plans for air attacks in Paris and London', including the possibility of the 'raining down of liquids containing chemicals or bacteria from various heights'. The following day in the House of Commons, incensed by the prospect of the German fleet's first visit to Britain since the First World War, Colonel Wedgwood asks 'the First Lord of the Admiralty when, and why' the Germans have been invited and whether it was 'not rather foolish to allow these people to come to London and Portsmouth'.

Also on 28 June, Benjamin Britten goes with a friend to the Apollo Theatre to see *Escape Me Never* and notes in his diary: 'Bergner is all that is said about her & more – I have never seen anyone like her.' Meanwhile in Westminster, an informal gathering of about seventy people takes place in the newly opened Warburg Institute on the ground floor of Thames House, a large office block by the river on Millbank.

On Saturday 30 June James G. McDonald is in London to address the Jewish crisis with some leading philanthropists. While having tea with Ernest Franklin, treasurer of the Board of Guardians for the Relief of the Jewish Poor, McDonald hears 'an announcement on the radio that [Kurt] v[on] Schleicher had been shot and [Ernst] Röhm arrested'. This is the beginning of the so-called 'Night of the Long Knives', during which in Bavaria the SS, acting on Hitler's orders, brutally kill Ernst Röhm and other Nazi leaders.

Chapter 3
London gains a library

In June, between then and now

A few days after the referendum about Britain's membership of the European Union in June 2016, the Warburg Institute, one of the world's most famous libraries and a bastion of international cooperation, was bathed in sunshine in the quiet corner of Bloomsbury that it has occupied since the late 1950s. The building is a solid five-storey structure of brown brick with straight rows of stone-framed windows. Its appearance recalls both the discreet elegance of the nineteenth-century terrace on the opposite side of the square and the modernist look of other academic buildings nearby. Its regular lines have an almost Germanic quality. After all, it was designed by Charles Holden, the same man who, in the early 1930s, created the white modernist skyscraper of Senate House, a building much admired by two German pioneers of modern design in Britain, Erich Mendelsohn and Nikolaus Pevsner.

As a research centre for the study of the history of culture and of the influence of classical antiquity on the visual arts, The Warburg Institute holds over 350,000 volumes and an extensive photographic archive. This unique collection originated in Hamburg as the private library of the Jewish art historian Aby Warburg at the end of the nineteenth century. In 1933 its safety was threatened by the National Socialist takeover and the library was transported in great haste to England, where it has remained ever since. Its adventurous arrival in London at the end of Hitler's first year in power was a triumph of humanity over brutality, and its life in a new country marked the beginning of a fruitful exchange between different worlds and scholarly traditions.

Above the institute's main entrance, an esoteric-looking symbol carved in pale stone invites the visitor to enter a realm that lies far beyond the gracious urbanity of Georgian Bloomsbury. The emblem, taken from the fifteenth-century woodcut of a work by the medieval Spanish theologian Isidore of Seville (560–636 CE), shows four concentric circles inside a round frame and, arranged within the symmetrical pattern of an uninterrupted line, the Latin names of the four elements (fire, air, water and earth), which in turn correspond to the four seasons and relative human temperaments. The connections between the human and the natural world suggest an arcane yet harmonious view of the universe and of man's place within it. A similar sense of the interrelation of all things governs the way in which the books are arranged, on open shelves, inside the library. The collection is still organized according to Warburg's own system of classification and, eschewing chronological order, it favours an unconventional thematic approach that mixes different genres and encourages readers to make serendipitous discoveries. In an ironic twist of fate, the theme of the interrelationship of all things seems to be confirmed by the curious fact that, at the end of the twentieth century, the Catholic Church declared Isidore of Seville the patron saint of the internet.

Figure 20 The emblem of the Warburg Institute.

Today, thoughts about the Warburg Institute entail a lingering concern about the impact of recent developments in the relationship between Britain and Europe upon an institution so deeply committed to the values of international associations. It is a question that brings to mind the time when the institute had to be transferred to England from Hamburg all those years ago. A statement issued by its former director, David Freedberg, in 2016 was reassuring regarding the possible effects of Britain's exit from the European Union on the Warburg Library. Yet in mentioning the institute's 'commitment to a Europe without border guards' Freedberg also alluded to the danger of creating barriers and evoked memories of a distant past when, having defied the power of the Nazi guards, this German institution began its new life, on a summer's day, on the banks of the Thames.

On Thursday 28 June 1934 staff at the institute celebrated its opening in London together with some of its English friends and benefactors. The party was a modest affair, held indoors, on the library's premises. It had been organized, rather hurriedly, by the mostly German members of staff. The institute's official opening had been barely advertised so as not to antagonize the Nazi authorities, but also because the Warburg scholars had no money to spend on publicity or lavish celebrations. The transfer to England had been an arduous task for everyone involved. The six members of staff who had accompanied the library to London worked hard for months to ensure a future for their institution, which they had opened to the public at the beginning of May. As Germany became engulfed by cruelty and chaos, another Germany in exile stood for tolerance and intellectual freedom. Both London and Britain as a whole were to be immensely enriched by the arrival of the Warburg Institute. This chapter tells the story of that arrival and of its main protagonists.

The Warburg Institute opens its doors

In a letter written from London on Friday 4 May 1934, the Austrian art historian Fritz Saxl invited the classical scholar and president of Corpus Christi College, Oxford, Richard Livingstone, to visit the newly opened Warburg Institute at Thames House. In his role as the library's director, Saxl expressed his gratitude towards Livingstone as one of the people responsible for its successful transfer from Hamburg a few months earlier. Saxl was looking to the future, and his optimism glossed over the trying experience of settling into a completely different environment: 'The Library is now installed and looks quite friendly, at least for our eyes. I need not emphasize how grateful we are to our English friends that we have got back our old surroundings, and that we can now start a new scientific life.'

The two men had known each other for some time. The British professor had lectured in Hamburg at the Kulturwissenschaftliche Bibliothek Warburg (Warburg Library for the Science of Culture), or KBW – as the first incarnation of the institute was called – four years earlier. He had met Saxl in London in the late 1920s, then again in 1930, when Saxl organized a series of lectures entitled *England and Antiquity*, and invited Livingstone and other British academics to Hamburg to speak about their country's relationship with the classical world.

The foreign visitors were impressed by the aims and rigour of their German colleagues. The Warburg scholars exemplified a new attitude towards the history of art. They championed an interdisciplinary study of visual culture and saw artworks not only as objects of aesthetic appreciation, but also as social and historical documents. To this purpose, the Warburg Library was founded as a collection of books pertaining to different fields, from philosophy, literature and mythology to anthropology, religion and astrology. At the same time, the Warburg approach privileged a specific perspective: the study of the lasting influence of the classics on the visual arts, which, in a literal translation from the German, is called the Afterlife of Antiquity. It concerned the dynamic relationship between the myths and symbols through which the Greeks and Romans had interpreted the world, and the visual permutations of those responses for centuries to come. The broad outlook and the narrow focus were not mutually exclusive, but rather closely related, as the study of the legacy of the classics became a means to explore the social and cultural roots of our civilization and their continued relevance in the modern world.

England and Antiquity had been Saxl's first international initiative and, in hindsight, an important step towards establishing a connection with the country to which the library would eventually migrate. In 1934, two years after the lectures' publication in Germany, the book was widely praised in Britain: an article in the *Classical Review* published at the time of Saxl's letter to Livingstone, for example, greeted this 'handsome volume as a welcome harbinger of the removal of the Warburg Library to England'.

In the spring of 1934, as the British academic community was beginning to welcome the new arrival, the Warburg's staff and scholars reorganized their library and illustrated its purpose for a British audience. In the words of Gertrud Bing, Saxl's assistant and life-partner and, like him, a key-figure in the history of the institute: 'it was vaguely known that it had a great reputation on the continent, but hardly anybody knew what its object really was'. There were hard tasks ahead for the newcomers, especially considering their financial concerns, the burden of being outsiders and the need to work in a foreign language. In a later account on the history of the library, Saxl remembered the strain of their first few months in London:

How could the six people who came over from Hamburg with the books set to work? The language in which they wrote – even if the words were English – was foreign because their habits of thought were un-English; and whom could one reach from this curious ground-floor Library in a gigantic office building, who would read what these few unknowns produced?

At first, Thames House, an imposing public building (now home to MI5), constructed on the north bank of the Thames on the site of a slum destroyed by floods in 1928, did not seem a suitable home for the institute. In January 1934, the correspondence between Sir Louis Vaughan, a British Army officer and managing director of the Thames House Estate, and Lord Lee of Fareham, the art collector, diplomat and former cabinet minister who had been instrumental in securing the premises for the new library, revealed the extent of the building work to be carried out before the institute could be installed. A letter from Sir Louis dated 8 January includes a detailed list of the outstanding tasks:

We are prepared to do the following work at our own expenses:

Partitions …
Doors.
Door furniture.
Locks.
Keys.
Architraves.
Skirtings.
Picture rails.
Dado rails.
Frames.
Distemper on walls.
Paint on joinery.

The cost of the following will be debitable to the Warburg Institute:

Partitioning other than normal.
Nameplates.
Signwriting.
Floor covering.
Letter Box.
Electrical: Special lead for Library
Fittings
Lamps
Switch Plates

Auxiliary Lighting Plugs,
Power Plugs.
Bells, Buzzers or any other special requirements.
Sink and Plumbing for Dark Room.

The following day, after Saxl agreed to settle a couple of 'small outstanding points' concerning 'the linoleum or other floor covering and the plumbing for the Photographic Dark Room', Lord Lee instructed Sir Louis to 'have the work taken in hand at once and completed at the earliest moment practicable'.

A few weeks later, Gertrud Bing wrote a progress report in English and a meticulous account of their current circumstances. Given the number of problems, she was remarkably positive, as her initial doubts over the suitability of the new premises gave way to optimism and to a grateful acceptance of the situation:

> Thanks to the disinterested help of our English friends the Library has found very good accommodation at Thames House, where a back ground floor has been divided up according to our special needs … The situation in London gave at first rise to some doubts, because there is no institute in the neighbourhood. It proved, however, not to be too bad, because twenty-five minutes['] bus ride brings us to the British Museum, and another bus from the back side of the house goes nearly to Portman Square, so that the way to the Courtauld Institute takes no longer than twenty-five minutes either.

Bing then went on to describe their plans for the layout of the library and its facilities:

> The premises comprise one large room which is going to be a reading room, as well as a lecture room; twenty seats for regular readers are provided … and if turned into a lecture room, 150 hearers can be accommodated, our authors' catalogue and one arranged according to subjects are going to be put into that room. There is a smaller room planned as a seminar room, also equipped with a lantern, so that, for instance, a university lecture might be held there without disturbing the readers in the reading room. A very favourable feature seems to us to be the easy accessibility of the books …There is a bookbindery and a photographic studio attached to the Library, for which we brought the technical machinery over from Germany.

Another leaflet included a floor plan and two photographs of the book stacks and reading room. The impression is that of a functional space built to provide the most effective research experience, an island of clarity and scholarship deep within the bowels of an institutional building in an area of London usually dominated by the business of government.

Interestingly, the architect who designed the new library's interior was Godfrey Samuel, a member of the avant-garde architectural practice Tecton, which counted some notable modernists among its members, such as Berthold Lubetkin and Francis Skinner. In 1932, one of the firm's first commissions had been the Gorilla House at London Zoo, a rounded, airy structure defined by clear lines and made of reinforced concrete – a precursor to Lubetkin's much celebrated Penguin Pool, also at London Zoo, a couple of years later.

It seems appropriate for the English home of a German institution to have been designed by an architect who championed a rational, modernist style. As Sir Louis Vaughan's letter to Lord Lee shows, Godfrey Samuel worked closely with Fritz Saxl and himself ('we have now been very thoroughly into the question of the layout for the accommodation of the Warburg Institute with Dr. Saxl and Mr. Samuel'). And the accuracy with which, on the printed floor plan, each section of the institute's interior is defined according to its purpose mirrors the clean lines of the library's windows, as well as its functional furniture and simple décor.

After opening the institute's doors in May, Saxl communicated the news of its English rebirth to members of the Warburg family in Hamburg and New York. On 7 May 1934, he informed one of Aby Warburg's nephews, Eric, that the reading room was beginning to populate ('naturally with our German friends at first') and that they had already held their first lecture. On 1 June, a long letter to Eric's uncle, Felix Warburg, contains a more detailed account of the library's progress in its new home and of the staff's activities:

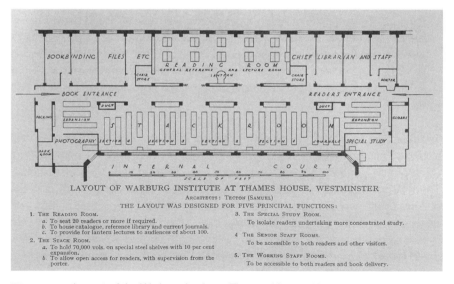

Figure 21 Layout of the Warburg Institute, Thames House, 1934.

Figure 22 The Warburg Institute at Thames House, Reading Room, 1934.

We have spent the last four weeks arranging the Library, a task which took all our energies. Fortunately the work is now more or less completed ... I have arranged a series of German lectures on the problems of the Warburg Institute, the audience of which too is mostly German, although a few English people who know German well enough, like to come too ... This series of lectures aims not only at creating a new circle of collaborators who are willing to work more or less along our lines with their research work, but above all to give these scattered compatriots of our [sic] a new centre where they can feel at home.

The passage illustrates the spirit with which a small group of émigrés managed to overcome enormous challenges. The six people who followed the library from Hamburg to London in 1933 were Fritz Saxl, Gertrud Bing, the art historian Edgar Wind, the librarian Hans Meier, the accountant Eva von Eckardt, and the photographer and bookbinder Otto Fein. From the moment they arrived and despite innumerable practical difficulties, they busied themselves trying to involve British students and academics while providing help and advice for their own exiled fellow citizens. They were all animated by a spirit that combined courage with a belief in the values of research and critical thinking and an unshakeable loyalty to the memory and methods of the library's founder.

Exceptional families

Aby Warburg was born in Hamburg in 1866 as the eldest son of seven children in a Jewish banking dynasty, whose presence in the region dated back to the mid seventeenth century. On his mother's side, Aby descended from a family of diamond merchants from Frankfurt, the Oppenheims. For centuries, both Hamburg and Frankfurt had been important centres of commerce, where the Jewish middle classes played a vital economic role and enjoyed a relative degree of social assimilation despite remaining committed to their own faith. In the case of Hamburg – a 'free city' since the twelfth century – its mercantile identity and cosmopolitan character were enhanced by its autonomous status. This meant that the city could determine its own foreign policy and trade agreements and maintain its independence from powerful neighbours such as Denmark and Prussia. More than any other German city, Hamburg boasted a solid civic tradition and a generally liberal attitude towards Jews, which resulted in one of the country's largest Jewish communities. In Hamburg, Jews were dominant in a highly influential group represented by financial giants such as the Warburgs (whose private bank, M. M. Warburg & Co., had been founded in 1798), and Albert Ballin, director of the world's largest shipping company, the Hamburg-America Line, and a friend and associate of Aby's brother, Max Warburg.

Both the Warburgs and the Oppenheims embodied a type of dynamism in which trade, religious observance and philanthropic activities went hand in hand with a sophisticated urbanity and a passionate commitment to high culture. Their social milieu combined business with an enlightened German-Jewish tradition founded on the ideal of *Bildung* as cultivation and self-improvement. Within the Oppenheim clan, for example, a love of music and a talent for languages coexisted with a strong work ethic and with an awareness of the family's privileged social standing.

Despite successful integration, for many Jews social empowerment was coupled with insecurity, because of an awareness of their own diversity, often exacerbated by the threat of anti-Semitism. The Warburg siblings, for example, were proud of their elders' achievements and endowed with a portentous sense of purpose (in a bold astrological analogy, they recognized themselves in the seven stars that form the constellation of the Plough), but also ambivalent about their Jewish identity. On the whole, the new generations were keen to assimilate more fully than their parents had done, and were willing to participate more actively in determining Germany's future.

During Aby's childhood, the family lived in affluent comfort in an idyllic neighbourhood near the Elbe River. At the time of the Franco-Prussian War in the early 1870s, the Warburgs contributed to the international loan that enabled France to pay reparations to Germany, a fact that marked the beginning of a prosperous period for the Warburg Bank. Three of the brothers, Max, Paul and Felix, grew up to become enormously influential in the world of business and high finance. As the head of M. M. Warburg & Co., Max was a prominent public figure in Hamburg and in his country as a whole, and played an important political role when he advised the Kaiser prior to Germany's involvement in the First World War. Paul and Felix, having married into two of the most powerful Jewish-American families, the Loebs and the Schiffs, became pivotal presences in US philanthropy and finance. Whereas Paul is remembered mainly as the founder of the American Federal Reserve Banking System, Felix raised funds for European Jews after the First World War and during the Great Depression as the leader of the American-Jewish Joint Distribution Committee.

The brothers' irrepressible blend of cleverness and charm shines through their photographs, in which an affectionate devotion to their elders and each other coincides with a sort of amused belief in their own individual strength. A well-known image of the five men portrays them at a table with the bookshelves of the Warburg Library behind them. Max is seated at the centre and, on his left, an ageing Aby is seen with his hands cupped in a supplicant gesture towards the brother who funded his lifelong passion for books. The photograph, dated 21 August 1929, was taken almost exactly two months before Aby Warburg's death.

Aby had been a sensitive and weakly child. He had contracted typhoid fever at the age of six, and when his mother also fell seriously ill with typhus not

Figure 23 The five Warburg brothers after the first official meeting of the KBW, 21 August 1929.

long after his recovery, he suffered a great deal and found respite in a fantasy world of books and stories. Despite his impressionable nature, the boy was brilliantly intelligent and very determined. He could be lively and witty, with the attractive yet despotic personality of a born leader. As the eldest son, Aby had been the first of the Warburg children to reject the family's religious observance. His wife, Mary Hertz, whom he married in 1897, to his relatives' consternation, was a gentile and an artist. Throughout Aby's life his loyalty lay with Germany and German culture rather than with his parents' Jewish orthodoxy. He did not become a rabbi, as his grandmother would have wanted, nor did he take over his father's role as head of the family firm. Instead, he became an art historian.

Not a beautiful flowery meadow

Aby Warburg studied history of art, archaeology and the history of religion at the University of Bonn, where two notable scholars, the philologist Hermann Usener and the historian Karl Lamprecht, introduced him to a broad understanding of history, which included the anthropological, religious and social aspects of human evolution. In the words of Ernst Gombrich, who published Warburg's *Intellectual Biography* in 1970, in their lectures Aby 'first came into touch with that powerful trend in nineteenth-century thought which tried to apply the findings of modern science to the subject matter of the humanities. Psychology and anthropology seemed to offer the key to the classics.'

Not long after encountering the use of evolutionary ideas in the understanding of cultural and historical processes, Warburg discovered Charles Darwin. During his stay in Florence in the autumn of 1888, reading Darwin's *The Expression of Emotions in Man and Animals*, which had been published in German the previous year, he wrote in his diary: 'At last a book which helps me.'

In his study, Darwin had explored the analogies between animals' reactions as necessary defence mechanisms (such as trembling to express fear) and similar human responses, which he saw as remnants of animal instincts and which happened independently of the will. Reading scientific evolutionism from an art-historical perspective, Warburg understood stylistic changes in artworks as reactions to earlier, more archaic forms of expression. In his interpretation of the Renaissance as a period of encounters between opposing forces – old and new, instinct and reason – he began to view history as a repository of images, often inherited from classical antiquity, that artists employed to express long-buried emotions. He saw art as an expression of control. By applying a scientific method to the study of images, Warburg revealed how the development of certain motifs followed a gradual process of emancipation from more primitive stages. He studied visual records from the past not only as aesthetic objects, but as human documents, which he read by retracing their literary, historical and psychological sources in order to unlock the social and emotional attitudes from which they originated.

Warburg put these ideas to the test in Florence, where he became absorbed in the artists of the Renaissance and began to question the superficial practices of art description and appreciation. Eventually, he chose to focus on Botticelli, whose paintings *The Birth of Venus* and *Primavera* became the subject of his dissertation, published in 1893. Aby based his interpretation of Botticelli's figures – such as the nymph who reaches to cover Venus with a billowing cloak in the first painting, and the nymph-like girl running from the wind in the second – on his own theories about the depiction of movement. He was especially interested in what he called 'animated accessories', in particular hair and garments.

Warburg examined Botticelli's divinities in the light of both classical and modern sources and concluded that the depiction of their flowing hair and drapery pointed to the revival of ancient motives. His choice of themes and methods illustrated the idea that 'God dwells in minutiae', and his thesis on Botticelli was his first, impressive attempt to see the universal in the particular. In his desire to explain these paintings, the young scholar went far beyond the confines of stylistic analysis and, through the scrutiny of seemingly incidental details, uncovered new layers of meaning. Warburg's thought is partly reminiscent of Nietzsche's view of classical Greece as marked by the opposing forces of the Apollonian and the Dionysian, of rational and irrational tendencies,

Figure 24 Sandro Botticelli, *Birth of Venus*, *c*. 1484, detail.

and his references to classical motifs in fifteenth-century Italian art led to an understanding of the Renaissance as an age traversed by primitive impulses. Through an accurate comparison of Botticelli's figures with similar images from ancient texts and artworks, Warburg concluded that the artist's representation of the young women's fluttering garments and flowing locks preserved the memory of earlier intense emotions that were then overcome. In Botticelli's use of ancient formulas to portray movement, Warburg recognized the symbolic representation of a tension between Christian imagery and pagan expressions, between the harmonious depiction of an ordered world and darker currents that lay beneath the surface. And when he compared Botticelli's twisting girls with 'a number of works of art showing maenads in a nymphlike costume of antique inspiration, about to strike at the recumbent figure of Orpheus', the billowing folds of drapery in the painting's nymphs and in Venus's blowing hair were suddenly revealed as modern intimations of ancient passions: the twisting movements of the maenads, Dionysus's ecstatic and murderous followers.

Aby's student years marked a turning point in his intellectual development. They also formed the basis of his scientific research methods. He had come to regard the study of art both as a topic of scientific enquiry and as a vital endeavour:

> Unfortunately so-called 'cultured' people look at art as if it were a beautiful flowery meadow, on to which they want to stroll of an evening silently to enjoy that splendid scent … We of the younger generation want to attempt to advance the science of art so far that anyone who talks in public about art without having specially and profoundly studied this science should be considered just as ridiculous as people are who dare to talk about medicine without being doctors.

Warburg's discovery of the Italian Renaissance represented his first foray into the question of the human tendency to rationalize man's most chaotic impulses. Despite the fragmentary nature of his writings, the majority of which remained unpublished during his lifetime, the lasting appeal of Warburg's thought lay in its ability to combine low and high culture, to uncover secret correspondences between the mundane and the sublime, between the world we inhabit and a distant past.

A centre for scholars of various descriptions

Aby Warburg's interest in the most varied aspects of art, history, anthropology and culture was reflected in the creation of his extraordinary library. He began to collect books as a very young man. According to a much-quoted anecdote, at the age of thirteen he offered his birthright to his brother Max in exchange for a life-long supply of books. Many years later Max Warburg remembered: 'After a brief pause for reflection, I consented. I told myself that when I was in the business I could, after all, always find the money to pay for the works of Schiller, Goethe, Lessing and perhaps also Klopstock, and so, unsuspecting, I gave him what I must now admit was a very large blank cheque.' As a student Aby was already keeping meticulous notes on all his book purchases. His collection expanded around him, almost organically, and soon became a necessary aspect of his life and research. From the earliest stages of its existence, his library encompassed all the elements that characterized his social and cultural background: the old Jewish tradition of scholarship and book collecting, the banker's sense of empirical knowledge and precision, and the scholarly rigour of the German academic.

The library began to grow extensively at the beginning of the new century, when Aby realized that he was buying books beyond his own research interests, and by 1904 it 'was sizeable enough and had taken a sufficiently definite shape for Warburg to make provisions for it to be handed over to a learned institution in the event of his death, with the proviso that it must be kept as a separate unit'.

Around the same time Aby, married and with two young children, returned to Hamburg from Florence. In Italy he had worked almost incessantly and in a state of nervous self-absorption, which exhausted him. Now in his early thirties, he was beginning to display all the signs of an instability that would cause his mental collapse in 1918. The frenzied and tormented manner in which he had pursued his studies while abroad did not abate once he was back in Hamburg. A year after his return from Italy, Warburg began to suffer from diabetes and hay fever. He complained of sleeplessness and bemoaned the fact that his need to find respite through work was often frustrated by his inability to concentrate unless completely alone.

Aby's library kept growing. By 1904 he had to employ a librarian to catalogue the collection. Despite his restlessness, or maybe as an attempt to banish his fears by seeking order through scholarly activity, he continued to amass new volumes. His compulsion to keep records of all his transactions, impressions and ideas was coupled with a distinctive sense of purpose and a gift for turning his personal responses into universal principles. Around 1907 he became drawn towards the occult. He delved into areas of knowledge in which he saw the symptoms of an ambiguity inherent to Renaissance culture, according to which – as he proved in a famous lecture on the arcane fifteenth-century frescoes in the Palazzo Schifanoia at Ferrara – the idealized gods of Olympus coexisted with the demons of medieval astrology. He studied astrological texts and tarot cards, sought their origins in classical mythology, and traced the evolution of their meanings through the centuries. At the end of 1909 he told his brother Felix that he had 'made his discoveries by buying fifteen hundred books on astrology the previous year'.

In the spring of that year, Aby, Mary and the children had moved to the house that the couple would occupy until the end of their lives, an art nouveau villa at 114 Heilwigstraße, in an affluent neighbourhood not far from the street where Aby had lived as a child. As his library took precedence over family life, the books were arranged on the ground floor and the dining room had to be moved upstairs. A visitor to the house noted: 'The sensitive wife, who really had to have space for her own work as a gifted sculptress, took these primitive events upon herself with touching patience, but the growing children looked full of wrath at the triumphal march of the hated books.'

In Aby's devotion to his library lay the seeds of his singular existence as private scholar and book collector. Although he was made honorary professor by the Hamburg Senate in 1912, he never held an academic appointment and was never affiliated to an institution. But his commitment to his work was unconditional. At the beginning of the new century, having gained a reputation as an art historian, he was working towards a definite aim, which, as he told a student, consisted in developing 'a new method of cultural science, whose basis is the "read" image'. Increasingly ambivalent about his prosperous background and about life in an often openly anti-Semitic environment, Warburg disliked any ostentation of material wealth, saw himself first and foremost as a scholar, and was confidently aware of his own role within his financially powerful family: 'In a favorite refrain, he would say that other rich families had their racing stables, while the Warburgs would have their library.'

When Fritz Saxl, then a twenty-one-year-old student from Vienna with a keen interest in astrology, met Aby Warburg for the first time in 1911, he was amazed at his immense erudition and magnetic personality. The following year, Aby's participation at a congress in Rome, which he had helped to organize and where he presented the findings of his work on the frescoes in the Palazzo Schifanoia, was a triumph widely recognized as a new departure in art-historical scholarship. Around the same time, a new librarian began working at Heilwigstraße, and in October 1913 Saxl was appointed as Warburg's research assistant. In his insatiable intellectual curiosity, Aby compiled long lists of book titles. At the time of his death, there were eighty boxes filled with separate cards for each book title.

It was with Saxl, on a sunny April day in 1914, on the way to see the Masaccio frescoes in the Brancacci Chapel in the Church of Santa Maria del Carmine in Florence, that Warburg discussed the idea of turning his library into a research institute. But his plan turned out to be far more difficult to realize than he imagined. It is a sad irony that Aby's project to create an institution devoted to the pursuit of human enlightenment should be thwarted by the advent of chaos: first through the onset of the First World War, then by his own mental breakdown.

Years of anguish at the horrors and absurdity of war, during which he gave up his studies in order to chronicle contemporary events by filing away inordinate quantities of newspaper cuttings, were followed by Aby's collapse, under the strain of enormous pressures, in October 1918. As ever receptive to the signs of moral and intellectual decline, he had been unable to conquer the force of his response to the torments of the world around him: 'The two preoccupations of his scholarly life, the expression of passion and the reaction to fear, were gripping him in the form of terrible tantrums and phobias, obsessions and delusions which ultimately made him a danger to himself and his surroundings.' After being committed to various institutions, Aby was interned at the Bellevue sanatorium on Lake Constance, where he remained until 1924. In the spring of 1923, in one of the most poignant episodes of his personal life and of his career as a scholar, he proved that he was capable of recovery by delivering a lecture to the clinic's patients and staff.

The talk, entitled 'Reminiscences from a Journey to the Pueblo Indians', concerned a topic closely related to Aby's work on the survival of pagan phenomena and to his own inner demons. Whereas his earlier studies had focused on art and led to conclusions about human psychology, he now examined the problem of wild instincts and of their modern equivalents from an anthropological perspective. In his discussion of the snake rituals through which the Pueblo Indians sought to control lightning and which he had witnessed during his visits to New Mexico and Arizona twenty-seven years earlier, he readdressed his speculations on the primitive use of mythological figures as substitutes for objects of fear. But he now viewed the polarity between such archaic responses and the modern science used by man to supplant ancient mythology more critically.

In remembering his American experience, Aby juxtaposed the snake's zigzag pattern, which symbolized lightning in Indian cultures, and the electric wires of a street in San Francisco, which he called 'Edison's copper serpent'. He saw electricity as the contemporary equivalent of a primitive reaction, and felt that man was going too far in his attempt to abolish the distance that separated him from nature, and that our urge to conquer the natural world risked 'lead[ing] the globe back into chaos'. Several decades later, Ernst Gombrich asked himself what Aby 'would have said to television from the moon'. Today, as we face the threat of global warming and are surrounded by the virtual, man-made space of internet technology, these questions are more relevant than ever.

During Aby's absence from Hamburg his family appointed Fritz Saxl as the institute's acting director and Gertrud Bing, a philosophy student who had joined the library staff in 1921, as his assistant. Saxl, a modest, reserved scholar though friendly and efficient, represented the antithesis to Aby's passionate and commanding personality. Yet Saxl's diplomatic and organizational skills worked wonders, as he transformed a private and in many ways very personal library into a highly functioning and widely respected research institute. According to Bing, Saxl achieved his purpose by moving forward 'on two fronts simultaneously: he made the library available to a larger public, and he invited scholars to lecture and publish under its auspices'.

The contents of Aby's library were ordered by subject according to his concept of human history as defined by four categories that today – with only a slight variation of Aby's plan – are still found in each one of the floors of the institute's premises. This is how Saxl described the original system:

> The books were housed on four floors. The first began with books on the general problems of expression and on the nature of symbols. From here one was led to anthropology and religion and from religion to philosophy and the history of science. The second floor contained books on expression in art, its theory and history. The third was devoted to language and literature, and the fourth to the social forms of human life – history, law, folklore, and so forth … what made it different from any other ready-made library system was the wealth of ideas in the divisions.

This unusual order followed Aby's idea about the library as an environment that nourished its readers' sense of discovery and intellectual enquiry in a way that was creative and fortuitous at the same time:

> Warburg … spoke of the 'law of the good neighbour'. The book of which one knew was in most cases not the book which one needed. The unknown neighbour on the shelf contained the vital information, although from its title one might not have guessed this. The overriding idea was that the books together … should by their titles guide the student to perceive the essential forces of the human mind and its history.

By the time of Aby's return from the sanatorium, the library, comprising nearly 25,000 volumes, had far outgrown its original premises:

> There was no lecture room, no reading room for the increased number of readers, and not even the most ingenious carpenter could invent new devices for producing more wall space. From floor to ceiling the walls were covered with books, the pantry became a stack room, heavy shelves were hanging dangerously over doors, the billiard room had been changed into an office, in the hall, on the landings, in the drawing-room of the family – everywhere books, books, books; and new books came in every day.

Since Aby required that his collection should remain whole, it was decided to move the library into the house built on the land adjoining the family home, which had been purchased with the other house fifteen years earlier. On 1 May 1926 the KBW was officially opened to the public in its new premises at 116 Heilwigstraße. It was a solemn occasion, at which the presence of the mayor and other officials as well as prominent academics (the philosopher Ernst Cassirer, future rector of Hamburg University, held the opening lecture) sanctioned the library's prestigious role in a city that had hitherto been known primarily as a centre of commerce rather than culture.

The new house, with an imposing red-brick exterior and clean geometrical lines, had been designed in a style that combined the look of traditional northern German buildings with stark modernist elements. The construction appeared as a daring mixture of old and new at the time, a visual disturbance in a quiet street and among its patrician neighbours (in the year of its inauguration, a local architect wrote a critical article about the building entitled 'Something Incomprehensible in the Heilwigstraße').

The back of the house had a whitewashed rounded exterior, which followed the elliptical shape of the library's main reading room. In Warburg's thought, the ellipse represented the movement of the cosmos and man's polarity of soul and intellect, so that the building of an institution devoted to the study of symbols was in itself a symbolic structure. On the front, the initials KBW in capital letters occupy a prominent place in between two rows of windows, while on both sides of the staircase two large lanterns could be seen as an allusion to the enlightened nature of the library's activities.

Mnemosyne

In the years between the opening of the new premises in 1926 and Aby Warburg's death on 26 October 1929, both Warburg and Saxl had been in charge of the institute, though rarely at the same time. Despite their bond and Warburg's role as the younger man's mentor, working together in close proximity proved difficult. In her memoir of Saxl, Gertrud Bing noted discreetly that he and Warburg 'agreed that it was useless to attempt to share responsibility for the Institute'. In fact, Warburg's despotic personality and a certain rivalry over their relationship with Bing impeded a close collaboration between the two scholars.

Saxl, who was unhappily married, had been linked romantically with Gertrud Bing since the early 1920s, and the two would go on to live together in London until his death in 1948. For her part, Bing – a self-possessed, emancipated and intelligent young woman – was intensely loyal to Warburg and, according to Kenneth Clark, looked after the great man with 'nun-like care'.

Despite some tension, this was a particularly productive period for both scholars. Saxl travelled extensively through Europe and in 1928 his prolonged research experience in England laid the basis for the future of the Warburg Institute in London after 1933. Warburg also travelled, most notably in Italy, in the company of Bing, in 1928 and 1929. Their second trip lasted ten months and culminated in Aby's now legendary lecture at the Hertziana Library in Rome on 19 January 1929. The talk went on for hours and enthralled an illustrious audience, which included several luminaries from the international academic community and a young Kenneth Clark, for whom the experience was a revelation:

> Dr. Steinmann, the director of the Herziana [*sic*], knowing that my German was imperfect, arranged for us to sit in the front row, and Warburg, who preferred to talk to an individual, directed the whole lecture at me. It lasted over two hours, and I understood about two thirds. But it was enough. Thenceforward my interest in 'connoisseurship' became no more than a kind of habit, and my mind was occupied in trying to answer the kind of questions that had occupied Warburg.

The lecture was part of a vast, unfinished research project, the *Mnemosyne Atlas*, which occupied Warburg during the last four years of his life. The work has no equal in the history of cultural studies. Named after the ancient Greek goddess of memory, it aimed to map, through images, the symbolic language of human expressions and emotions, which first appeared in Greek and Roman antiquity and then re-emerged throughout the centuries, from the Middle Ages to 1920s Germany. *Mnemosyne* was meant as a great archive of the social-cultural memory of the western world, whereby the word 'Atlas' illustrated Warburg's intention to produce a visual map, a historical encyclopedia of images, which would chart the gestures, themes and forms that shaped our culture. To this aim, Warburg used wooden panels covered in black cloth, onto which he pinned a series of black and white pictures, which ranged from artworks to astrological images and newspaper clippings.

For example, in one of the panels Warburg juxtaposed various representations of nymphs, establishing that the same figure could have opposing meanings: it could symbolize protection when it appeared in the guise of a guardian angel (as in a painting by a fifteenth-century Florentine artist), or destruction if portrayed as a head hunter (as the deuterocanonical Judith in an etching from the same period). On another panel, representations of the planet Mars in astrological form – such as those by the seventeenth-century astronomer Johannes Kepler – were flanked by a symbol of the modern conquest of space, the airship *Graf Zeppelin*, whose photograph Aby had cut out of a contemporary newspaper.

Figure 25 Aby Warburg (centre) and Gertrud Bing with Warburg's personal assistant, Franz Alber, in Rome, 1929. Visible on the wall behind them are some of the panels for Warburg's *Mnemosyne* lecture.

Figure 26 Examples of Warburg's panels for his *Mnemosyne Atlas*, Panel A.

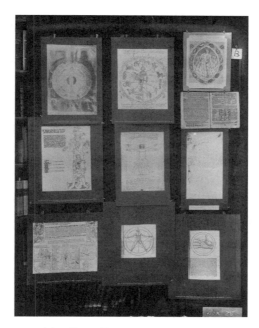

Figure 27 *Mnemosyne Atlas*, Panel B.

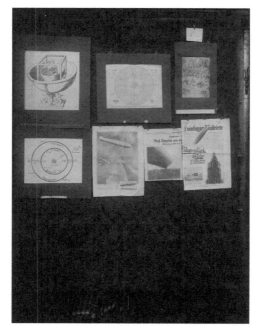

Figure 28 *Mnemosyne Atlas*, Panel C. The panel shows representations of Mars and *Graf Zeppelin*.

A scholarly pantheon

From its inception, the KBW was at the centre of Hamburg's intellectual community. It was also closely linked with the city's new university, whose founding had been financially supported by the Warburgs. Moreover, all the personalities from the coterie of philosophers and art historians that became known as the Hamburg School of Art History were associated with Warburg's Library.

The KBW embraced different disciplines and offered invaluable tools for researchers, but it also remained a private library and a reflection of its founder's personality and ideas. When Saxl reorganized the institute during Warburg's absence in the early 1920s, students and academics began to use the collection and to participate in the newly established lecture programme, yet on the whole the KBW's role within the German cultural landscape was unique. Its singularity reflects Hamburg's own identity as a free city with its own laws and rich commercial tradition. On the one hand, the city was not traditionally known as a thriving cultural centre, because it lacked the state-funded museums and institutions that abounded in places such as Berlin, Munich and Frankfurt. On the other hand, the enterprising spirit and international connections of Hamburg's merchant families ensured the flourishing of a liberal humanism, founded on the philanthropic spirit, enlightened beliefs and cultivated taste of a cosmopolitan Jewish elite.

The majority of the scholars who worked in Warburg's library came from affluent Jewish backgrounds and had been educated in the classical tradition. They had all attended the *Gymnasium*, the most advanced type of secondary school in the German education system and an establishment that placed great emphasis on the study of Latin, Greek and history and, more generally, on the humanistic ideal of self-cultivation. They belonged to the educated urban middle class and loved art, books and classical music. Like Aby himself, the men in these families usually married independent-minded and talented women who – although bound by domestic obligations and often eclipsed by the men's prestige – shared their husband's intellectual interests.

The biography of the philosopher Ernst Cassirer, one of the most prominent figures in Warburg's circle, is a case in point. He was born in 1874 to a wealthy Jewish dynasty, and counted three leading figures of Weimar Germany – the publisher Bruno Cassirer, the art dealer Paul Cassirer and the neurologist Richard Cassirer – among his closest relatives. In 1902, he married his first cousin, the Viennese Toni Bondy, an intelligent and attractive young woman, whose privileged, cultured background mirrored Ernst's own.

Ernst Cassirer studied philosophy in Berlin with the sociologist Georg Simmel and then at Marburg with the neo-Kantian scholar Hermann Cohen, the first

Figure 29 Ernst Cassirer, 1931. Portrait by Transocean.

unconverted German Jew to hold a full university professorship. At first, anti-Semitism hindered Cassirer's academic career and he could only work as a private lecturer. Yet he was a brilliant and original thinker, who would go on to become one of the foremost German philosophers of the twentieth century. In a simplified explanation of his impact, he can be remembered as a representative of a philosophy of culture that reconciled scientific thought as a product of human creativity and reason with all the other areas of cultural life, including myth and artistic expression.

Appointed professor at the University of Hamburg in 1919, Cassirer came into contact with the KBW the following year. His encounter with Warburg's world came at a crucial stage of his development and culminated in the publication of his major work, *The Philosophy of Symbolic Forms* (1923–9). According to Saxl's recollection of Cassirer's first visit to the library, the place made a tremendous impression on the philosopher, who later remembered: 'the philosophical problems involved are close to my own, but the concrete historical material which Warburg has collected is overwhelming'.

The experience of Warburg's collection partly inspired Cassirer's comprehensive view of human culture as defined by symbolic patterns through which man interprets the world. These enable the individual to progress 'from animal reactions to human responses' and comprise creativity, mythology and language. In his essay 'The Problem of Symbol and Its Place in the System of Philosophy' (1927), Cassirer described the experience of looking at a drawing in terms of a transition from a 'simple lived-experience of perception' to the moment when one grasps it 'as something timeless'. This moment not only coincides with the realization of the drawing 'as an excerpt and expression of an artistic language' in its stylistic and historical peculiarity, but is also tinged with 'magical enchantment'. The idea echoes Warburg's belief in art as a symbolic activity through which we produce meaning and express feelings – an activity both prosaic and magic, human and divine. This ambivalence was exemplified in the complex structure of Warburg's library, and it is not surprising that Cassirer saw Aby's collection as an uncanny reflection of his own thoughts.

Cassirer visited Warburg at the clinic shortly before the patient's release and became one of the most assiduous users of his library. At the KBW, the philosopher often ordered new books for his own use – a welcome luxury in those years of inflation. Apparently they were sent straight to his house, and 'every summer Fritz Saxl had all the volumes – which amounted to more than one hundred – collected in great laundry baskets' from the Cassirers' home.

The other scholar 'most seduced by the Library's magic' was the art historian Erwin Panofsky. Like Cassirer, he shared Warburg's idea of art as the expression of human concerns and an interest in the secret connection between

Figure 30 Erwin Panofsky, 1966.

visual representation and individual experience. Panofsky, too, advocated an iconological reading of images that refers to the 'branch of the history of art which concerns itself with the subject matter or meaning of works of art, as opposed to their form'.

In practice, the process consisted in identifying an artwork's themes, in examining their development over time and reading them in the light of cultural, historical and religious factors. According to Panofsky, this happened through a threefold distinction among a simple acknowledgement of an artwork's visual elements ('primary or natural subject matter'), their subsequent identification as themes and concepts ('secondary subject matter') and a more sophisticated level of interpretation ('intrinsic meaning or content'). In some ways, the process is similar to Cassirer's idea of aesthetic experience as described in 'The Problem of Symbol', where a drawing was at first simply perceived and then recognized as a more complex example of artistic expression. Panofsky was deeply influenced by Cassirer's thought, as is clear from a groundbreaking early work, *Perspective as a Symbolic Form* (1927), in which Panofsky identified perspective, symbolically, as an element of the human mind.

Eighteen years younger than Cassirer, in 1920 Erwin Panofsky was called to the University of Hamburg, where he began his career as a private lecturer in the department of art history. At this time, he had already married the Jewish art historian Dora Mosse, of the prestigious Mosse family, whose newspaper empire was one of the liberal authorities of Weimar Berlin. Six years later, Panofsky was appointed full professor, one of three Jewish art historians in the whole of Germany to hold a permanent academic position in their field before 1933.

One of the most talented young scholars of his generation, in 1915 the twenty-three-year-old Panofsky travelled to Hamburg and was introduced to the KBW. Warburg opened his library to him, and it is clear from the tone and frequency of their early correspondence that the scholar had cast a spell over his young guest. From that moment onward, Panofsky formed far-reaching ties with Aby and his circle.

Towards the end of its life in Germany, the library's prestige was aided by the presence and activities of other talented scholars, two of whom would go on to play a central role in ensuring the institute's transfer to London: Raymond Klibansky and Edgar Wind. Both became eminent figures outside Germany after they left the country in 1933, and their backgrounds, early influences and schooling experiences reveal the usual similarities, for they were both cosmopolitan German Jews from well-to-do families and highly educated.

In 1926 Klibansky was invited to Hamburg by his mentor, Ernst Cassirer, who introduced him to Warburg. The meeting was a pivotal moment in the life of the philosophy student, who described Aby's library as a 'labyrinthine paradise'. Many decades later, a ninety-eight-year-old Klibansky described the encounter in a video interview and remembered when Warburg first asked him to work in his library: 'It was a library dear to my heart … books which were linked by some thought … of the survival of Antiquity … when you heard him, as I did, you had the impression that this was not a man who had lost his way in the labyrinth.'

Klibansky spoke without hyperbole, in a quiet voice, his bright blue eyes still lively. In the interview, he illustrated Warburg's ideas about art as a filter and a connection between rational thought and elemental forces. One of his own major works, written with Saxl and Panofsky in the late 1920s and published in 1964, is the seminal study on the historical, philosophical and philological context behind Albrecht Dürer's famous engraving *Melencolia I* (1514). A masterpiece of the history of ideas in the Warburg tradition, the book bears all the marks of Klibansky's extensive knowledge of ancient and medieval philosophy.

When the Nazis came to power, Klibansky, who was teaching philosophy at Heidelberg, lost his post. He left for Britain in the summer of 1933 and lectured in London, Oxford and Liverpool before moving to Canada after the war, where he taught philosophy for almost three decades. He became a British citizen in 1938. During the war, he worked as an intelligence officer at the time of the Allied invasion of Italy, when – as rumour has it – he persuaded Sir Arthur 'Bomber' Harris not to bomb the town of Kues in the Moselle Valley, the birthplace of the Renaissance philosopher and theologian Nicolas of Cusa, whose works Klibansky had edited. At the time, he also happened to find Mussolini's memoirs, which he published in a critically annotated edition.

The range of Klibansky's interests was indeed very wide. And he must have translated something of the humanistic principles of tolerance and civility into real life, for he was liked by many and remembered as a committed humanitarian and animal lover. According to a colleague, Klibansky 'kept fit, had old world manners, dressed elegantly, favoured blue bow ties that enhanced the blueness of his shiny eyes, and cultivated a long mane that earned him the nickname "The mad Russian" among the students'.

Edgar Wind did not possess Klibansky's charm, but he was equally eminent and revered as a scholar. After completing his doctorate under the supervision of Panofsky and Cassirer at the University of Hamburg in 1922, Wind lived in the United States during the time of the German inflation and, having met Warburg in the summer of 1927, became his research assistant at the KBW. Between 1930 and 1933, Wind taught at Hamburg as a private lecturer, specializing in studies – such as his seminal work on English eighteenth-century painters – that combined his interest in art theory with a Warburgian emphasis on a broader cultural and philosophical context.

Dismissed from the university in 1933, Wind organized the transfer of the Warburg Library to England thanks to his useful connections in London. Henrietta Franklin (née Montagu), who had been a protagonist of the women's suffrage movement and would go on to support German refugees throughout the 1930s, was a relative, and introduced Wind to the chemist and educationalist Sir Philip

Hartog. Through Hartog, Wind met Dr C. S. Gibson, professor of chemistry at Guy's Hospital, who, as secretary of the Academic Assistance Council, was able to endorse the KBW's move to England. Between 1934 and 1939 Edgar Wind was deputy director of the new Warburg Institute. Thereafter, for more than a decade, he taught at several American universities before returning to Europe for good in 1955, the year he was appointed to the first chair of art history at the University of Oxford, which he had helped to create.

In a photograph probably taken sometime after 1933, a middle-aged Wind looks contented and self-assured as he stands erect in a double-breasted suit and round rimless glasses, his dark hair, straight nose and full mouth a reminder of his South American ancestry. A few examples from his published work, as well as radio broadcasts and contemporaries' recollections, create a portrait of an eminent scholar and a strong-minded, if somewhat belligerent, man.

There is, for instance, his introduction to the *Bibliography on the Survival of the Classics*, an important reference work published in German in 1931 and in English three years later, in which Wind summed up Warburg's ideas about antique symbols as the key to unlocking 'the drama of civilisation'. And there are the stories of his disagreements with Saxl and Bing over their different understanding of the future role of the institute after Warburg's death. The contrasts rankled at least until Wind resigned as deputy director of the institute after the war. He had always seen himself as 'the crown prince in the intellectual succession to Warburg', disapproving of Saxl's apolitical stance and of his 'tendency ... toward the conventional'. Finally, in 1971, came Wind's attack on Ernst Gombrich's biography of Warburg, whose personality he thought had been distorted by Gombrich's interpretation.

But Edgar Wind is also remembered for his undisputed fame as 'a magician with words', for his reputation as a wonderful lecturer, commanding and accessible at the same time. The English art historian John Pope-Hennessy recalled him at Oxford: 'The sense of form throughout his lectures was impeccable, and at the lectern he was a magician ... His range was very great – it extended from Michelangelo to Matisse – and his manner was intimate and confidential; one's mind moved alongside his own.'

Pope-Hennessy also felt that, despite Wind's academic brilliance, he was 'an unnerving colleague' and 'seemed very foreign' in Oxford. Whether this judgement stemmed from envy or resentment at a foreigner's prestige is hard to say, but on the whole Edgar Wind's immense authority in his field is undisputed. From the available recordings of his 1960 Reith Lectures on *Art and Anarchy*, about the forces that shape our attitude to art in the modern world, it is possible that his heavy German accent and phenomenal display of erudition might have startled his English audience. Yet his well-modulated voice sounds confident, and the brilliance of his artistic knowledge and use of poetic allusions are exhilarating.

Man is at the centre and history is alive

By the mid 1920s, through the towering figures of Cassirer and Panofsky, through Saxl's and Bing's tireless energy, and thanks to the work of younger scholars of Wind's and Klibansky's stature, Warburg's ambition to create a centre in the humanities as 'the observation tower of the academic world' had been fulfilled. His collection was a product of Hamburg as a liberal-minded city, of the Warburg family's civilized traditions and, above all, of a firm belief in humanism as a living value. It is a terrible irony that this pinnacle of cultural achievement should have been thwarted by the advent of the Nazis so soon after being reached.

One of the most inspiring characteristics of Warburg's intellectual circle is the fact that these scholars' work, though scientifically rigorous and often concerned with obscure topics, does not feel remote, but rather alive and relevant. Their interest in humanism as an academic pursuit revived the past for the present. For example, in an essay entitled 'The History of Art as a Humanistic Discipline' (1940), Panofsky compared the medieval idea of *humanitas* as human frailty with the thought of the Renaissance philosophers, for whom man had been placed 'in the centre of the universe so that he might be conscious of where he stands, and therefore free to decide "where to turn"'. In a lecture held in Hamburg in 1925, Fritz Saxl also explored concepts about the freedom and dignity of man, when he said that Hans Holbein, as opposed to Luther, wanted 'the individual mind to be independent and not submerged in God'.

This belief in human autonomy implied an interest in the continued vitality of human records. The idea formed the basis of a collection of essays entitled *Philosophy and History*, presented to Ernst Cassirer on his sixtieth birthday and published in England in 1936. In his contribution, Klibansky addressed the question of the meaning of history with great poignancy. He argued that the study of history should be not a mere chronicle of past events and customs, but rather 'a force stirring the foundations of life itself'. He advocated 'knowledge of the historical picture in its fullness of reality' and maintained a view of history not as a catalogue of facts, places and figures, but as a meaningful record of real life and thought. From this perspective, an immersion into the past is relevant to the future and – in an acknowledgement of Warburg's teachings – it is also a celebration of the human power of memory.

The humanistic vision of the Warburg scholars also emerged through playful learned allusions in their personal correspondence, as brief glimpses into their private voices illuminate the links between their life and work. Their letters, even those dating from their exhausting first months in London, display an irony that enlivened mundane subjects such as bureaucratic matters, financial worries and the packing of book boxes. For instance, their nicknames for each other usually referred to mythological characters or to their love for Italy and the Renaissance. Gertrud Bing was often called 'Bingia', and Saxl 'Signor Sassetti'. The latter was an allusion to the fifteenth-century banker and art patron Francesco Sassetti, to whom the eponymous chapel in the Church of Santa Trinita in Florence is dedicated. The name evoked an abundance of associations in their circle, as Warburg had worked extensively on Sassetti, as well as on Domenico Ghirlandaio, the Florentine painter who had adorned the chapel. In a letter dated 26 July 1933, Klibansky informed Bing of Saxl's progress with the British academics who were visiting Hamburg with a view to considering the library's move to London, and wrote that 'Sgr. Sassetti' was just having dinner with 'your little chemical friend' (Professor C. S. Gibson at Guy's Hospital) 'and his art-historical colleague' (W. G. Constable, then director of the Courtauld Institute). In a similar vein, Saxl was sometimes also referred to as 'Federigo', while Edgar Wind's surname was translated into Italian ('Vento'). In October 1933, alluding to the possibility of the latter being offered a teaching post at Cambridge, Klibansky closed a letter to Bing with a handwritten note: 'What about the Vento's Cambridge matter? I hope we shall succeed in this case.' A couple of months later, a report about the adventurous transport of the library's contents is humorously compared (probably by Saxl) to Hölderlin's interpretation of Sophocles' idea of 'tragic transport' in Greek tragedy, a sort of ecstatic feeling that affects the spectators of ancient drama. More famously, Panofsky was known to his friends as 'Pan'. This was both an abbreviation of his name and a reference to the wild Greek god worshipped in Arcadia, a subject dear to the scholar. In a doubling of the pun, the couple Erwin and Dora Panofsky, who went on to co-author a seminal study on the mythical symbol of Pandora's box, were affectionately known as 'Pan-Dora'.

In some cases, as in the letters sent from Nazi Germany in 1933, the use of nicknames was as much a private jargon as a way of foiling the censors. And yet this world of humorous epithets and learned allusions provides a window into the depth of a commitment to scholarship as part of these scholars' innermost being. They displayed a strong sense of identity. Their German-Jewish background combined a belief in the moral value of learning with a secular faith in personal cultivation and urbanity. It was partly this confidence in their scholarly mission that enabled them to put down roots in a new country without sacrificing their own heritage. In this respect, they performed a rare feat, especially if compared to other German-speaking exiles in London, for whom assimilation into British society (let alone British institutions) proved difficult and often impossible. And it is not surprising that in a letter written from London in February 1934, in which she informed a friend in Hamburg of the first meeting with the British Committee for the Management of the Warburg Institute, Gertrud Bing jokingly stated her intention to frighten the English 'with the profound thoroughness of our scholarship, so as to discourage them from meddling too much into our affairs'.

The Warburg scholars' identity was human and intellectual rather than ethnic or religious. They never defined themselves as Jews or refugees, but rather emphasized their supportive role towards other émigrés, almost as if they did not shared a similar predicament. Aby Warburg himself was ambivalent towards his Jewish roots. Far from denying them, he felt nonetheless that he was above all a German national. His intellectual personality, though very much indebted to the Jewish traditions of scholarship and philanthropy, was decidedly secular. The same could be said of his nephew's, as shown in a note that Eric Warburg wrote to Saxl a few days before the official opening of the institute in London. Eric's advice about the librarians' move to England included a warning against publicizing the institute's Jewish background: '1 – Do nothing rash 2 – Do nothing with Zionists or with Jewish flags.' Ernst Gombrich, an illustrious associate and future director of the institute, also disapproved of emphasizing 'race and religion', and considered 'all forms of nationalism and chauvinism as unfortunate aberrations'.

Bad times for a German library

Despite their secularism, from the late 1920s onwards the Warburg scholars faced the animosity of German anti-Jewish sentiments. The death of the then foreign minister, Gustav Stresemann, on 3 October 1929 – an event that Aby Warburg described, three weeks before his own death, as a 'loss of incalculably dark consequences' – and the Wall Street stock-market crash at the end of the month dealt a devastating blow to German democracy. An intolerant climate began to take hold. Nationalism intensified and anti-Semitism spread, especially within the universities. The Nazi Party registered substantial gains at the polls in 1930 and in the 1932 federal election. In Hamburg, hostility towards the Jews ran high, and Cassirer encountered considerable opposition as rector of the university. The economic crisis took its toll on the Warburg family firm and, consequently, on the library, whose funds dwindled. At the beginning of 1932, Saxl contemplated the possibility of moving the collection to Rome or to the United States. In March of that year, Gertrud Bing complained of cuts to their budget. She was not concerned about a reduction of her own pay or a move to a smaller flat, but lamented the lack of funds to buy books. A year later, with Hitler in power, the library's financial problems worsened further.

On 9 March 1933, Panofsky wrote to an American friend:

As for the Warburg budget, I really don't know myself. Things look pretty bad, for Felix Warburg wanted to 'talk it over' with me (meaning to inform me about the cuts he thinks necessary), but did not do it as yet ... Here is a bank-crisis, too … and the Nazi-victory will not encourage him to invest more money in a Hamburg Library.

A few weeks later, following the passing of the Law that excluded 'non-Aryans' from German universities, both Cassirer and Panofsky relinquished their posts and were considering careers abroad. On 6 May, reporting that fewer and fewer students were visiting the library because their supervisors had left, Saxl asked to meet with Max Warburg to discuss the future of the KBW. This is when the story of the library's transfer from Hamburg to London begins. It has a happy ending, but it entailed many months of travels and negotiations, and of copious, often coded, correspondence. Since it was imperative to keep the plan a secret from the German authorities, the Warburg scholars referred to the move as a project for a manuscript catalogue.

One of Saxl's initial steps towards finding a new home for the library outside Germany was a trip to England in May 1933. At first he thought that there would be no need for another art-historical institution in London, as the Courtauld Institute of Art had opened the previous year. But a letter from Wind soon reassured him that the Courtauld people would not have presented an obstacle, since they had only 'some very beautiful paintings (especially French Impressionists) and surprisingly few books (just over 3,000)'. And so the search for a London home continued, while the links with English academia became progressively more useful. On 25 May, Wind's aunt, Mrs Franklin, wrote to William Beveridge, who had just founded the Academic Assistance Council. Thanks to her recommendation, Wind was able to contact Sir Edwin Deller, principal of University College London who, in turn, introduced Wind to W. G. Constable and C. S. Gibson. This string of contacts proved effective. On 31 May, Wind had a long telephone conversation with the Academic Assistance Council, during which he explained the aims and organization of the Warburg scholars and their library. He emphasized the political reasons behind their decision to emigrate. On 6 June, he sent a confident note to Gertrud Bing in Hamburg ('Things are too good to be true') and a long memorandum to Edwin Deller with a detailed description of the 'Purpose of the Institute'.

In July 1933 Wind travelled to Holland. On his return he wrote to Saxl, in code, that the air in England was 'much fresher than in Holland' and that everybody agreed with the plan for the manuscript edition. This meant that the English had approved the move to London. A few weeks later, after Gibson's and Constable's successful trip to Hamburg, where they visited the library and had dinner with members of the Warburg family at Max's house, it was decided that Aby's collection should be transferred to London as soon as possible for a period of three years.

The Warburgs were unable to shoulder all the costs, and money was still a problem. But at the end of September 1933 things began to look up, when Lord

Lee of Fareham agreed to finance the library, anonymously, for a sum of £3,000 a year for three years. On 28 September Gertrud Bing, calm and efficient as usual, wrote to Eric Warburg:

> We find that it would be most unadvisable [*sic*] for Saxl to return to Hamburg now. He has gained the confidence of Constable and Gibson ... is able to influence the [Academic Assistance] Council's activities and is consulted on the appointments of German scholars ... It has not yet been decided who will be called to work at the Library in London. A committee in charge of finding suitable library premises will be formed soon. As agreed, we are ready to close the Library to the public on 1 October.

Nothing stood in the way of the library's transfer to London. The delicate matter of bypassing the German authorities had been addressed four months earlier, when the American consul in Berlin informed Eric that the KBW's main shareholders were his uncles Paul and Felix in New York, and that its 'majority ownership interest and maintenance was therefore in the hands of American citizens' – a fact that allowed the Warburg family to decide on the library's future independently of Nazi intrusion.

On 10 November 1933, Lord Lee of Fareham wrote a letter to the undersecretary of state at the Home Office explaining the situation: 'Owing to the present political situation in Germany a state of affairs has arisen which makes it necessary for the above Institute ... either to remain closed or to transfer its entire activities to a country where independent research can be carried out without political interference.' He also asked whether the British government 'would be willing to permit a skeleton staff of the Institute' to carry on its work in London. The matter, he added, was 'one of great importance and urgency, particularly in view of the fact that Dr. Saxl's present Home Office "Permit" to remain in England expires on November 20'. Lord Lee's request was granted. After Saxl left a statement with the Ministry of Labour on the purpose and activities of the Warburg Institute and visited Thames House, MI5 sent a file to the Home Office with a succinct note on the cover that read: 'We have nothing against the Institute or any of its personnel.'

Although the American Warburgs still hoped that the KBW might be transferred to the United States, the matter was decided in favour of relocating to London. Meanwhile, in Hamburg, preparations intensified. The local authorities had agreed to the move on condition that the Warburg family prevent the foreign press from publishing anything regarding the transfer of the library to England and that the collection return to Germany after three years. The move had to happen quickly and without publicity. Apart from a short news item published in the *New York Times* on 22 November 1933, which Eric Warburg immediately asked to be retracted, it did.

Hermia afloat

The next part of the story is fascinating, a heroic feat. An entire library was shipped from Hamburg to London overnight, while its guardians worked at both ends to ensure its safe arrival. It was as if the civilized world were floating away from Nazi Germany towards a place where, revived by a different culture, it could flourish afresh.

At the beginning of December 1933 Fritz Saxl was in England and in charge of the organization for the library's arrival, while Gertrud Bing coordinated the move from Hamburg. This involved arranging the removal of about 60,000 books and thousands of photographs and slides, as well as furniture and technical equipment. It was no easy task, and the enormous practical challenge was coupled with a considerable degree of psychological adjustment. An interesting document in this respect is a memorandum that Max Warburg sent to Bing on 26 November, almost exactly two weeks before the move. It was meant to prepare the staff for the encounter with a foreign culture, to serve as a sort code of conduct for their successful assimilation into the British way of life. Max advocated diplomacy and discretion, and encouraged an unobtrusive demeanour. His text is also a window into a German perception of British mentality:

> 1. Library staff should avoid voicing political opinion (Right or wrong, my country). 2. Members of staff should appear reserved, dignified, strong and unpretentious in every way. 3. Research should be carried on as before. Scholars, and especially ordinary readers, should be given clear instructions and, in particular, complicated explanations should be avoided. The English are passionate about simple, straightforward statements. 4. It is important to emphasise the fact that the relocation of part of the Library to London is only a loan. No one knows what will happen at the end of the three-year period etc.

Max's advice highlights the librarians' role as the collection's chaperones. This was a library's journey to safety, and the people who accompanied it had to behave as unobtrusively as possible. In a unique occurrence in the history of the emigration from Nazi Germany, the main protagonists of this escape abroad were not individuals but books. As Fritz Saxl noted several years later, 'travelling adventures are not so common in the life of learned institutions. These are stable by nature, rooted to the spot by massive buildings or heavy equipment, and requiring a tranquil environment in which to develop.' The library's move to London appears as a reversal of the public book-burning spectacularly staged by the Nazis in every German city a few months earlier. The transfer of Aby's books symbolized the rescue of knowledge and freedom of expression.

Four days after Max Warburg sent his memorandum, removal companies had been chosen and booked in both cities, and on 10 December the steamship

Hermia was already waiting for its cargo in Hamburg's harbour (on the Warburg Institute website we read that the steamer in question was in fact called *Jessica*). At 116 Heilwigstraße there was fevered activity. Books, slides and photographs were packed first; the furniture would follow in a separate shipment in January. Although Bing's records of the removal men's wages show that some of them had been packing boxes for well over a month, it all happened swiftly. In his account of the move, Eric Warburg offered a poignant tableau of one of its last moments: 'The final scene in Hamburg was enacted in the bare elliptical Reading Room which Professor Warburg had built six or seven years earlier; here his widow offered tea, on trestles and planks, to the staunchly anti-Nazi packers who had completed the move in record time.' In hindsight, the moment was rendered all the more touching by the fact that Mary Warburg, who died almost exactly a year later, on 4 December 1934, was seeing her husband's books for the last time. By Wednesday 11 December 1933, everything was ready. The boxes were taken to the port. The following day Saxl received a telegram from his colleagues in Hamburg with the momentous message: 'Hermia afloat.'

Meanwhile, in London, Saxl was writing to the director of the Hamburg removal firm to thank him for his services. He also thought of keeping the empty cartons after the books had been unpacked, since 'the future of the library is still uncertain and we don't want to have to order new boxes if we can avoid it'. His mood oscillated between relief at the successful transfer of Warburg's collection and doubts about its future in a foreign country. On 16 December Gertrud Bing, who had joined Saxl in England, announced to her Hamburg colleagues that the boat had arrived safely, despite minor damage to some of the boxes. She and Saxl spent Christmas together in London where, given the number of problems to be solved, they kept seasonal celebrations to a minimum.

The weather promised a fairly mild holiday with light winds and moderate temperatures that year, and London, expecting 'more traffic and bustle than usual' because Christmas fell close to a weekend, was made to look festive ('Paddington is decked with lanterns and gauze and steamers, together with a large Christmas tree[,] and a forest of illuminated Christmas trees has sprung up among other decorations at Euston'). Meanwhile, Saxl and Bing worked to ensure the success of a very delicate operation. In their desire to strengthen their ties with the local art-historical community, they sent Christmas cards to British colleagues. The Warburg Institute Archive preserves a note in which Kenneth Clark – who was about to begin his post as director of the National Gallery – thanked them both 'for the beautiful card which the Institute sent me this Christmas'. The library faced obstacles on several fronts, and although Saxl and Bing could count on the help of powerful allies such as Lord Lee and Lord Melchett, they must have been under considerable physical and mental strain (the latter was a Jewish philanthropist, director of Imperial Chemical Industries and owner of Thames House).

On Boxing Day 1933, Saxl reported to Eric Warburg that everything was running 'smoothly and according to plan' and that he would hold his first lecture at the end of January. But he also complained of the high customs tariffs (eventually paid by a friend of Lord Lee's) and of an anti-Semitic incident at Thames House, where an American member of the board had disapproved of the low rent the new tenants were paying for the library premises. This last problem was also solved: 'as Chairman of the Board, Melchett has successfully challenged the question and told off his people, so that now they don't know how politely they should treat us'. Other questions concerned the search for a good and affordable English publisher for the institute's publications, the ongoing building work at Thames House – which was likely to last until February – and, last but not least, the constant financial pressures.

'An incalculable gain to English scholarship'

Sometime after Christmas, Gertrud Bing travelled back to Hamburg to oversee the packing and transport of the library's furniture. Bizarrely, this also included a motorbike, which had just been repaired and would be used in London to deliver books to other institutions. Though she became ill with influenza during her short stay, Bing did not lose her pragmatic spirit and dealt with several matters before returning to London two weeks later. As ever concerned for others, she helped many friends and colleagues in need throughout those difficult years. In Hamburg that winter, for instance, she decided that Otto Fein should join the library staff in London as photographer and bookbinder, and she praised a young colleague, Walter Solmitz, for his work in the old premises at Heilwigstraße ('Hall, reading room and cellar are a fantastic picture, as everything in there is piled up'). She was also worried about Claire Lachmann, a doctoral student of Panofsky and Saxl who had been working at the library and who, being Jewish, was in a hurry to leave Germany. In the end, Claire Lachmann immigrated to Palestine, but Bing's concern – as expressed in her letter to Saxl – shows that the Warburg circle was not only a scholarly institution, but also something resembling a family:

> I would ask you to consider once again the possibility of us all renting a furnished house for the next few months, which Mrs Lachmann could run for us. It would be a great relief to her, though we should not base our decision only on this. I am also thinking that her presence might help Miss von Eckardt while she settles in and grapples with the new language. Please let me have your definitive answer soon, since Mrs Lachmann needs to know whether this is a possibility.

Not long after writing this, Bing returned to London and began to write the first English-language report on the activities of the new institute. Both she and Saxl worked incessantly to lay the foundations of Warburg's library in exile. They lived not far from each other at the time, in north-west London, a long bus ride away from the centre of town. The area was Hampstead Garden Suburb, and part of a recent residential development in East Finchley, just north of Hampstead Heath. It was a typically English urban landscape, a mixture of red-brick houses and more modest semi-detached two-storey cottages with large bay windows and pitched roofs, neat front gardens, small wooden gates and thick green hedges to separate the houses from the street. Saxl and Bing, a ten-minute walk away from each other, lived in rented rooms in two of the smaller properties. Saxl's house, at 52 Erskine Hill, is very similar to 31 Brookland Rise, where Bing was a lodger. But their living arrangements were less than ideal. Months later Bing wrote to a friend that her landlady had declared that 'she'd rather eat dry bread all her life than keep me any longer in her house', and that Bing, Saxl and other friends were planning to share a furnished house in Bromley, south London. This would have solved the question of unfriendly landlords, a recurring problem in the life of the émigrés.

Saxl and Bing did not spend much time at home during those hectic first months in London. January was especially busy. Their activity revolved around two major tasks: securing funds for the library and its staff, and publicizing their presence as a new cultural asset while trying to play down their foreignness. There were also other, more menial demands, such as delivering books to other libraries on the motorbike that they had shipped over from Germany – a task often carried out by Saxl himself.

On 1 January Saxl was pondering the question of how to finance Otto Fein's post and help Claire Lachmann. The following day he was weighing the options for Panofsky's future in Europe in a letter to Professor Constable of the Courtauld Institute (Panofsky, who eventually settled in the United States, resented Saxl and Bing for failing to include him in their London plans and felt that they favoured Klibansky). On 6 January Kenneth Clark, as well as acknowledging Saxl's and Bing's Christmas greetings, asked Saxl for help in deciphering a detail of a painting from the National Gallery collection. More importantly, he praised the Warburg Institute as 'an incalculable gain to English scholarship'.

Saxl's next two days were devoted to a survey of the new library premises at Thames House with Lord Lee and the building manager. This was followed by discussions about floor space and estimates of building costs. On the evening of 21 January Saxl missed an appointment with Klibansky, who waited in vain for over an hour outside a Lyons' Corner House, tried to ring him ten times without success, and finally wrote him a concerned letter ('am quite worried. "Che c'è?" [Italian for 'What is the matter?']'). A couple of days later Saxl received a note from Eric Warburg, who was arriving in London on the morning of Friday 26

January. As a representative of the Warburg family, Eric monitored the library's progress and examined its financial situation. On 30 January, Saxl sent him a detailed list of expenditures and a progress report on the institute's forthcoming publications, while informing him of the need to find money to pay the salary of Edgar Wind, whom Saxl regarded as 'indispensable for keeping up the contact … with London University'. When Cassirer wrote to Saxl from Oxford on 29 January to inform him that he was going to be in London in two days' time, he seemed aware of his friend's exacting schedule: 'you can find me the day after tomorrow (Wednesday) in the British Museum reading room between 11 and 12. But please come only if you were going there anyway.'

February was just as busy. The pressure to complete the refurbishment of Thames House mounted, as Saxl and Bing hoped to be able to show the library 'in all its splendour' in time for Lord Lee's return from holiday at the end of March. On 13 February Klibansky invited Saxl to an evening lecture at the 'British Institute of Philosophy', but feared that the latter might be too exhausted. Saxl, who was attending a conference at the Courtauld Institute at the time, would certainly have been tired.

Bing was also overworked. That month she completed her report. The document is a good example of her and her colleagues' Germanic precision and intellectual robustness. After expressing gratitude to their hosts ('Thanks to the disinterested help of our English friends'), she illustrated the whole range of their library's services, such as open shelves, borrowing facilities, an extensive photographic collection and extended opening hours, which were unavailable in the major English libraries. She then went on to present details of the institute's internal organization, financial position and research activities, before concluding with a powerful metaphor: 'As we are now, we seem to resemble a large hospital run by a staff of efficient doctors beautifully equipped with all technical contrivances, but having no nurses, and being unable to take in patients because the funds for feeding and medicine are missing.' The medical comparison was apt. In envisaging Thames House as an empty hospital, in which a handful of doctors were busy arranging their tools for a major operation, Bing was also describing the library's impact upon British art history.

Put boldly, there was no serious art-historical department in Britain before the arrival of the Warburg scholars. As several émigrés recognized at the time, the English were generally suspicious of theories and considered art mainly as a matter of visual enjoyment rather than as a subject of philosophical speculation. In a letter to a friend written at the beginning of January 1934, Panofsky defined the English as 'a matter of fact people', unimpressed by rhetoric. Around the same time, Saxl also expressed his doubts about the English by stating that he found their rhythm very slow and that 'he had learnt to be patient and to affect a sort of old man's resignation'. Years later, Ernst Gombrich recalled in an amusing anecdote that some English art historians 'distanced themselves from the Germanic way' and, sceptical of the scientific methods of the Warburg scholars, mockingly used the word *Forschen*, from the German *Kunstforschung* (art research), which they thought sounded funny 'and so pronounced it in a certain way: "I must do Forschen"'.

In 1930s Britain the study of art was still based on connoisseurship and aesthetic appreciation in the style of Ruskin and Pater, and eschewed rigorous methods and intellectual enquiry. However, some critics were aware of the problem, and there were changes on the horizon. Writing in February 1934, at the very time Saxl and Bing were busy creating what they hoped would become 'a centre for a study of history of art' in the German sense of the word, the artist – and Bloomsbury member – Roger Fry published a piece in the *Burlington Magazine*, in which he pleaded for 'the advent of the trained art historian', who could bring order into a world of 'chaotic and capricious attributions'. The newly arrived Warburg scholars were about to achieve much more than this. They were turning the fledgling field of British art history into a serious academic discipline, in which cross-cultural connections were made and artworks were not merely described, but rather were examined from the point of view of their place in history and according to exact philological methods.

Saxl, Bing and their small circle of friends and colleagues were aware of their intellectual advantage, and their efforts to establish the institute's reputation in England reveal a strong sense of purpose. For a time, their daily existence was devoted to countless practical and bureaucratic tasks concerning the library. Yet despite the inevitable mixture of hope and anxiety, their activities were informed by a cheerful determination to succeed and did not seem impaired by a longing for the country that they had lost. The Warburg scholars were driven by a moral imperative for the sake of humanity and knowledge. This is probably one of the reasons why they never gave the impression of being defeated by the hardship of a life of hard work and exile.

The faces of humane scholarship

Even though Edgar Wind had established contacts with influential British sponsors, the library's move to England would not have been as successful without the commitment of Fritz Saxl and Gertrud Bing. Neither the generosity of the British nor the prestige of the famous scholars associated with the Warburg circle would have sufficed to ensure the smooth transition of a whole institution to a new country in such a short time.

In their quiet and unassuming way, within a couple of months Saxl and Bing had raised money; arranged meetings; drafted reports; and supervised library staff, building work, and the unpacking and sorting of books, slides and photographs. They organized lectures and publication series, answered queries, travelled,

Figure 31 The house on Erskine Hill where Fritz Saxl lodged in 1933 and 1934.

fostered ties with colleagues and other academics, and dealt with the British authorities. They had only three years to prove that the Warburg Institute was an indispensable asset to British culture and they knew that three years would pass quickly. But they never wavered. Their attitude and work ethics are encapsulated in Bing's description of Saxl's surge of energy after the transfer to London:

> For Saxl the situation was not unlike that of twelve years earlier [when he had turned Warburg's library into a public research institution]. He had again to explain himself, to explore opportunities and to administer for the unforeseen. This time he had the advantage of his experience and the Institute with its excellent library as a solid reality behind him – if only he could find people to make use of it. He did not mind having to make this fresh beginning: on the contrary, he almost welcomed it as an enforced breaking away from the rut. Another ten years, and he would say: 'It almost seems a pity that the Institute is now finally settled. What fun it would have been to start all over again.'

Saxl was resilient and everybody seemed to like and respect him, but there was also a mercurial unpredictability about his character. As Bing recalled: 'more than once, when people were trying to find a formula for him, they hit independently upon a comparison with Mercury, the airy, fast-moving, mischievous messenger

Figure 32 Fritz Saxl in the 1920s.

of the gods, tutelary deity of travellers, scholars and craftsmen'. He was a modest and quiet man, but also jovial and good-natured, and an energetic organizer (Aby Warburg jokingly called him 'Saxl à vapeur' because of his tireless activity). A meticulous researcher and indefatigable traveller, Saxl was at home in many of the European libraries he had been visiting since his student days. His appearance somewhat belied his enormous capacity for energy. He was slight, with dark hair, a tall forehead, a straight prominent nose and a pointed chin. A notable characteristic in every photograph is the hint of a smile in his heavy-lidded, penetrating eyes and on the mouth, half-hidden by a small moustache. Apparently, when he was a child, his teachers at school could not bring themselves to punish him for playing truant, because they found that he had 'such a laughing face that it makes you smile'. As an adult, he retained something of that impish quality, perhaps a sign of his Austrian Jewish sense of irony.

There was a reassuring and very human quality in his gaze. Perhaps this is what Gertrud Bing defined as 'the almost magical spell of his personality, his understanding of men, his capacity to absorb shocks and turn setbacks into opportunities'. Moreover, 'he hated all formality, institutions and dignities because they fettered the individual spirit'.

Saxl was reserved and did not like to talk about himself. He revealed very little of his personal life. His wife Elise, whom he had married in his early twenties and who suffered from nervous complaints for most of her adult life, hardly features in his correspondence. And of his romantic attachment to Bing, who, in her letters, addressed him with the formal 'Sie' as late as 1933, is shrouded in mystery. For years, after the time spent in rented rooms in the first months of exile, they shared a house in the genteel surroundings of Dulwich, in south-east London, where Saxl liked to tend to their garden at weekends, as he did until the day before he died, suddenly, on Monday 22 March 1948.

While it is true that Saxl and Bing lived for their work and led a quiet life, they were not bookish recluses, had many friends and were generous, witty and convivial. They regarded intellectual endeavour as something vital. In Saxl's case, his passion for learning went back to the Jewish tradition of religious scholarship, coupled with a sort of understated brilliance and a dry Viennese humour. He came from a family of shopkeepers from the eastern provinces of the Austro-Hungarian Empire, and always remembered how 'his grandfather used to study the Talmud in a backroom during leisure hours spared from making a scant living'.

Whereas Saxl was above all a scholar, who described himself as 'a vagrant, a wanderer through the museums and libraries of Europe', Gertrud Bing published very little and devoted her life to assisting other scholars and keeping alive the memory of Aby Warburg and his collection. To a wider audience, she may have been an almost invisible character among the great figures associated with the Warburg Institute. Her relative obscurity is a result of her own choices and the consequence of being a woman in a very masculine world. But her personality shines bright in this story. She was a pivotal presence at the heart of the library for a long time, first as Warburg's closest assistant, then as one of the main organizing forces during and after the move to London, and finally as the institute's director after Saxl's death and until her own passing in 1964.

A tribute volume to her memory published by friends and colleagues after her death contains moving accounts of her remarkable personality. She emerges from these recollections as kind, sensible, clever, funny and immensely knowledgeable, a brilliant conversationalist and a truly engaging woman. Bing was not particularly fond of England, was rather indifferent to Germany and loved Italy above all. As opposed to most émigrés, she did not strive for assimilation and was not interested in becoming anglicized. This is likely to have facilitated her life in exile, as she never struggled to conform but always remained herself, a true cosmopolitan.

In person, the first impression of her – according to Gombrich – was one of severity and distance ('she had a great skill in keeping herself out of the picture'). A handful of photographs show a simply dressed woman of medium height with short dark hair, thick eyebrows and round rimless glasses. The Renaissance scholar D. J. Gordon penned a vivid portrait of her as stern yet rather brilliant: 'If Saxl alarmed me, Bing frightened me. She was the image of severity … dark cropped hair, the endless cigarettes, the dark austere clothes, the use of surnames, her quickness, the sharpness of her questions: all to me … suggested the advanced woman of the Twenties.' Behind her plain appearance was a person of sophisticated intelligence with surprising reserves of strength. And behind her seemingly cold exterior was a gift for communication, a sympathetic

Figure 33 Gertrud Bing in the 1950s.

outlook on life and the authenticity of a balanced personality. Her biographical memoir of Saxl, for instance, is not only profound and vividly written, but also reveals the extent of Bing's skills as a judge of character.

And it is possible to imagine that some of the traits she attributed to Saxl – his instinctive sense of pragmatic solutions, his way of making himself useful to others, his ability to adapt to new surroundings – could also be applied to Bing herself.

Of all the exiles from Nazi Germany in 1930s London, Fritz Saxl and Gertrud Bing were among the least concerned about their outsider status. Surprisingly, they chose to settle in Dulwich, an area not usually associated with refugees. As D. J. Gordon wrote in his tribute: 'I never thought of Saxl and Bing as "refugees" at all. The unmistakable smell of exile was never in that house.' The same could be said of the Warburg Institute. Its staff was mainly German, as were many of its early visitors, yet the library was not a place of exile and displacement, but a haven of independent scholarship with an Anglo-German identity.

The unimaginable becomes real

At the beginning of 1934 rumours were spreading in London about the new library. In February Klibansky informed Saxl that 'at Bedford College (for women) everybody was asking about the Warburg Library and whether I was connected with it'. Less than a month later, Saxl was finally able to work from Thames House where, as he wrote to Eric Warburg, it was 'all still very messy, but at least most of the bookshelves have been installed and we are planning to fill them next week'. Soon they began to send books to their readers. Their services were efficient and included inter-library loans from England and abroad. On 10 April, Saxl ordered a volume on Latin proverbs from the Prussian State Library in Berlin for the scholar, and librarian and keeper of the papers at the Foreign Office, Sir Stephen Gaselee, who gratefully acknowledged its arrival nine days later. The following week Bing, writing to a friend from Thames House, felt relieved at the thought of what they had achieved: 'one can once again believe in possibilities which until now would have been unimaginable'.

The institute opened its doors for the first time at the beginning of May, when the librarians' main task was to find new means of publicity. Saxl was hopeful and as ever optimistically inclined. On 4 May Saxl and Bing invited many of their English friends and colleagues, such as Professor Livingstone and Kenneth Clark, to see the new library. The latter wrote to Bing that he was on his way to Venice and disappointed to be unable to visit: 'I should have liked to have been one of the first to use the Institute. We come back in the middle of June, and I hope it will be possible to see you immediately.'

Several people accepted their invitation and on 7 May Saxl informed Eric Warburg that the reading room was already well attended, albeit mainly by Germans, and that they had already held a lecture. 'I am optimistic about anything that doesn't cost money', he concluded. Despite permanent financial worries and his and Bing's intense involvement on behalf of less fortunate émigrés, Saxl did have reasons to be cheerful. The institute's first initiatives were going well and a lecture by Cassirer, sometime in late May, seems to have been a memorable occasion.

On Saturday 2 June, a notice appeared as far away as Scotland, where the *Aberdeen Press and Journal* reported that 'a notable addition to London's libraries' had 'just been made by the transference of the famous Warburg Library and Institute to London'. More importantly, on 10 June, the *Observer* ran an article entitled 'A Library of Civilisation: Warburg Institute in London. 70,000 Volumes', in which a special correspondent described the significance and aims of this extraordinary new institution:

a library of a kind not yet known in this country. Here is a library in which the books – whether they are first editions of immense value or cheap reprints – are in open shelves where the student can go and root to his heart's content. The books are arranged in the shelves more according to the practice of a museum than a library: arranged, that is to say, with their psychological effect on the student as much in mind as the necessity of scientific classification.

A significant step towards establishing the library as a London institution was to be the party at Thames House on 28 June. It had been Lord Lee's idea, and the Warburg scholars and librarians, wishing to comply with English social etiquette, set out to organize the event at very short notice. Invitations were printed and posted two weeks before the party. This was going to be an 'At Home', a closed and rather informal gathering, a sort of 'open house' inauguration for friends, associates and other British academics. As well as the main supporters of the institute and members of the Warburg Committee – Lord Lee of Fareham; Professors Gibson, Constable and Livingstone – those invited included Ernst and Toni Cassirer, who came from Oxford; Kenneth Clark, who attended with his wife; Sir Stephen Gaselee, who was unable to join them 'because of a previous engagement'; and the assistant keeper of Greek and Roman antiquities at the British Museum, Roger Hinks, who gratefully accepted. On 17 June, Professor Gibson asked Gertrud Bing to send invitations to the scientists, and secretaries of the Royal Society, Sir Henry H. Dale and Sir Frank E. Smith; to the surgeon T. B. Layton, a colleague at Guy's Hospital; to the marchioness of Donegall; and to a Mrs Brocklebank. Gibson himself invited the assistant secretary of the Academic Assistance Council, Charles Milne Skepper. Gibson, who had cared about the library's plight since his visit to Hamburg the previous summer and was aware of its tight budget, was particularly keen for the event to succeed. On the day before the party, he offered to provide flowers for the occasion, which Bing accepted, noting that they would 'certainly do much to exhilarate the somewhat austere surroundings of the Library'.

On 15 June, Saxl explained in a letter to Professor Livingstone how the idea of the tea party had come about:

> As we do not propose to open the Library with an official ceremony, Lord Lee thought that a tea party would be a simple way of marking the occasion.
>
> We have had to make these arrangements rather hurriedly, but we very much hope that you, as a Member of the Committee, will be able to come and assist in making the function a success.

Nine days later Livingstone, who had already arranged to visit his sister in Chichester, declined the invitation. Yet plenty of people attended, and the Warburg Institute's first official occasion was a success. In London, Thursday 28 June was an average summer's day, mainly fair and moderately warm, after bouts of rain the previous afternoon had disrupted a cricket match at Lord's and the Wimbledon tennis tournament. Saxl was pleased. On 2 and 3 July he wrote to both Eric and Felix Warburg, in Amsterdam and New York respectively, that their 'At Home' had been attended by 'about seventy guests, quite a number of important people among them', and that they had printed and distributed an informative leaflet about the library, which he was enclosing.

The most poignant comment about the event came from Cassirer on 9 July. In a letter to Saxl from Vienna, the philosopher recalled wistfully that 'harmonious reception' and felt as if the party had 'occurred an eternity ago'. There was a reason for his sombre mood. Two days after the Warburg Institute's 'At Home', which had been attended by many of those who had helped to secure the library's future and brightened up by Gibson's flowers, Hitler's Germany – and Europe as a whole – was shaken by the events of the so-called 'Night of the Long Knives', one of the most shocking crimes of the Nazi regime's early years. The contrast between the two circumstances reminded the exiles associated with the Warburg Library of the horrors from which they had just escaped, and distanced them further from their homeland.

Once the reception was over, the Warburg staff resumed their usual activities. On 5 July, Gibson informed Saxl that he had secured substantial grants from the Academic Assistance Council for Raymond Klibansky and Rudolf Wittkower (the latter was a thirty-three-year-old German art historian who had recently joined the Warburg Institute and would go on to become professor of fine art at the Slade School in London before embarking on an illustrious career in the United States). The following week, Saxl corresponded with Roger Hinks about a 'semi-archeological matter' involving Rome's early Christian basilicas, and worked with Klibansky on a study of Saturn, which formed the basis for their – and Panofsky's – seminal book on the ancient origins of melancholia, published thirty years later as *Saturn and Melancholy: Studies in the History of Natural Philosophy, Religion and Art*. On 16 July, at 8.15 p.m., Saxl and Bing joined Kenneth and Jane Clark for dinner at the Clarks' grand home at 30 Portland Place. And on 25 July Bing informed Lord Lee that they were planning to close the library during the summer break, leaving only one member of staff to deal with urgent requests.

Before leaving for the summer, the Warburg scholars became involved in yet another plan to enhance the institute's reputation by publicizing their methods and their research. Between 30 July and 4 August 1934 they invited participants of the International Congress of Anthropological and Ethnological Sciences, which was then taking place in London, to visit the library. Here, they had set up twenty black panels (presumably the same ones that Warburg had used for his *Mnemosyne* project), on which – as Bing explained in a letter to Eric Warburg – they showed examples of 'the afterlife and transmutations of visual symbols from the Primitives (which should interest the anthropologists) to more complex layers of civilisation, e.g. the serpent as symbol of evil on the one hand and of salvation on the other'.

In just over seven months, Saxl, Bing and the other members of the Warburg circle had resurrected a great German library and gone a long way in promoting it as a London institution. Now they were taking some time off, although their holidays were mostly dedicated to scholarly work. In August, Bing spent a few weeks in the Swiss Alps before travelling to Italy to join Saxl, who was doing some research in Venice, at the beginning of September. By this time, the library in London had reopened. On 15 September, Klibansky wrote complaining of having to welcome readers on his own, and asked Saxl to enlist the help of Edgar Wind, who was on a family holiday in Ireland. Klibansky argued that it was important to have someone there at all times, so as to 'offer foreign scholars the possibility of intellectual exchange'.

By the end of its first English summer, the institute, though by no means financially secure, was doing well. On 26 September Saxl wrote to Professor Livingstone that the library had 're-opened after its August holidays' and that it was 'visited by an increasing number of English scholars'. Two months earlier, the buoyancy with which Saxl and Bing informed the Warburg family in Hamburg of the institute's increasing popularity in its host country had been met with a humorous reply from Max Warburg. He was pleased to hear the good news and, in a typically witty remark, replied that there always seemed to be 'a certain overestimation of German scholars'. But these scholars, who were also the guardians of a unique collection of books and photographs, could not be overestimated.

The interest that, in 1931, had led a small group of German intellectuals to explore the British relationship with the classics was reignited during their first decade in London. Through their study of art, history and culture, the Warburg scholars built bridges. This became evident in 1941, when, at the height of Britain's war against Nazi Germany, Fritz Saxl and Rudolf Wittkower organized an exhibition entitled *British Art and the Mediterranean* and drew attention to the cultural roots that bound England to Europe. The following year, as the institute became involved in a campaign to photograph buildings and works of art that were in danger of being bombed, an article in the *Architectural Review* stated: 'the Warburg Institute is proving more and more of a blessing to live archaeology and history in England'. And it is heartening to think that a German institution should have been responsible for emphasizing the links between Britain and continental Europe at such a tragic historical moment. When the institute was officially incorporated into the University of London in 1944, an article published in the *Observer* on Christmas Eve called the event 'the nation's best Christmas present of the year' and reaffirmed its role as a symbol of cultural cooperation.

Many years later, in 2010, the Warburg Institute was to be threatened again, when budget cuts and a planned merger with the University of London jeopardized its independence and threatened to disperse its collection or force its relocation abroad. This caused public outrage. Petitions were signed and articles appeared in major newspapers, magazines and scholarly journals, until finally, in November 2014, the dispute was settled and the High Court ruled in favour of the institute. Eight decades after the *Jessica*'s risky voyage from Hamburg to London, the library was given another lease of life. As a postscript to this story, two years later, the result of the British referendum to leave the European Union came to pose a new threat to the ideals embodied by Aby Warburg's creation.

July–September

The Austrian director Berthold Viertel and the actors Conrad Veidt and Fritz Kortner work on some popular English films

On 3 July 1934, the architect Maxwell Fry writes to Walter Gropius inviting him to work in England and to live 'in a studio flat at Lawn Road with service and meals for six months or whatever time is needed'.

That same day, two German citizens, identified as Dr Phil Max Thimann, aged thirty-one, and Ursula Klee, aged twenty-one, are found dead in a room at the Grosvenor Hotel near Victoria Station. An inquest establishes that they poisoned themselves by drinking cyanide of potassium. 'The Coroner, summing up, said that it was only right to say that statements had appeared in the Press that these two unfortunate people were refugees from the Nazi Government, but they had not the slightest evidence of that fact.'

On 7 July, Richard Tauber lands at Croydon from Paris and moves into the Hyde Park Hotel. Two days later, he attends a special midnight premiere of the romantic musical *Blossom Time*, in which he starred as Franz Schubert, at the Regal Cinema, Marble Arch.

On 9 July, in Hampstead, Edith Tudor-Hart provides a photographic record of the opening of the Lawn Road flats.

On 13 July, a meeting of the local group of Nazi Party members takes place at Porchester Hall, London W2. The next day a group of people protesting outside the German Embassy in Carlton House Terrace attempt 'to present a petition for the release of Thälmann and Torgler', two of the Communists detained by the German authorities in connection with the Reichstag fire.

On 25 July, news that armed Nazis disguised as soldiers attacked the chancellery in Vienna reaches the Austrian ambassador in London, Baron

Franckenstein, as he is leaving the Wimbledon tennis championships. The following Monday, Lotte Altmann, Stefan Zweig's secretary and future wife, informs Zweig that she has contracted the 'Wimbledon Throat', an infection similar to diphtheria that mysteriously affected several tennis players that summer, leaving them unable to speak.

On 11 August, Princess Elizabeth Bibesco, daughter of former prime minister Herbert Henry Asquith, sends a letter to the editor of *The Times*, published on 16 August, in which she calls for the 'mobilizing of public indignation' over the appallingly cruel methods employed by the German government to silence its political opponents. She comments: 'The Nazi régime benefits from the fact that its atrocities overstep the limits of credibility.'

On the evening of Wednesday 22 August, the avant-garde Communist composer Hanns Eisler, newly arrived in England and a guest of the Piccadilly Hotel on Regent Street, encourages Bertolt Brecht to join him in London as soon as possible.

On 1 September, Mischa Spoliansky, the cabaret composer who had emigrated from Berlin in 1933 and is now 'residing at Berkeley Court Baker Street', signs a copyright agreement with Alexander Korda's London Films to write the music for *Sanders of the River*, a film about British rule in Nigeria.

On 18 September, Walter Gropius, who, despite his fame and connections, is no longer willing to work in Germany under Nazi rule, replies positively to Maxwell Fry's invitation: 'I am looking forward to work [sic] with you hoping that my lacking knowledge of building customs in England will not bring much trouble to you. But I am really glad to have found the opportunity to work again after a long involuntary rest.'

On 26 September in Glasgow, the queen, accompanied by the king, the prince of Wales and Mrs Wallis Simpson, launches the new Cunard liner, the 'Queen Mary', in front of 250,000 spectators: 'It was one of the very few occasions on which she had spoken in public and many people were shocked to hear how Germanic she sounded.'

The month closes with a much-anticipated London premiere on 28 September, when C. B. Cochran's latest revue, *Streamline*, opens at the Palace Theatre. It is a four-hour spectacle in twenty-six acts, designed by Cecil Beaton and with splendid costumes by couturier Charles James. The show's main attraction is the celebrated Austrian dancer Tilly Losch, whose scandalous divorce from aristocrat Edward James had been on all the British front pages at the end of June.

Chapter 4
'Spell your name'

German-speaking exiles in British film studios

Three kings

For a brief period in 1934, three eminent figures of the German stage and screen lived a few hundred yards from each other in rented apartments near Hyde Park, in the centre of London. They were the actors Fritz Kortner and Conrad Veidt, and the poet, theatre and film director Berthold Viertel.

Viertel's flat, at 19 Basil Street, Knightsbridge, was expensive but small and stuffy and, according to Christopher Isherwood, his collaborator at the time, it reeked of 'tobacco, buttered toast and white paint'. Viertel occupied it for several months between November 1933 and the summer of the following year while working on the film *Little Friend*, his English directorial debut. Around the same time, both Kortner and Veidt were staying at Grosvenor House on Park Lane, a modern development overlooking the park that – when it opened in 1929 – boasted 'the finest position in London and the finest service flats in Europe'.

Fritz Kortner, who had emigrated from Germany in 1933, benefited little from the comfort of his new home, as the struggle to adapt to a foreign environment and to the English language filled him with sadness and fear. Three letters to a friend written in the summer of 1934 illustrate how 'the loss of the mother tongue' meant a kind of death to the exiled performer, who found acting in a foreign language not just frightening, but an experience that 'touched on the dark regions of insanity'.

Conrad Veidt's predicament was less gloomy, because he had become a favourite with British audiences. A typewritten note addressed to a Mr Madden, who had suggested something the actor did not have time for ('Unfortunately I am engaged for so long a period that I am unable to interest myself with your proposition at present'), places Veidt at Grosvenor House in February 1934.

That must have been a temporary address, as he and his wife, Lilli Prager, soon moved to the suburban affluence of north-west London. Three years later, a long illustrated feature in the *Film Pictorial* magazine shows him posing informally in several rooms of an elegantly furnished suburban villa on Platts Lane, a stone's throw from Hampstead Heath.

The three men were bound by deeper connections than the coincidence of living in the same neighbourhood. Their paths had already crossed during their careers in Germany and they would do so again in exile. Berthold Viertel once wrote that German artists and intellectuals 'went into exile like deposed kings' – a metaphor that describes the predicament of all the men and women who had a successful career suddenly cut short by a flight into the unknown. Their influence and fame thwarted by the necessities of exile and by the difficulties of a new beginning in a country in which their previous high status counted very little, Viertel, Kortner and Veidt – once at the top of their profession – experienced the frustrations of a diminishing reputation. And although Veidt rose to the pinnacle of the British star system, he never quite regained the enigmatic allure of his Berlin days.

Viertel, Kortner and Veidt had been 'kings' also because they had embodied – each in his own individual fashion – the cultural vitality and creative brilliance of Austria and Weimar Germany in the decade after the First World War. In the 1920s they had been at the forefront of the German entertainment industry, and they had all worked abroad in the years before Hitler came to power. Viertel and Veidt had accepted substantial contracts in Hollywood, and Kortner had been involved in an important English film production. Yet they had never seriously considered a permanent career away from Germany and always knew that they would eventually return to Berlin.

Veidt first travelled to America in September 1926, when John Barrymore invited him to act in *The Beloved Rogue*, a historical drama in which the German star played King Louis XI to Barrymore's François Villon. Veidt then worked on three more Hollywood pictures, the most remarkable of which, *The Man who Laughs* (1928), directed by the German Paul Leni, was an adaptation of a novel by Victor Hugo set in seventeenth-century England. The arresting image of Veidt as the orphan Gwynplaine, a character who was disfigured as a child and condemned to smile forever in a grotesquely wide grin, is a typical example of the actor's expressive possibilities. The mesmerizing combination of a nobility of character with a frightening exterior was perfectly captured by Leni, one of the pioneers of Expressionist cinema and a master of a visionary approach to film.

One of the main factors that contributed to Veidt's mystique was the unusual contrast between his haunting screen presence and his utterly charming personality in real life. In the words of Michael Powell, who directed him in three major films in the late 1930s:

He was such an overpowering personality that directors were afraid of him. He was tall, over six feet two inches, lean and bony. He had magnetic blue eyes, black hair and eyebrows, beautiful, strong hands, and a mouth with sardonic, not to say satanic, lines to it. In private life … he was the sweetest and most easy of human beings.

In home movie footage shot for the German market sometime after 1926, audiences were given a glimpse of the actor at his Hollywood home, enjoying a sunny afternoon in the company of family and friends. 'There is a swimming-pool in the Veidts' garden', reads a caption, 'and the famous Dorothy Mackaill comes for a swim'. Greta Garbo is there, too, sitting on the edge of the lawn and throwing a ball to Veidt's young daughter, Viola, nicknamed Kicki. Then it's time for a ping-pong tournament: Garbo, relaxed and smiling behind dark glasses, plays a match with Dorothy Mackaill. The host is also filmed at the ping-pong table. Veidt ('Connie' to his family and friends) is tall, slender and impeccably dressed in light-coloured trousers and shirt, with a dark blazer and tie. His hair neatly swept back on his high forehead, he has a patrician look, yet appears gentle, open, at ease with himself and the world. Other stars come into the frame: Lya De Putti having fun with a small monkey perched on her arm, Dolores Del Río posing in a cloche hat, a cheerful Emil Jannings during a game of tennis.

But the lighthearted glamour of the privileged Californian lifestyle, which Veidt shared with several European colleagues, was not enough to keep him in America for long, and in February 1929 he sailed back to Europe. The decision was partly determined by the difficulty of employing foreign actors after the advent of talking pictures. Moreover Veidt, like many of his compatriots, was uninspired by the American film world, which was heavily controlled by the moral and commercial demands of the big Hollywood studios. And he missed Berlin.

In December 1929 Christopher Isherwood, then living in the city that he immortalized in his Berlin stories, glimpsed the actor as a guest at a costume ball for men. In a later book of memoirs Isherwood penned a portrait of Veidt, encapsulating his allure:

The respectability of the ball was open to doubt. But it did have one dazzling guest: Conrad Veidt. The great film star sat apart at his own table, impeccable in evening tails. He watched the dancing benevolently through his monocle as he sipped champagne and smoked a cigarette in a long holder. He seemed a supernatural figure, the guardian god of these festivities, who was graciously manifesting himself to his devotees. A few favoured ones approached and talked to him but without presuming to sit down.

In the summer of the same year, Fritz Kortner spent several weeks at Elstree studios playing one of the protagonists in *Atlantik* (1929), a German-language disaster movie produced in England and based on a play loosely inspired by the sinking of the *Titanic*. It was a time of dynamic international exchange within the film world, especially since the recent transition to sound meant that the same story would often be produced in different languages. This had been the case with *Atlantik*, not only the first multiple-language movie in cinema history, but also the first '100 per cent German talking film'.

Kortner enjoyed working at Elstree and was impressed by the technical novelty of sound, but he refused the offer of another contract in England. He dreaded the thought of living away from home and of having to learn a new language. Kortner's panic about his inability to speak well during his London exile began at this time, when he felt that to work in an English-speaking country would mean becoming, in his own expression, a 'language clown'. Yet his decision not to go abroad also depended on his strong identity as a German actor and on his attachment to Berlin:

Yes, I refused, although disturbing news was coming out of Germany. Today I find my refusal difficult to understand. I remember telling myself that expulsion [as a Jew] was a thing of the past ... So we travelled back to Berlin, with our still unborn daughter. I wanted to go back to my euphorically beautiful, ravishingly effervescent, dazzling, poisonous, magnetic Berlin.

Veidt and Kortner had shared the screen in several early films, for example in silent classics such as Murnau's now lost trilogy *Satan* (1920), with Veidt as Satan, and in Robert Wiene's dark psychological thriller *The Hands of Orlac* (1924). Both actors were mesmerizing in their own way. Whereas Veidt's handsome face and tall figure suggested an aristocratic – if somewhat sinister – physical presence, Kortner's small stature, his deep-set eyes, wide mouth and strong nose were suited for exotic and menacing parts. He often played Middle Eastern rulers, Jewish characters – such as Shylock, the part for which he will always be remembered – and generally fearsome strangers.

The third protagonist in this German-speaking cinematic trinity in 1930s London, Berthold Viertel, never quite enjoyed the star status of Kortner and Veidt, partly because he was not a famous actor, but also because of his difficult, rather tormented personality. But he was a significant and well-regarded figure as a poet, scriptwriter, theatre director and filmmaker. Like Kortner, Viertel was an Austrian Jew who had thrived within Vienna's rich theatrical world from an early age and had moved on to the equally prestigious, if more progressive, stages of Weimar Berlin. Like Veidt, he also went to Hollywood, where he enjoyed the friendship of many German-speaking actors and intellectuals, including Veidt himself, Emily Jannings, Ernst Lubitsch, and Erika and Klaus Mann.

Figure 34 Berthold Viertel (centre) with Matheson Lang and Nova Pilbeam on the set of *Little Friend*, 1934.

Viertel had been invited to the United States in 1927 by the renowned German director F. W. Murnau, for whom he wrote scripts and who had procured him a contract with Fox Film Corporation. Yet although he lived with his family in an idyllic setting in Santa Monica, and although he went on to direct several films for Paramount after Fox's demise in 1930, the hopelessly European Viertel soon tired of America. In July 1932, after leaving his wife and three children behind, he boarded the aptly named ocean liner *Europa* and returned to the old continent.

The way to England

Viertel's first stop on his journey back from America was Paris, where he met Alexander Korda to discuss a film project. He then travelled to Vienna to be near his dying father. Months later, a day after Hitler's rise to power, Viertel was in Berlin to direct the screen version of *Little Man, What Now?*, the novel in which Hans Fallada had depicted the hard life of a young, ordinary German couple against the chaotic backdrop of the city during the final years of the Weimar Republic. However, abiding promptly by the new government's racist rules, the film company appointed a non-Jewish director and reduced Viertel's pay. Then the Reichstag fire in the night between 27 and 28 February 1933 marked the moment when, for Berthold Viertel as for other prominent Jews and left-wing activists, the thought of leaving Nazi Germany became a necessity and, for those who were lucky enough to escape, a reality.

Viertel fled to Prague and went back to Paris and London before rejoining his family in Santa Monica in the summer, but his peregrinations would last for years.

His nervous temperament and commitment to a poetic calling that had very little in common with the commercial world of Hollywood drew him back to Europe. In October 1933 he left his wife and children in the United States and moved to London. The meeting with Korda the previous year had resulted in a contract to direct a film for the British Gaumont Company. The picture was to be entitled *Little Friend*. It was an unusual story, from a novel by the Austrian author Ernst Lothar, about a young girl traumatized by her parents' separation. Though not a particularly interesting proposition for Viertel, this was a good offer, and he hoped that life in London would be a decent compromise between the frivolity of the Californian lifestyle and the gloom that had engulfed Germany and would soon envelop Austria as well.

As it turned out, his hopes for a literary career in London came to nothing. Instead, as Isherwood's fictional account of Viertel's first English directorial experience shows, the older man retreated into his smoky Knightsbridge flat, worried about being away from his family, agonized over the increasingly difficult political situation in Austria and often raged against his crew when on set. At first, Viertel did not adjust well to the English way of life, but he began a romantic relationship with British actress Beatrix Lehmann and worked in London for years to come. He also met old friends from the past, some of whom were in an even more difficult predicament than his own. One of these was Fritz Kortner.

In his autobiography, Kortner recalls that when news broke of Hitler's election as German chancellor, he was on his way to Copenhagen to star in *The Merchant of Venice*. Two other members of the company, who were fervent Nazis but also Kortner's admirers, warned him against returning to Germany. Their report after a consultation with the Nazi authorities about the possibility of Kortner's repatriation was chillingly clear: 'K. should not come.'

This is how Fritz Kortner, one of the greatest actors in the German language, was forced into exile. Later that year, he was reunited with his wife, the actress Johanna Hofer, and two children in Vienna. There, he spent suspenseful hours at the train station as he waited for their delayed train from Germany, where Jews were routinely retained at the border and prevented from leaving the country. Yet they arrived. Spotting his family through the crowd, Kortner imagined that Johanna's blonde hair had saved them from the suspicions of the Nazi guards. Eventually, the four of them settled in England ('Months later the doll's pram was passed out of the train window in London'), where Kortner had found work on the strength of his international reputation. But his fight with the English language and his inner struggle with the new surroundings never abated.

Conrad Veidt's transition to life abroad had been much easier by comparison, as he was already fêted as a celebrity in London by the time Viertel and Kortner arrived in 1933 ('Women fight for Conrad Veidt' was a well-known slogan in the 1930s). Veidt's English career had begun three years earlier, when he was offered a part in the German version of the British drama *Cape Forlorn* (released in America as *The Love Storm*), which had been shot at Elstree Studios and in which, ironically, he played a minor role alongside Fritz Kortner, who was one of the protagonists. But, as opposed to Kortner, Veidt soon became a familiar presence in British cinema.

At a film premiere in 1932, King George congratulated Veidt for his 'fifteen years of film work' and Queen Mary confessed to having enjoyed *The Congress Dances*, a farcical romantic drama recently released in England, in which the actor starred as a cunningly angular Prince Metternich. There were other notable successes that year: the expensively produced *Rome Express*, the first film from Gaumont British Studios, with Veidt as the master-crook Zurta, whom he endowed 'with a quite magnificent strength and ruthlessness'; and the biographical German drama *Rasputin, Demon with Women*, in which Veidt's performance as the devilish monk is said to have reminded Rasputin's own daughter of the image of her 'father in the flesh'.

By this stage of his career Conrad Veidt, now almost forty years old, was an actor whose fame no longer depended on his legendary roles from the early days of the Weimar era (his murderous Cesare in *The Cabinet of Dr Caligari* comes to mind). Veidt often worked in England after Hitler rose to power, not because he needed to escape Nazi Germany, but as a star who earned handsomely abroad. Like many other German actors and technicians employed in the British film industry at the time, Veidt was first an economic rather than a political migrant. Nazi Germany did not pose a threat for him, because he was a gentile and not particularly interested in politics. According to director Victor Saville, one evening in 1933 the actor received a personal phone call from Goebbels. The Nazi minister of propaganda was hoping to entice him back to Germany and even promised to solve the problem of Veidt's half-Jewish wife by making her 'one hundred per cent Aryan'. Yet Veidt was a man of moral and artistic integrity. Not only had he married a Jewish woman, he had also antagonized the authorities by speaking out against the party's control over the German film industry. Moreover, he is said to have declared himself to be Jewish on an official document in order to spite the Nazis. This may be only a rumour, but it is a good indication of the courage that eventually drove Veidt away from Germany and its new rulers.

In the spring of 1933 Connie and his wife were granted permission to travel from Berlin to London, where they arrived on 6 April. The head of production for Gaumont British, Michael Balcon, had offered Veidt a major role in Saville's *I Was a Spy*, a film set in the First World War and based on the autobiographical account by the Belgian nurse and secret agent Marthe McKenna. The story opens with quotes from Winston Churchill's letters and ends with an appeal for peace, and its setting, tense plot and pacifist message revealed England's nervousness about a Teutonic threat at a time when the prospect of an all-powerful Germany was becoming real. *I Was a Spy* earned considerable success and was hailed by *Film Weekly* as the film of the year. Veidt played a German commanding officer, whose impeccable demeanour barely concealed an undercurrent of steely determination and a strong erotic appeal. The character, which anticipated one of Connie's best-known roles, Major Strasser in *Casablanca* (1942), secured him a long-term contract with Gaumont and sealed his fate as one of the most beguiling male leads in British cinema. His fame in the English-speaking world was now assured. As Michael Balcon said: 'Veidt is a dominant personality. Every time I go out with him in the West End I am mobbed.'

In Berlin, *I Was a Spy* was criticized by the Nazis because of its unfavourable portrayal of German characters. Around the same time, Veidt's reputation within his own country was further damaged by his decision to play the lead in *The Wandering Jew*, an ambitious epic directed by Maurice Elvey and produced by the German-born Julius Hagen at Twickenham Studios. The plot was a sympathetic representation of Jewish destiny through the myth of the merchant who mocked Jesus on the way to the crucifixion and was condemned to wander the earth, alone, until Christ's return. Conrad Veidt as Matathias, the Jew of the title, delivered a powerful performance and was praised for the subtlety of his portrayal. The film was soon to be followed by another philo-Semitic story, produced by Gaumont and entitled *Jew Süss*, from the eponymous novel by the German Jewish author Lion Feuchtwanger.

Conrad Veidt's roles were an affront to Hitler's regime, and his association with acting roles opposed to National Socialist ideals led to his sudden imprisonment in Berlin sometime between the final months of 1933 and the beginning of the following year. Veidt had gone back to Germany to star in a remake of *Wilhelm Tell*, a silent movie in which he had appeared ten years earlier. But he was inexplicably arrested in Bavaria, where the film was being shot, and prevented from returning to London. Under the vague excuse that Veidt was ill and unable to travel, the authorities detained him for an indefinite period without charge. Only when the British Foreign Office intervened and Michael Balcon sent a doctor to Germany to ascertain the real state of Veidt's health was the actor released. In the spring of 1934, Connie was safely in London. He would never set foot in his country again.

A London summer

The weather was unusually warm that summer. On Wednesday 11 July 1934, *The Times* informed its readers that 'over most of the British Isles the day was again brilliantly fine with practically continuous sunshine'. In London, a warm front had approached at the end of June and a fortnight later the heatwave was still holding sway. Such conditions drove crowds into Hyde Park on a Sunday afternoon. The place came to life – families lay out picnic blankets, women pushed their babies in black-hooded prams, bathers of all ages swam in the Serpentine Lido, people walked their dogs, children fed ducks and pigeons by the Round Pond, and 'an ancient man with a white beard often fed crumbs to sparrows'. Couples strolled, lounged on deck chairs under the shade of the trees and rested on the warm grass at sunset. In the words of a contemporary observer: 'they forget themselves, and are blessed, at peace, sensuality, too diffuse to be restless, dissolves their spirits'.

Grazing sheep were another characteristic sight in the park during spring and summer. Every year since 1920 a shepherd called George Donald and his dog had brought down a flock of sheep from Aberdeenshire to mow the grass in London's green spaces. Wolf Suschitzky immortalized Donald's sheep in Hyde Park twice, once on a lawn, with a smart-looking young woman seated on a deck chair on what could be a hazy summer's afternoon, and once with the shepherd and his dog, as the man conversed with a policeman while his curly-fleeced flock grazed in the distance. The tops of some of the fashionable new buildings on Park Lane are just visible above the plane trees.

Hyde Park and its environs must have bemused the continental foreigner through a bizarre, and very English, combination of modern urbanity and rural idyll. Yet possibly even more surprising was the proximity of another unique landmark of that particular London setting: Speakers' Corner, a small section of land on the north-eastern edge of the park where impromptu orators gave

Figure 35 Wolfgang Suschitzky, *Sheep in Hyde Park*, London, 1934.

speeches and held debates. While the park itself exemplified the pastoral nature of English life, and its surrounding areas displayed all the signs of a prosperous modern metropolis, Speakers' Corner was something entirely different. It was a platform open to all. To a foreign observer, and especially to a refugee from Nazi Germany, this piece of central London was an example of civil equality and freedom. This is how the journalist Malcolm Muggeridge saw it on one of those warm afternoons in 1934:

> Lenin's Corner, Freedom's Corner, Peace's Corner, an infinite variety of Known and Unknown Gods' Corners. From little platforms, each labelled, words overflow, like cascades of water from fountains … Beneath a red flag a communist orates … a cheerful round-faced Irishman in a black soft hat with an immense brim attracts a large crowd … Three Jews mournfully erect a platform. One of them mounts it to complain of the wrongs of his people. The other two listen. He is shaggy and unkempt, with swollen features, eyes and mouth large and indeterminate, voice mellow with despair … When he is spent, another of the three takes his place … We have to thank Hitler for forcing thousands of Jews who had become ashamed of their race to acknowledge it. We owe him a debt of gratitude. His voice rises and falls as he describes century after century of suffering, of wandering, of restlessness … Now it is almost dark. The crowds in Hyde Park melt away; platforms are folded up and removed … Soon there is nothing except darkness, and lovers lying in the grass, and stars, and the three Jews complaining of the wrongs of their people.

That summer, the peaceful occasion of a sunny day in the park was in stark contrast with the conflicts played out at Speakers' Corner. Londoners seemed torn between the desire to enjoy their city in that radiant weather and the fear of a threat to their freedom. On 30 June, the 'Night of the Long Knives' shocked Britain and the world. Throughout June and July, German pacifists campaigned in the pages of the *Manchester Guardian* to alert the British public to the Nazi crimes, and rumours circulated everywhere about Germany's secret rearmament. In the words of an anonymous journalist: 'There are references to war in the conversations of our friends … War. War. Always this preparation for a war which nobody wants.'

Meanwhile, the numbers of refugees entering Britain continued to rise. On 27 June reports were published of an increase of nearly 1,000 German visitors, at which the London correspondent for the *Manchester Guardian* quipped: 'It is just possible that many Germans have a desire to see what it is like to live again for a little in a free country.' At the end of July, the assassination in Vienna of Chancellor Dollfuss by a band of Austrian Nazis intensified the anxiety about Germany's expansionist plans in Europe. On 2 August, the announcement of

President von Hindenburg's death was swiftly followed by news that Hitler had succeeded him. Adolf Hitler had now become both head of state and chancellor of Germany; he was also commander-in-chief of the Reich's armed forces.

In hindsight, the publication of Evelyn Waugh's novel *A Handful of Dust* on 3 September 1934 could be seen to reflect the fears around the destructive potential of a menace coming from Germany that had pervaded London and the whole of Britain for months. When Waugh's protagonist, Tony Last, travels to Brazil after the sudden death of his son and his wife's desertion, he is accompanied by an eccentric explorer with a German-sounding surname, Dr Messinger, and the vaguely sinister toy mice 'the size of large rats' with which the latter hopes to bribe the local people are 'of German manufacture'. More significantly, the embodiment of chaotic forces in the novel, the creepy recluse who enslaves Tony and prevents him from returning home, is a Mr Todd, whose name is a veiled allusion to the German word for death (*Tod*).

In the early 1930s, similarly oblique references to a darkness beyond human control could be found in the work of émigré filmmakers, who often noticed the signs of impending doom far more clearly than the English. Exiles were expected to produce entertaining, commercial pictures for the British market, yet their films occasionally hinted at an engagement with the most pressing aspects of contemporary reality. These films' subject matter and high technical accomplishment revealed their continental background. This transpired through an allusive use of light and darkness; through a plot dense with daring political undertones; or simply through the casting of exotic-looking, foreign-sounding actors such as Kortner and Veidt. Émigré filmmakers shared a heritage marked by the traumas of the First World War (a recent study on Weimar film is cleverly entitled *Shell Shock Cinema*), and they all came from countries affected by profound social and institutional conflicts.

At the same time, émigré actors, directors and technicians represented a kind of artistic freedom that was new to Britain, because their earlier films had challenged the roles of gender and the themes of sexuality, mental illness, religion and education far more radically than their English equivalents. German cinema had always addressed controversial social and psychological issues. As early as 1919, Conrad Veidt had been a dark and brooding presence as the homosexual violinist who falls in love with one of his students in the drama *Different from the Others*. And in 1923 Berthold Viertel's silent film *Nora* was a screen adaptation of Ibsen's feminist classic *A Doll's House*, in which none other than Fritz Kortner starred as the dishonest lawyer Krogstad, a creepy character well suited to the actor's brilliant ability to project an aura of danger and unease.

Herein lies an important reason for the frustration experienced by many German-speaking film practitioners in London at the time: they felt lonely and misunderstood in an environment that lacked the cosmopolitan flair and professional opportunities that they had left behind and that the Nazis were eradicating. Yet many émigrés also grew to love England as a safe and tolerant place. The exiles came from a world in turmoil. After the First World War Austria had shrunk from a great empire to a fairly insignificant state, and Germany was a country marked by political and economic volatility. In Britain, on the other hand, the exiles encountered a society keen to retain its identity and a culture that, on the whole, appeared to resist the temptations of modernity.

Little Friend: creative teamwork

On Wednesday 11 July 1934, during that sweltering spell and sometime after the completion of *Little Friend*, Berthold Viertel typed a letter to his producer, Michael Balcon:

> After finishing 'Little Friend' and before leaving the country, I want to express my gratitude for your confidence. I know exactly how big your risk is and understood, throughout the whole time, that to let me choose this subject and to let me go along with it the whole long-winded way meant all the courage on your side, and this obliged me to put in as much risk and effort myself as there was available in my system. I hope that 'Little Friend' will do well and win the sympathy of the audience to a degree which will make it worthwhile for you and the company to have helped with all your efforts to call Felicity [the film's protagonist] into life.

Viertel, a headstrong, impractical man with a nervous disposition, was anxious about the picture's impending release, on which hinged his future collaboration with British Gaumont. He also agonized, as usual, over his own writing, which he pursued tirelessly but for which he lacked both time and an appreciative readership (as Christopher Isherwood put it: 'Viertel thought of himself as a poet, first and foremost, and it was depressing for him to find himself almost without an audience in England'). That Wednesday in July he was probably restless, chainsmoking in his tiny flat, troubled by the symptoms of his diabetes, rehearsing lines of poetry, as ever conflicted between his artistic calling and the need to work for money. Or maybe he wandered the streets in his shirt sleeves, his large head and greying mane a curious sight in his Knightsbridge neighbourhood. He must have been keen to settle his affairs in London before travelling to see his family in California at the end of the week. He also had various projects in mind, and thoughts of Germany and Austria were a source of constant misery.

The film adaptation of the Austrian novel on which *Little Friend* was based had been Viertel's idea, and yet at times he tired of it, because he found the project insignificant now that tragic historical events plagued his country and threatened the whole of Europe. According to Christopher Isherwood:

For hours, Viertel would talk of anything, everything except 'Little Friend' – of the Reichstag fire trial, then in progress (he imitated Dimitrov defying Goering); of his productions for [the theatre company] 'Die Truppe' in Berlin during the 1920s … of the poetry of Hoelderlin; of the awful future in store for the world; of the nature of woman. It was then that the grimly grinning, sparkling-eyed Clown surpassed himself … Sometimes he saw Christopher and himself as heroic rebels against bourgeois culture … Sometimes he discovered a deep significance in the story, decided that it was even perhaps a kind of masterpiece. He philosophized over it, quoting Marx, Freud, Nietzsche, and his own elected Socrates, Karl Kraus … But such high moods of optimism didn't survive the daylight.

In her memoirs, Salka Viertel is also eloquent about her husband's choleric temperament and his fanatic attachment to the values of European culture. As a commentary on Viertel's first English movie, Isherwood's words emphasize the idea of the director as representing a whole group of European émigrés, who lived in the shadows in 1930s London and struggled to survive. But it is also important to remember that Viertel's work during that time made a significant contribution to British cinema.

In this respect, *Little Friend* is a remarkable achievement. As a domestic drama about a young girl disturbed by her parents' estrangement, the film eschews serious psychological enquiry in favour of a sentimental and implausible happy ending. Nevertheless, it was a bold choice of subject in the unadventurous world of British film at the time, and the final result is an interesting hybrid of an English context and a Germanic sensibility.

The film's compelling opening sequence, for example, must have been a surprise to English-speaking audiences, for everything about it – music, lighting, subject matter and overall visual impact – is artistic and reminiscent of German Expressionist cinema. The first two minutes of *Little Friend* consist of a fast-moving, accelerating visionary landscape, in which everyday objects attain a symbolic meaning and a nightmarish quality. The romantic orchestral music that accompanies the initial credits gives way to a frenzied score as the story begins. Percussive rhythms and the increasing beat of high-pitched wooden sounds compete with a flow of indistinct bright images. Smoke and flames dance on a dark background. When a small, white spot emerges and circles the light in time with the thumping cadences, a candle's flame comes into focus against a pitch-black backdrop and brightly lit objects start parading before our eyes: hyacinths in glass vases; a translucent goldfish bowl; soft toys; an eerie doll staring blankly ahead; a huge white tooth; a fast-moving film reel; a faceless girl with her mouth wide open; a white-robed dentist wielding a long tool; a child's scooter flying through the fog; the large, gloved hand of a policeman and his stony face, spouting admonitions; a girl on a scooter; a thin, bespectacled gentleman in black; an angry-looking charwoman brandishing a broom; a female teacher shaking her pince-nez. In the end, this intimidating group of authority figures is seen bending over the child, whose head is resting on her pillow, just as she is woken up by the sound of her parents arguing in the next room.

In the following frame, seated upright in bed, the girl directs an anxious glance towards the door, while the striped diagonal pattern of the light shining through the window behind her creates an optical enhancement of the subconscious drama that disturbed her sleep. The child's name is Felicity, played by the fourteen-year-old English actress Nova Pilbeam in her first screen role. Despite her inexperience, Pilbeam (who would become one of Alfred Hitchcock's favourite female leads for a time) carried her part with great assurance. Her expression in the scene that follows the dream, for example, reveals a great emotional intelligence, because her look of genuine alarm is fully human and contrasts effectively with the surreal quality of the nightmare sequence.

Dreams are at the core of *Little Friend* in more than one sense. Apparently Viertel intended to portray the whole story of the upheaval in Felicity's life caused by her parents' discord as a dream episode. Although not immediately obvious to the viewer, the film's main plot is framed by two bed-scenes and could indeed be read as a long nightmare with a happy outcome. Viertel's Viennese heritage and his interest in psychoanalysis undoubtedly played a role in his intention to show a young person's emotional struggle through the lens of subconscious fears and desires. In *Prater Violet*, Isherwood relates a rather comical episode that sees Viertel's fictional counterpart, Dr Friedrich Bergmann, entertaining a young tobacconist's assistant with stories about a foreign doctor who believed in the secret meaning of dreams:

> Bergmann had told her of a doctor, somewhere abroad, who said that your dreams don't mean what you think they mean. He had seemed to regard this as a scientific discovery, which had amused the girl and made her feel somewhat superior, because she'd always known that. She has a book at home which used to belong to her aunt. It was called 'The Queen of Sheba's Dream Dictionary', and it had been written long before the doctor was born.

Whether fictional or based on a real event, the anecdote captures the contrast between Viertel's attachment to high culture and the prosaic nature of his everyday life in London. His frequent bouts of dissatisfaction were also caused by the gulf that separated the demands of the director's role within a British film production and his uncompromising identity as an Austrian intellectual. Viertel's devotion to poetry, his interest in psychoanalysis, his vast experience in the German theatre and his dismissive attitude towards film as – in Bertolt Brecht's words – necessary but ultimately inferior 'bread and butter work' made his first English experience particularly disheartening. And there is no doubt that *Little Friend*, which in Viertel's hands had become a dreamlike tale with elements of social critique, was different from any film produced in Britain at the time.

Little Friend is now largely forgotten. It can be watched online, but is out of print and only mentioned in specialist publications. The plot – with its sentimental streak and predictable outcome – is likely to irritate a modern audience, and its bourgeois setting, so steeped in the social habits and rituals of the rich in 1930s London, may seem irrelevant to modern viewers. But the film is in many respects remarkable. It has dramatic pace, a compelling musical score and a strong central performance from its young protagonist, and is, above all, visually stunning.

Its unique charm derives from the collaboration of several distinguished German-speaking émigrés. As well as Berthold Viertel as its director and script adaptor, the film boasts photography by Günther Krampf, art direction by Alfred Junge, music by Ernst Toch and an acting cameo from Fritz Kortner.

The exchange of skills between German and English filmmakers began in the days of silent cinema, increased with the advent of the talkies and the custom of shooting multiple-language versions of the same movie, and became standard practice with the introduction of the Cinematograph Films Act in 1927. The legislation stipulated that British film distributors and cinema owners were obliged to buy and show a minimum quota of British films. It had been established to boost domestic film production, which until then had been mediocre and thwarted by the power of the Hollywood studios. On the one hand, the Films Act proved to be detrimental to the quality of British movies, as the required percentage of films (which became known as 'quota quickies') resulted in the release of shoddily made, inferior pictures. On the other hand, it also created a boom in the production and popularity of high-quality films. The movies suddenly became big business, and the emergence of ambitious production companies such as Korda's London Films and Balcon's Gaumont British put English filmmaking on the international map. The immense success of Korda's *The Private Life of Henry VIII* in 1933 marked a triumph for domestic cinema, and the following year saw the release of several outstanding productions, most of which benefited from the expertise of Mitteleuropean cast and crew members.

The resurgence of British filmmaking in the early 1930s would be unthinkable without the input of continental directors, actors and technicians. Since England's movie industry had long suffered under Hollywood's stranglehold, the country lacked a substantial body of skilled film workers. The migration of foreign personnel to Britain began in the late 1920s and was mainly driven by the German monetary inflation and by a crisis sparked by the advent of the talkies. Yet from 1933 onwards, Hitler's political and racial persecutions led film workers to seek work abroad. The influx of highly trained technicians from places with an advanced cinematic tradition – such as Germany and Russia – partly contributed to the quality and popularity of domestic pictures in the decade following the establishment of the Films Act. For example, during the 1930s, 'six foreign designers took art director credits on British films ... the German Alfred Junge, Austrian Oscar Friedrich Werndorff, Hungarians Vincent Korda and Ernö Metzner and Russians Andre Andrejew and Lazare Meerson'.

Compared to British designers, who lacked a distinctive aesthetic vision and saw sets as mere backdrops, foreign technicians worked more closely with directors and photographers and developed imaginative designs. Under their influence, British films acquired a new look and a new sense of elegance and style. This was apparent both in the elaborate scenery and costumes of the lavish historical productions that became so fashionable in the early 1930s, and in the shadowy sets of thrillers such as Hitchcock's *The Man who Knew Too Much* (1934). In this particular instance, the eerily lit, scarred face of Peter Lorre and Alfred Junge's grotesque sets created a highly atmospheric visual style, the likes of which British cinemagoers had never seen before.

The association between Berthold Viertel and several German and Austrian professionals on the set of *Little Friend* is another case in point. Viertel, who had left behind an illustrious career as a theatre director, knew that filmmaking was a collective effort. In his first British venture, he surrounded himself with German-speakers. Isherwood, who had been involved in the project because he spoke the language, described the director's occasional need to express himself in his own tongue. Salka Viertel, too, remembered her husband's impatience towards the working habits of the English, whom he considered slow and disorganized ('the phlegmatic tempo of the studio, with the long decision-delaying weekends and tea breaks, got on his nerves'). As a result, *Little Friend* possesses some uniquely Germanic traits, from lighting, camera work and sets to music and emotional content. Its success, considerable on both sides of the Atlantic, was probably due to the more sentimental aspects of Felicity's story. Yet the film's content and its overall look are unusual by the standards of British cinema at the time.

In the opening sequence, the optical wizardry achieved by Günther Krampf's photography and Alfred Junge's use of props and models synchronizes with the frantic rhythms of the music composed by the Austrian Ernst Toch, and helps to convey Viertel's conception of the story as a dream. In the scene that follows, Felicity wakes up in the middle of her nightmare at the sound of her parents' raised voices. Once she closes her eyes again, a long, smooth sweep of the camera focuses on every object in her room, on every shadow, every corner of the girl's familiar world of toys, furniture and pictures. Now the music is less frenzied than it was during the nightmare sequence, but it still communicates occasional bouts of turmoil as the rhythm accelerates. Towards the end of the scene, the frenetic quality of the percussion turns seamlessly into the fixed cadences of the metronome that accompanies Felicity's piano lesson in the morning.

In a later scene, the girl is in the park with her governess. She has just run into her mother and her lover horse-riding together, and tries the governess's patience by stepping deliberately into the pond before darting off on her scooter towards the park's gates. At this point the action is shown through a quick succession of isolated tableaux: a dramatic close up of the governess's fearful expression as she shouts 'Stop!', the oncoming cars on the road outside, Felicity's uncontrollable ride, a delivery boy on his bicycle, the alarmed face of a driver hooting his horn and the head-shot of Felicity screaming before the inevitable accident. The culmination of all this commotion is rendered effectively by the image of a spinning bicycle wheel and, in the next frame, by the close view of the girl lying motionless on the ground before being helped up by the young cyclist.

There is no music in this scene and the dramatic progression towards the accident's climax is reached through a combination of clever editing and arresting camera work. Music is used sparingly in *Little Friend*. The story progresses naturalistically over long stretches of film, only to be complemented by Toch's score as a commentary on Felicity's moods and as a signal of emotional danger when the camera lingers on the silent world of interiors and domestic objects.

The overall style of *Little Friend* can be described as polished and progressive. The filmmakers used sophisticated visual techniques and musical effects to deliver a social commentary, as in the motif of the class divisions between Felicity's privileged existence and the working-class milieu of errand-boy Leonard, and in the theme of marital discord. Above all, *Little Friend* documents the complex psychology and the emotional deprivation of a young person in a world whose stability – despite the sugary ending – is only apparent and probably short-lived. Disturbing elements abound thanks to Günther Krampf's mobile camera and unsettling close-ups, to Alfred Junge's symbolic sets and props, and to Ernst Toch's insistent and occasionally menacing music.

All these men had the German language and heritage in common. As far as we know, they lacked Viertel's flamboyant personality and yet – to use a phrase coined by Isherwood in *Prater Violet* to describe the director's fictional counterpart – they had, like him, 'the face of a political situation, of an epoch. The face of Central Europe.' They were lucky to be employed, but also anxious about an unfamiliar present and troubled by thoughts of an uncertain future. Some – such as Alfred Junge and Günther Krampf, who were already established in the British film studios and whose talents did not rely too heavily on a good knowledge of the English language – found it easier to adapt and thrive. Others – for example Kortner, Toch and Viertel – struggled, because the next job was never assured and because their fame at home had become almost irrelevant in their new life. While Viertel described himself and his fellow exiles as deposed kings, Toch used the metaphor of the dachshund that had been a Saint Bernard in the old country.

Some personalities can be difficult to gauge and many remained largely invisible. Berthold Viertel, whose temperament emerges from the accounts of those who knew him, is a towering figure. His voice is still audible and his appearance – the grey leonine mane, his bushy eyebrows and prominent nose – is clearly recognizable in our mind's eye. Others are harder to visualize, but inevitably, these men had some common traits that made them stand out in 1930s Britain. They were: a devotion to culture, advanced technical skills and an openness towards the modern world.

In Toch's case, work on *Little Friend* was only a stopgap between his escape from Nazi Germany in the spring of 1933 and his emigration to the United States in the autumn of the following year. Both Krampf and Junge, on the other hand, had joined Balcon's team at Gaumont British long before the birth of the Third Reich. Günther Krampf (who changed his name to Gunther in Britain) first went to London to work on two 'quota quickies' and then joined Conrad Veidt on the set of *Rome Express*, where he employed his extraordinary skills to reproduce the effect of a moving train on screen. Junge had worked in England after the establishment of the Films Act and finally settled at Gaumont British in 1932, when he became supervising art director, thus influencing the company's visual style, most notably in Hitchcock's early thrillers.

In their youth, Toch, Junge and Krampf had all trained and gained experience in Germany, within institutions – be they orchestras, theatres or film studios – that excelled in their respective fields. All three men were at the vanguard of their professions, because they embraced aesthetic principles that combined outstanding quality with openness towards the most striking phenomena of contemporary society, from street culture to psychoanalysis, from modern transport to geometric abstraction.

In *Little Friend*, the sounds of Toch's score give the impression that Felicity's subconscious fears are feeding on the cacophonous confusion of the real world, while Junge's concept of 'total design' – based on the functionality of the German modernist tradition – is evident in a set defined by sharp chromatic contrasts, clear patterns and simple lines. Junge saw filmmaking as a comprehensive process, whereby the overall appearance of a movie – from furnishings to lighting and costumes – was carefully conceived and visually coherent. He achieved his aim by planning camera set-ups and sources of light in his preparatory drawings – a novel approach at a time when art direction played a minor role in British movies. Krampf, too, considered film to be an art form, and his famously obsessive desire to obtain the perfect lighting revealed the integrity of a professional for whom authenticity, not entertainment, was the main goal.

Shylock as a pantomime villain

In *Little Friend*, a notable example of the viewer being drawn into Felicity's own perception of the outside world is the episode in which her father takes her to the theatre to see the Christmas pantomime of *Jack and the Beanstalk*.

The show opens with a puppet horse and a pretty blonde girl alarmed by the arrival of the giant, whose refrain is heard booming from behind the scenes. It is a low, slow 'Fee-fi-fo-fum, I smell the blood of an Englishman', spoken with a slight foreign accent – the last syllable of 'Englishman' pronounced with a German doubling of the final 'n'. The young actress exaggerates her expression of fear, screams and raises her hands over her head. In her box, Felicity is frightened, a serious look of concentration on her pale features, one hand clasped tight before her. Introduced by an excited 'Here he comes!' from a boy in the stalls, the giant makes his entrance preceded by a raucous laugh and by the heavy thump of his enormous boots. He is dressed in leather, wears a chain of what looks like small white bones around his neck and is sharpening a big knife. He has long, unkempt hair, a prominent nose and slanted eyes set below a pair of bushy eyebrows. He speaks the lines 'horseflesh doesn't taste so good' in a deep guttural voice and pauses before adding 'as human flesh and human blood', with an emphasis on the word 'human'. He gives a sort of gasp after each noun, a chomping sound at the end of the sentence, a low, throaty laugh and finally a loud 'Boo!', which makes the children in the audience shrink back in their seats. He then licks the knife with an evil glint in his eyes before putting a foot on the barrel in which his victim is trying to hide. At this point the camera alternates between the action on stage and Felicity's alarmed expression as she stares fixedly ahead. The monster has picked up the tiny-looking barrel in his big hands, is shaking it as if it were a toy and chuckling in amusement at the shrieks of the girl trapped inside.

The actor who plays the giant is Fritz Kortner and the whole episode lasts barely one minute. A nightmarish vision of this terrifying figure recurs in one of Felicity's dreams later on, as he booms a drawn-out 'You will die, my child, you will die', shortly before the girl's failed suicide attempt which will finally reunite her parents. The pantomime scene is Kortner's only appearance in Viertel's English film debut.

This was not Kortner's first role after his arrival in London in 1933. A more substantial engagement had been a leading part in the screen version of a popular musical by the Australian actor and director Oscar Asche, based on the story of Ali Baba and the Forty Thieves and entitled *Chu Chin Chow*. Here, Kortner played the robber Abu Hassan, who masquerades as the wealthy Chinese merchant of the title, whom he has murdered in order to steal Ali Baba's fortune. The film, produced by Michael Balcon for Gaumont British, aimed to repeat the success of recent costume dramas. It was also one of Balcon's first attempts to branch out into the international scene. After its release in the United States, a reviewer in the *New York Times* saw *Chu Chin Chow* in terms of a possible British 'invasion of the American film market'.

Celebrated as a 'central and outstanding figure in the creation of … the British film Industry' and a tireless promoter of the idea of a national cinema, Balcon, the son of Jewish immigrants from Eastern Europe, employed a large number of émigrés from the Third Reich. His connections with Germany reached back to the 1920s, when he travelled to Berlin to secure the British release of German films, discuss British–German coproductions and hire experienced technicians. Balcon was aware of the commercial potential of foreign stars and keen to build an efficient art department 'on modern German lines'. His desire to create a strong and distinctive British film industry went hand in hand with his willingness to engage continental actors and filmmakers. Balcon's plan worked, for his company benefited from the presence of European stars and artists, mostly from Germany, Austria and Hungary, throughout the 1930s.

In 1934, a momentous year for Gaumont British, Balcon produced twenty-six features, some of which were not only well received at the time, but are still regarded as classics of their genre. A good example is Hitchcock's *The Man who Knew Too Much*. The film, photographed by Curt Courant (another famous name from Berlin), with Alfred Junge as art director and Peter Lorre as the villain, established Hitchcock as a master of suspense and dark atmospheres, whose unique combination of realism and stylization was indebted to the German cinematic tradition.

Chu Chin Chow, on the other hand, although moderately successful, failed to launch Fritz Kortner into a flourishing career in British cinema. As well as Kortner and the Chinese-American star Anna May Wong in the main roles, other foreign professionals involved in the making of the film were the German photographer Mutz Greenbaum, and Ernö Metzner. The latter was a Jewish art director from Hungary with ample experience on the film sets of Berlin, where he was associated with several important names, including Ernst Lubitsch, Karl Grune and W. G. Pabst. But *Chu Chin Chow*, for which he created magnificent and unusually elaborate pseudo-oriental sets, was not a complete success for Metzner. He resented the fact that in Britain art directors were less powerful than they would have been in Germany, and the uncomfortable conditions in the unwelcoming Gainsborough Studios – nicknamed 'Siberia' because of their extreme temperatures – made Metzner's work during the shooting of *Chu Chin Chow* particularly difficult.

It is also possible that his style was too distinctive for audiences unaccustomed to the creative licence of continental technicians (the same could be said of Mutz Greenbaum's atmospheric photography). Soon after the film's release, a reviewer in *The Times* acknowledged that 'the Eastern settings [had] been reconstructed with unusual accuracy', but complained about the sets being shrouded 'in a dim twilight which even the desert sun at midday is powerless to dispel'. The production was considered to be an English pantomime, in which the robbers were 'heartily operatic, and their leader (Mr. Fritz Kortner) exaggerated his own villany with an evidently humorous intention'. Along the same lines, the reviewer in the *Manchester Guardian* argued that Kortner was impressive, yet described the film as 'a child's pantomime'.

The references to pantomime are thought-provoking, especially considering that in Kortner's work schedule *Chu Chin Chow*'s Abu Hassan was followed by the cameo of *Jack and the Beanstalk*'s giant in *Little Friend*. Although his performances were praised, his British film roles never reached beyond the realm of parody, because they merely exploited the man's exuberant persona and the exotic sound of his stilted accent. After 1933, the extraordinary talent of one of Europe's greatest actors was only good for pantomime villains.

Kortner's participation in *Chu Chin Chow* had been announced enthusiastically in the British press. On 11 February 1934, the *Observer* published a particularly flattering portrayal:

Germany's losses in the theatre and cinema continue to be our gain. The latest recruit to the British film studios is Fritz Kortner … probably the greatest living player of Shakespeare and Schiller roles, and now to play the part of Chu Chin Chow in England.

Kortner is barely known to film audiences in this country, and to theatre audiences not at all … But in Germany every man, woman, and child knows the name of Kortner. He is famous as stage actor, screen star, and radio artist. At forty-two, with a repertory of all the classical parts at his finger-tips, he is one of the youngest of the great German players …

When I went to interview him yesterday, almost the first thing he said was, 'Why do people laugh when I mention Chu Chin Chow? To me it is a great opportunity, a great widening of experience. After all, this great bandit-robber-murderer-whatever you like to call him – is not so far remote from modern times. He is a gangster – what is the name of the great gangster in America? – Yes, Al Capone – he is the Al Capone of China' … 'He seems to us rather an odd choice for a great Shakespearean actor', I said … 'To me not at all … I think it is a good choice for a foreigner's first venture in a strange tongue … It would be still too difficult for me to work in a problematical film in this country. I should be oppressed by the strange idiom, self-conscious. In a film like "Chu Chin Chow" I can play with broad, strong outlines, and concentrate on the mastery of the speech.'

Kortner has a voice with extraordinary modulations, very soft and swift in ordinary conversation, with a perfect control. He speaks now a mixture of German and almost accentless English – that peculiarly pure and beautiful English that seems to come easily only to a foreigner.

The journalist seemed oblivious to the enormous difficulties that beset Kortner's relationship with the English language, but his description of the actor's remarkable voice and skill is accurate. Kortner was well known for his ability to express emotions through the tone and modulation of his speech. He was a virtuoso of gestures and spoken sound and this, in turn, explains his interest in mime and his aptitude for playing pantomime characters (he was a great admirer of Charlie Chaplin).

As a very young man, Kortner had learnt the value of expressive acting from the plays produced by the theatre impresario Otto Brahm in Berlin's Deutsches Theater at the turn of the century. In Germany, Brahm had been the principal promoter of naturalism as a style that aimed at a truthful representation of a character's life and feelings through both physical and emotional means. He had freed theatre from the declamatory style of star performers and viewed drama as a comprehensive process, which embraced every aspect of a production, down to minor parts and details.

Another formative experience for Kortner had been, at the same theatre, Max Reinhardt's production of *Hamlet* with Alexander Moissi in the title role. This time the young Kortner felt that theatre had suddenly 'come alive'. There may have been more talented Hamlets in the past, but the originality of Reinhardt's production and the almost magical quality of Moissi's subdued, melancholic delivery alerted the budding actor to the importance of inhabiting a role and portraying characters from within.

At the age of nineteen, Kortner was engaged by Reinhardt at Berlin's Deutsches Theater, where he only played small roles and which he left after two years. In 1913, he achieved his first success in Vienna under the direction of none other than Berthold Viertel, who was then artistic director of the Wiener Volksbühne. Six years later, in a country traumatized by the war that had just come to an end, Kortner triumphed in Berlin as the protagonist of Ernst Toller's Expressionist drama *Transfiguration* (1919), in which the actors' ability to portray the story through gestures and a strong display of emotion were paramount. Kortner was the ideal performer for such tasks, the play was a triumph and his fame was sealed. He became known for the full range of his vocal and mimic virtuosity. Alfred Kerr, Weimar Germany's most authoritative theatre critic, devoted the closing lines of his exuberant review to the young talent: 'The director was helped above all by actor Fritz Kortner. His vocal impetus is fused with feeling. A new man. A new treasure.' Kortner was the man of the future. From a newcomer whose unseemly physique seemed to preclude a distinguished theatrical career, he became the talk of Berlin, the embodiment of a new kind of performer, who acted with his whole self and whose energy was utterly arresting.

The role for which Kortner will always be remembered is Shylock. He played the character for the first time in Vienna in 1916, then again in Berlin in 1923 under Viertel's direction for the theatre company that they had cofounded,

Die Truppe. The following year, Max Reinhardt directed Kortner in another Viennese production of *The Merchant of Venice*. Yet the definitive portrayal of the character took place in November 1927, in Jürgen Fehling's version at Berlin's Staatstheater. This time Kortner created a completely new Shylock. His interpretation went against the wishes of the director, who wanted a humane and mild merchant to counteract the growing waves of anti-Semitism. The actor became a furious Shylock, a reflection of, rather than a contrast to, the racial hatred that was spreading through the German-speaking world. Kortner himself was clear about the political nature of his intentions: '*The Merchant of Venice* seemed frighteningly modern. Its allusions to the racism of a power-hungry fascism electrified both friends and enemies.'

The upheaval that, five years later, changed the course of Kortner's life reflects a sadly familiar story. When the Nazis came to power he stood at the pinnacle of his fame. It is a cruel irony of fate that such an extraordinary actor should end up playing pantomime villains in a language that he never made his own, and that his Shylock's fury should turn into the clownish greed of two-dimensional characters such as Abu Hassan and a fairy-tale giant.

Hidden politics

Kortner failed to become established in London because his personality was too deeply rooted in his own culture. His acting style was too unfamiliar to British audiences. As early as 1924, the drama critic of *The Times* commented sarcastically on the excesses of Expressionist drama ('always wanting to make our flesh creep') and on the emotional mode of acting championed by 'Teutonic favourites Fritz Kortner and Werner Krause [*sic*]', who shouted and gesticulated instead of simply performing a role.

Kortner himself was aware of the differences between his own style and that of his British colleagues. He thought that the English kept their emotions to themselves, that they were too reserved, on stage as in life. He had encountered the proverbial 'stiff upper lip' and called it 'anaemia of expression' ('Ausdrucksanämie'). Kortner felt that such restraint reflected a habit of underacting on the British stage, which, 'excluding the great actors Laughton, Richardson and Gielgud, who had nothing to do with the mediocrity of a theatre that eschewed emotions', offered no more than charming small talk.

There was a fundamental difference between Kortner's understanding of the actor's role and the British attitude to theatre and film. He regarded stage and cinema as platforms for the expression of concerns about the contemporary world, and acting as the reflection of a powerful emotional experience as opposed to mere entertainment. Both his interpretation of Shylock as a response to Germany's descent into racism and his comparison between the robber chief in *Chu Chin Chow* and Al Capone's reign of terror show that he regarded acting as something relevant to real life and to the turbulence of one's own time.

Despite his struggle with the language, Kortner could count on a steady stream of work, and his wife and children were soon settled into a comfortable British existence. In a letter dated 2 June 1934, around the time of his appearance as the giant in *Little Friend*, he wrote encouragingly about their new circumstances:

> The grip to the throat has loosened, I am free of nightmares sometimes. – Hanna has overcome everything quite marvellously. Peter is at a temporary school. He learns English with spellbinding energy. The school is an hour away from London – a true paradise for boys. Hanna and her equally resilient daughter live near him.

Kortner was finding his feet in an alien environment, was curious about British customs and made the most of his time in London. Like many émigrés, he was torn between a fruitless pining for the past and a desire to assimilate into the life of his host country. Perhaps inevitably, these feelings were mingled with the seeds of an identity crisis:

> I was now drawn to shows that did not require knowledge of the language and that I never found particularly interesting before… I added tennis to my old passion for boxing … In the Davis-Cup Wimbledon final, the American Budge competed against the still formidable German von Cramm. – Apart from our interest in the sport, we went to see it in order to witness the defeat of a representative of Hitler's Germany.
>
> The 'Thousand Year Reich' now triumphed on all possible fronts. The German head of state … was beginning to gain the admiration of the appropriate circles abroad through a blood-soaked display of his power … Europe found him both threatening and fascinating … And yet, in the middle of the fight, as the initially stronger von Cramm weakened, I was dismayed to notice that I feared for him, and that my sympathy was being conquered by the aristocratic and detached German player.

This memory refers to the Davis Cup final at Wimbledon in July 1937, but sentiments of a similar nature assailed Kortner throughout his time in London. This must have been especially true in the summer of 1934, when the actor was trying to establish himself in England yet missed the Continent and was disturbed by the threat posed by an increasingly aggressive Third Reich. A sense of political urgency explains his choice of role in the film on which he worked after *Chu Chin Chow*, a historical allegory of Fascism entitled *Abdul the Damned*. Kortner was now resigned to work for the screen. Cinema had become the only possible source of income for most émigré actors, as theatre posed the problem of translation and performing in English on stage, which was for many an impossible task.

On 1 July 1934 Kortner travelled to France, Switzerland and Austria. In a letter written before his departure, the thought of a visit to his family in Vienna steadied his nerves as he was preparing to play what he called 'my last big scene in the second film'. This is likely to have been *Evensong*, a romantic musical loosely based on the story of the soprano Nellie Melba, with Kortner as Kober, the star's domineering manager. At the end of September, he was back in London to work on *Abdul the Damned* (then provisionally titled *Abdul Hamid*) and to attend the premiere of *Evensong*. He was exhausted. He had sold the script of *Abdul Hamid* – from a story by Robert Neumann – to Gaumont British, and *Evensong* had been a personal triumph, but Kortner was unhappy and pined for the Continent ('Still battling with the English language. My head and my imagination are not free to develop ideas. I feel heavy and old and unable to register new things').

It seems that Kortner's success as a screen actor and his financial security were not worth the mental and psychological efforts necessary to sustain an involvement in projects that did not interest him, in a country that was not his own. The strain eventually drove him to America in 1937 and back to Germany twelve years later, when he became a celebrated stage director.

In *Abdul the Damned*, which was shot at Elstree and on location in Turkey from December 1934 and released in Britain the following March, Kortner played yet another disturbing figure of authority. The role carried a deliberately anti-Fascist message. The film is a melodrama about the nineteenth-century Turkish sultan Abdul Hamid II, a despotic ruler haunted by a paranoid fear of assassination, who was responsible for the atrocities committed by the Turks against the Armenians in the 1890s. The plot centres around the theme of the dictator's political and personal demise, conveyed by Kortner in the kind of exotic and menacing role at which he excelled. This time, the story was a reference to Fascism and the sultan a parody of Adolf Hitler, with whom the Turkish tyrant shared his initials.

Financed largely by Max Schach, an Austro-Hungarian producer, *Abdul the Damned* was a product of the British German-speaking community in exile. The idea came from Kortner and Robert Neumann. The two men had met in London sometime in 1934, when Neumann was a lodger at Loo Hardy's boarding house in Cleveland Square and Kortner a regular visitor. The actor's fame and the writer's standing in the German-speaking literary world counted little in their new life, where everybody seemed to be looking for work. Kortner and Neumann mulled over suitable subjects and marketable ideas in the hope of breaking into the British film industry. Kortner's reputation and exuberant personality must have made him a welcome guest at Cleveland Square, and his anecdotes amused the lodgers of this peculiar German microcosm in the heart of London:

Figure 36 Fritz Kortner plays dual roles in a scene from *Abdul the Damned*.

Fritz Kortner dropped in often to tell his 'Spell your name' story which later on became a play he wrote together with Dorothy Thompson [*Another Sun*, 1940], but actually everybody there had the same experience. Yesterday they were still famous and everybody knew their names; and now they had to start all over again to make their gifts and talents known to directors, agents, and publishers.

A project originated in refugee circles would have had a slim chance of being accepted by a major film company in 1930s London, but *Abdul Hamid* was the exception. According to one of its producers, Walter C. Mycroft, only a stroke of luck led to the making of the film. Mycroft had been given Neumann's story by an agent, read it in one sitting, enjoyed the depiction of the tyrant as 'cruel and cunning, yet pitiful in his attempts to extricate himself from the net of vicious intrigue which he himself had woven', and decided to have it adapted for the screen. This may seem strange, as Mycroft was reportedly 'a small German sympathiser, enthusiastic about the Nazis'. But it is likely that, once again, the choice of a historical subject was determined by financial considerations and by a desire to repeat the success of films such as *The Private Life of Henry VIII*.

Abdul the Damned, released in March 1935, was a very continental affair. Its director was the Austrian Karl Grune and the script, which followed Neumann's story, had been adapted into English from a treatment by Emeric Pressburger and Curt Siodmak. The picture also boasted spectacular cinematography from another virtuoso photographer in exile, Otto Kanturek, and the costumes were by another resident of Loo Hardy's boarding house, Joe Strassner, the most celebrated costume designer of the Weimar era. Hanns Eisler had written the music, although he loathed having to resort to film work for money and had reported indignantly to his friend Bertolt Brecht that he thought the picture was 'politically respectful but unfortunately still rubbish'.

Abdul the Damned did indeed exemplify the shortcomings of many Anglo-German collaborations at the time. Their technical and visual brilliance notwithstanding, most of these films were an uneven combination of two diverging sensibilities: a central European eagerness to use cinema as a medium to reflect on the current historical situation on the one hand and, on the other, a need to produce good-quality British entertainment for commercial purposes. In the case of *Abdul the Damned*, the allusions to Nazi Germany are confined mainly to Kortner's portrayal of Hamid's disturbed personality, while a romantic subplot concerning a Viennese singer who joins the Sultan's harem to save the life of her lover provides a sentimentality that weakens the film's impact.

The desire to advance financial interests resulted in sumptuously executed pictures with charismatic, foreign-sounding actors and sometimes – as in *Abdul the Damned* – a hidden anti-Nazi agenda. Many émigrés longed to make a political point through their art, but this went unnoticed by the vast majority of the British public. The situation changed in the late 1930s, when the German threat became apparent and British films more politicized. The release of Michael Powell and Emeric Pressburger's *The Spy in Black* in 1939 and, a year later, *Contraband*, both with Conrad Veidt in the lead, are good examples of this.

In 1934, among the most politically insightful observers were the country's leading film producer, Alexander Korda, who had enlisted Winston Churchill as 'an Editor, Associate Producer and Advisor' on a series of topical short films in the spring of that year, and Michael Balcon, who had always employed foreign actors and technicians and who, as a Jew, was aware of the Nazis' nefarious tactics.

British cinema audiences liked light, romantic entertainment. Interestingly, German-speaking exiles were also responsible for the greatest successes in this field. One of the most popular films of the year was *Blossom Time*, a musical subtitled *A Romance to the Music of Franz Schubert*, released in London on the same day as *Little Friend* and a week after *Chu Chin Chow*. Adapted for the screen from a popular Austrian operetta about the composer's love life, it starred Richard Tauber, a Jewish exile with an enthusiastic British following. The film's director, Paul L. Stein, was also an Austrian émigré, as was its cinematographer, Otto Kanturek, who would go on to photograph *Abdul the Damned*.

As the exclusion of Jewish actors and technicians from the National Socialist film industry began to take its toll (on 15 August of that year, *The Times* had announced a sharp 'decline in German film exports'), English film studios teemed with exiles who adapted their talents to market demands. The summer of 1934 – a particularly fortunate time for British cinema – was an anxious yet busy time for many of them.

The Making of *Jew Süss*

Abdul the Damned, a story conceived as an anti-Nazi tale, was not perceived as such by the public and did not cause a stir in Germany. The film was generally well reviewed and Kortner's performance praised as usual, but the political message was barely noticed. *Jew Süss*, on the other hand, made a huge impact both in Britain and abroad. While *Abdul the Damned* had been mainly the product of émigré circles, *Jew Süss* reflected a British agenda. As in the case of *I Was a Spy*, *Jew Süss* mirrored a critical attitude towards the Nazi government and a more diffuse preoccupation with the prospect of German aggression. The film was particularly relevant as a response to the anti-Semitism that had swept through Germany after Hitler's rise to power.

Jew Süss underwent a long development process, and the path to its much-publicized release at the Tivoli Cinema in London on 4 October 1934 had not been smooth. After years of negotiations and opposition from the censors, who requested changes to the more harrowing sections of the script, the project was approved because it was a costume drama based on a popular book. Production of *Jew Süss* could finally go ahead in November 1933.

The film was to be directed by Lothar Mendes who, according to the press releases, had been interested in the subject since seeing a stage version of Feuchtwanger's novel in New York in 1929. Mendes was German, had had a modest career as a director in Berlin's Ufa studios and had worked in the United States since 1926, when he married the actress Dorothy Mackaill (the one who was filmed playing ping-pong with Greta Garbo in Conrad Veidt's Hollywood home).

The person most closely involved in the promotion of a film version of *Jew Süss* was Michael Balcon. Both he and the other owners of Gaumont British, the brothers Isidore, Maurice and Mark Ostrer, also Jewish, were instrumental in the advancement of the project. On the one hand, the story was suitable for a lucrative historical epic on a grand scale; on the other, it presented the opportunity to address the burning question of anti-Semitism. Like the Hollywood movie *The House of Rothschild*, released in the spring of 1934, *Jew Süss* was a reaction to the increasing threat of institutional racism in Germany, where the organized

Jewish boycott had shown the world the troubling scale of racial discrimination. As we know, plans for a production of *Jew Süss* had antagonized the German authorities who, already incensed by the release of *The Wandering Jew* in November 1933, had tried to detain Conrad Veidt to prevent him from returning to England. The writer Heinrich Fraenkel, who was working on the script of *Jew Süss* at the time, recalls that: 'Veidt refused to discuss coming to Britain to play the part fearing that his phone was tapped, and … negotiations were eventually conducted in an hour-long phone conversation between [Fraenkel] and Mendes at Shepherd's Bush Studios and Veidt in Prague.'

In the end, Balcon invested around £120,000 into the film, an enormous sum in those days. Originally written in 1921–2 and published in Germany in 1925, Lion Feuchtwanger's *Jew Süss* was its author's first bestseller. An English translation appeared in 1926, the book became a literary sensation and its popularity marked the beginning of a new fashion for historical fiction. A year later, a title in *The Sunday Times* announced: 'Everybody is reading *Jew Süss*.'

Vividly told, with clearly drawn characters and a good dramatic pace, Feuchtwanger's novel deals with the subject of anti-Semitism, although its main theme is the protagonist's transition from assimilation and wealth to a rediscovery of his Jewish identity. The book reflects the politically charged atmosphere of the Weimar Republic. Feuchtwanger had already written the story of Süss for the theatre in 1916–17, but the play had been a flop, and he had put the project aside before picking it up again some years later. By 1922, the author's interest in the figure of Joseph Süss Oppenheimer had become a response to the Jewish question in his own time. That same year, the assassination of the foreign minister Walther Rathenau – the Jewish industrialist and intellectual who advocated the complete assimilation of Jews into German society – revealed the full extent of the racial tensions weakening Weimar democracy.

Joseph Süss Oppenheimer (1698–1738) was a Jewish courtier who rose from the ghetto in eighteenth-century Germany, became a powerful advisor to the duke of Württemberg and was brutally executed after the duke's death. While the novel is a psychological study into the trappings of power, the film presents a more obvious denunciation of inhumanity and racism. The script's first stage direction reads: 'In 1730, Württemberg – now a part of Germany – was and independent Duchy. Then, as now, the Jews were judged differently from other men.' In its setting of the historical situation, the film's opening title reinforces the same message: 'It was a time of brutality and universal intolerance and the Jews above all suffered oppression and boycott.'

The word 'boycott', absent in the novel, is a contemporary reference to the discriminatory practices of the Hitler government. Similarly, the titles that introduce the film's protagonist as 'a man of human frailty, whose work remained unfinished' characterize Süss as a hero from the outset. On his first appearance in the script, Süss is presented as 'a very distinguished-looking gentleman', and his hand, adorned with a large solitaire diamond, is seen opening the door of an elegant carriage. In the novel, on the other hand, Feuchtwanger's initial description of Süss emphasizes the man's lust for power, his greed and the seductive quality of his physical appearance ('large brown eyes ... ripe red mouth'). Whereas in the book Süss's motives appear as selfish striving for personal advancement, in the film his ambition is shown as a yearning for equality ('I'm going to show them a Jew can hold his head as high as any other man').

After becoming advisor to Duke Karl Alexander of Württemberg, an impoverished Catholic nobleman in line for the throne, Süss Oppenheimer sacrificed everything to the pursuit of power as a means to vindicate Jewish oppression. The film opens in a Jewish classroom. When one of the young pupils asks why they are confined to the ghetto, his teacher's reply is a lesson on the ideals of human tolerance and equality.

One of the story's subplots concerns Süss's daughter, fifteen-year-old Naemi. When the unscrupulous, lecherous duke drives the girl to suicide, Süss plots a scheme to avenge her death. In the end, his revenge becomes his own downfall. After Karl Alexander dies, Süss is put on trial and sentenced to death by hanging on the pretext that he had fallen in love with a German woman and was therefore guilty of contravening an ancient law that forbade carnal relations between Jews and gentiles. Süss heroically accepts his fate. In the final scene, he is hoisted into a cage that suspends him high above the scaffold. The film closes with a poignant shot of Süss's tearstreaked face as he recites the holy prayer in English ('One and Eternal is Jehovah Adonai!'), then in Hebrew, echoed by the chants of the old Jews and the crowds.

In Britain, *Jew Süss* was one of the most successful films of the year. Despite some scepticism about its length and extravagant budget, it was praised in the press, especially for the exceptional quality of the acting, and recognized as a response to Germany's racial policies. Some dissenting voices, such as that of Caroline A. Lejeune in the *Observer*, argued that although *Jew Süss* was to be admired as 'a plea for sympathy with an oppressed people', it would have been better for British cinema to concentrate on domestic problems, such as unemployment, mining and farming, rather than on 'a little German municipality of two hundred years ago'.

In some respects, Lejeune's comments are understandable, both because the spectacle of such an elaborate costume epic tends to distance the viewer from the human content of the story, and because *Jew Süss* was perceived in many ways as a piece of continental, rather than British, filmmaking. As well as Mendes and Veidt, the cast included Paul Graetz, another German exile, erstwhile comedian and brilliant cabaret artist, in the role of Süss's friend Landauer. Also, the film was photographed by Günther Krampf, with art direction by Alfred Junge. The latter's sketches for the set of the gallows, reproduced in the English edition of the script, display a clear sense of perspective and the clean lines of Bauhaus aesthetics, while his drawings of the ghetto evoke the stylized shadow-play of Expressionist scenery.

Jew Süss mirrored a German idea of cinema as an art form, and the most startling feature of the film was Conrad Veidt's affecting performance. The actor embodied the worldly sophistication of Weimar cinema. As Michael Powell recalled: 'Emeric [Pressburger], like me, looked upon Conrad Veidt as a legendary figure. For us, he "was" the great German cinema. For us, he was invention, control, imagination, irony and elegance. He was the master technician of the camera, who knew where every light was placed.'

A genuine living being: Conrad Veidt's *Jew Süss*

On 13 February 1934, the casting of Veidt as the lead character in *Jew Süss* was disclosed in *The Times*, in the same article that announced the making of *Chu Chin Chow*. A publicity campaign for the film had been set in motion months before the official announcement. On 7 December 1933, a small photograph printed on the picture page of *The Times* showed the actors Mary Clare and Paul Graetz on the set of *Jew Süss* at Shepherd's Bush Gaumont studios. On the same day, the magazine *Film Weekly* featured an interview with Conrad Veidt. The piece's opening lines and a close-up of the actor, looking suitably inscrutable as Süss, perpetuated the popular image of the German star as a mix of stylish composure and effortless charm: 'Jew Suss [*sic*], magnificent in powdered peruque and dressing-gown, lowered his six-feet-something into a canvas chair marked "Connie" and waved an inviting hand towards the chair next to it.'

The role of Süss promised to add a new complexity to Veidt's acting abilities. As he told his interviewer:

> I don't want character parts. Or rather I do want them, because they're easy to play … But when I think about things seriously I realise that what I should consider a really satisfying part is one in which I should have to struggle and give every effort to express the inner thoughts and desires of a genuine living being.

A month later, another British film magazine, *Picture Show*, featured an article entitled 'An Actor who Lives His Part', whose author praised Veidt's ability to inhabit his character and predicted that 'Veidt, as the Jew in "Jew Süss", will startle the world.' That week British newspapers were printing similar articles about Elisabeth Bergner and her inspired performance on the London stage. Thanks to method acting, today this kind of total immersion into a fictional

Figure 37 Conrad Veidt in *Jew Süss*.

character is far more familiar to theatre- and cinema-goers than it was at the time, when the British public was still unaccustomed to the intense symbiosis between actors and their roles. German-speaking performers added emotional power to their parts. Interestingly, around the same time a young Alistair Cooke, then film reviewer for *The Listener*, wrote of the 'tireless German sincerity, which reassures you that the story is happening in the middle of real life'.

Veidt, like Bergner and Kortner, had learnt his craft with Max Reinhardt and on the sets of Expressionist films. His first contract with Reinhardt in Berlin, dated 1 September 1913, when Connie was twenty years old, now rests in the archives of the British Film Institute in London. His second contract is also there, a three-year agreement with the Deutsches Theater between September 1914 and August 1917. The young Veidt rose through the ranks of a school of acting that privileged a complete absorption in the plot, in the character's mind, body and spatial surroundings.

Christopher Isherwood remembers an occasion during the filming of *Little Friend* when he witnessed Veidt in *Jew Süss*, which was being shot in the same studios at Shepherd's Bush:

Two memories remain. My first is of a scene in which Veidt had to read a letter of bad news and, at a certain point, burst into tears. There were three successive takes and in each one – despite the intermediate fussing of the technicians and the makeup man – Veidt wept right on cue, the great drops rolling down his cheeks as if released from a tap … My second memory is of the beginning of the scene of Süss's execution. Veidt sat in a cart, his hands manacled, on his way to death – a wealthy and powerful man ruined, alone. However, just as the filming was about to begin, something went wrong with the lights. There was to be a delay of five minutes. Veidt stayed in the cart. And now a stenographer came up to him and offered him a piece of candy. Some stars … would have ignored the stenographer. Others would have chatted and joked with her … Veidt did neither. He remained Süss, and through the eyes of Süss he looked down from the cart upon this sweet Christian girl, the only human being in this cruel city who had the heart and the courage to show kindness to a condemned Jew. His eyes filled with tears. With his manacled hands he took the candy from her and tried to eat it – for her sake, to show his gratitude to her. But he couldn't. He was beyond hunger, too near death. And his emotion was too great. He began to sob. He turned his face away.

At the risk of being too theatrical, Veidt maintained the energy of his performance throughout the film. In a scene between Süss and Magdalena Weissensee, the woman whom Süss loves but fails to protect from the advances of the duke, he tells her of the suffering he has endured, for the sake of power, since his childhood days in the ghetto. Veidt's eyes are closed as he speaks, his voice almost a whisper in his strangely melodic German inflection until, at the word 'power', he opens his eyes wide and stares at her with hypnotic yet fully human intensity. Similarly, in the moments before his death, when Süss is looking up to the sky as the snow begins to cover the top of the gallows and he is being hoisted into the cage, he smiles faintly, closes his eyes and then reopens them, fixing an invisible point somewhere beyond this world.

Veidt's performance in *Jew Süss* marked a departure from the roles of his previous English films. He acted with the same force and emotional intelligence as in his other parts, but this character was different. In Süss he was portraying an outsider, a man who became a victim of persecution and social exclusion. True, Veidt had often been cast in similar roles, but whereas his early parts displayed the excesses of Expressionist acting, his performances in his English movies are more nuanced and more real. In this respect, Veidt's portrayal of Joseph Süss symbolizes not only the historical tragedy of a single individual, but also a universal drama of exile and exclusion. Around the time of his involvement in *The Wandering Jew*, the actor denied that the film was concerned with politics or propaganda, and both Michael Balcon and Lothar Mendes echoed his remarks with regard to *Jew Süss*. And yet it is impossible to watch Veidt's Süss without making a connection between his character and the tensions that hung over Europe at the time of filming.

Through the eyes of a stranger

Veidt's next major role in a British movie reinforced his reputation as one of the most magnetic screen personalities of the era. The film in question, entitled *The Passing of the Third Floor Back*, is an adaptation of the eponymous play by Jerome K. Jerome about the arrival of an unknown man in a London boarding house, the inhabitants of which are troubled individuals eventually saved by the stranger's healing ways. Released in London just over a year after *Little Friend*, the film was Berthold Viertel's second project with Gaumont British. Once again, his task as the foreign director of an English movie was relieved by the presence on set of other exiles and of Britons with whom he could speak his own language. This time, apart from Conrad Veidt and Viertel's lover Beatrix Lehmann, who spoke German, the film's associate producer was Ivor Montagu, another German-speaker and left-wing intellectual. There were also two Jewish émigrés: the German cameraman Curt Courant and the Austrian art director Oscar Friedrich Werndorff, who had recently worked with Hitchcock on *The 39 Steps*.

The Passing of the Third Floor Back is an unusual film and an interesting example of continental filmmaking in a British setting. The story takes place in a Bloomsbury boarding house, but also outdoors, and is in many ways an accurate portrayal of London life. At the same time, the film has a timeless quality and moments of lyrical intensity.

The house is inhabited by a cast of very British types: a timid maid, an ageing spinster, a beautiful girl forced into a loveless marriage by her socially ambitious parents. The sudden arrival of the nameless Stranger brings an exotic element into this group, a peculiar blend of mystery and goodness. Veidt's enigmatic charm holds the story together as a suspenseful cross between a noir thriller and a dreamlike fairy tale. His performance is restrained, charismatic and authoritative, and his sophisticated elegance evokes memories of his mythical reputation in Weimar Berlin. The Stranger alleviates the other characters' troubles through an almost otherworldly ability to defeat evil – in the guise of the rapacious Mr Wright – and bring peace into their lives. His status as an outsider grants the Stranger a privileged perspective. As he says in his soft, accented English towards the beginning of the film: 'I am a stranger to you. And because of that I am able to see you more clearly than you see yourselves.'

The Passing of the Third Floor Back is an unconventional movie because it combines elements of social drama with mystical overtones. It is not political, yet its distinctive look – realistic and strange at the same time, enhanced by Courant's atmospheric photography – and the towering presence of Veidt as a noble cosmopolitan figure add another dimension to Viertel's second English picture: the dimension of exile.

The outlandishness of the Stranger and the landlady's sneering remarks against foreigners make this a story about diversity in more than one sense. As the tale of the outcast who is able see more deeply into a new environment, *The Passing of the Third Floor Back* can be read as an allegory of exile. This remarkable film is an indirect comment on a time of uncertainty, when displaced people came to England and appeared conspicuous because of their different ways. As the product of émigré filmmakers, this movie shows that those different ways threw light onto aspects of British life and culture that were usually taken for granted by the British themselves. In this particular case, ordinary existence in 1930s London, with all its social conflicts and daily rituals, is shown through the intensity of a foreigner's gaze.

After 1934

Kortner, Veidt and Viertel were among the privileged émigrés who could afford to leave the country in the summer months. Kortner left London on 1 July, and Veidt almost certainly vacated his Park Lane apartment around the same time. Viertel stayed at his flat in Knightsbridge for another two weeks and then boarded the *Britannic* from London to New York. On his return, he moved into another temporary home across the park, at 20 Hyde Park Place in Bayswater, and to an apartment in the modernist High Point Tower, Highgate, the following year. Kortner had gone to Paris and Vienna. Veidt and his wife may have travelled to Switzerland or to the south of France.

On his way to join his family in California, Viertel felt relieved because work on *Little Friend* was over, but he was restless, concerned that the film might be a flop and anxious about the future. Hoping for another contract, he was also busy planning new film scenarios, and a letter to Balcon dated 14 July 1934 showed his desire to consolidate his affiliation with the company ('I feel so much connected with you and G[aumont] B[ritish] that it was not easy to leave. I would have liked indeed to talk further about future plans').

At the end of September, Kortner was back in London and busy preparing for *Abdul Hamid*. The London and New York openings of *Jew Süss* on 4 October 1934 promised to be the main cinematic events of the new season. Veidt attended the London premiere, at which Prince George was the guest of honour, whereas Viertel joined Einstein and Charlie Chaplin for the opening in New York. Viertel returned to London sometime that autumn to work on *The Passing of the Third Floor Back*.

Eventually, all three men left England. Kortner returned to Germany for good in 1947. Veidt became a British citizen in 1939, but signed a contract with MGM and settled in America in April of the following year. He felt a debt of gratitude towards Britain. In September 1939, he and his wife welcomed four boys who had been evacuated from the East End into their Hampstead home ('Mr. Veidt in the Role of Uncle', read the title of an article in the *Daily Herald*), and the actor later donated his entire fortune to the British government and the British war relief. Conrad Veidt died of a heart attack, playing golf in Hollywood, in 1943. In one of the bizarre twists of fate typical of the itinerance of exile, his ashes were brought back to London from the United States and interred at Golders Green Cemetery in 1998.

An exile to the end, Viertel continued to lead a nomadic existence. After the collapse of Gaumont British in 1937, work in London dried up almost completely and in 1939 he left the country. Eventually, he was appointed stage director at the Zürich Schauspielhaus, and finally guest stage director at the Akademietheater and at the Burgtheater in Vienna, where he died in 1953.

On the whole, life in London was rewarding for the three men, and 1934 marked the peak of their English careers. In Veidt's case, his British image was carefully controlled and very different from that of his Berlin days. The actor portrayed in the English film weeklies did not reflect his ambiguous screen persona. The monocled figure sitting alone at a ball for men in one of Berlin's less reputable dance halls had become a respectable married gentleman who returned home to his wife after a long day on set and went to bed early. In England, Veidt's politeness became as legendary as the sincerity with which he inhabited his characters. Like Bergner, he shed the psychological complexity and sexual ambiguity that defined his earlier career and adapted quite successfully to the puritan demands of the anglophone world.

Kortner and Viertel found the transition into exile more difficult and never recovered the professional standing they had enjoyed before 1933. Kortner's problems with the English language reflected a more fundamental distrust in people's ability to communicate with each other. Once, on a grey morning in London, on his way to his daily English lesson, he read the news of some Nazi atrocity in a newspaper and was baffled by his teacher's indifference as he told her about it. The woman 'was non-committal … her truly or seemingly impassible face was the face of England: polite, hospitable, even helpful, but non-committal'.

Kortner was lucky enough to work in England, yet he missed the joy of spontaneous human interaction in a country that appeared to be cool and indifferent to the wider world. He and Viertel shared the fiery temperament of their Eastern European Jewish roots and were similarly troubled by the apparent placidity of the English.

Salka Viertel, who visited her husband in London in 1935, thought that Berthold did not suit the neat coolness of the English scenery, and that he 'seemed a stranger in this green and well-groomed landscape, in which even the hedges, the parks and the meadows were lovely but foreign'. But she also conceded that he had made England his home. His relationship with Beatrix Lehmann had certainly something to do with his decision to remain in London. Beatrix was cultured, spoke German, and shared with Viertel a love of theatre and cinema. Yet his restlessness never abated. In this respect, John Lehmann's description of Viertel is almost as effective as Isherwood's famous evocation of Viertel/Bergman as 'the face of Central Europe':

Physically he was small and stockily built, a small shaggy bear of a man, of enormous energy, much persuasive charm and finely receptive intellect, capable of talking with brilliant wit and imagination for hours as he paced up and down his working-room in his dressing-gown, in and out of the huge pile of half-read books that always littered the floor; equally capable of changing his mood with the speed of lightning and growling with rage at some slight he detected, or imagined he detected, in the way he himself or one of his friends had been treated by the obtuse film-bosses with whom he had to work.

Viertel's frustration found an outlet in his writing. Exile meant homelessness, and the only place where he – as many others who shared his fate – felt truly at home was the German language. Viertel's exile poems brim with thoughts of his own country: his schooldays, the alleyways of Vienna, a Christmas market seen through the eyes of Jewish children, his parents, an old garden, and two minutes' silence on the day of the Nazis' annexation of Austria. There are also several poems about his places of exile, but these, too, are rarely free from the memories of his old life. In one example, a stranger who approached him at a London theatre turned out to be a childhood acquaintance from Vienna who had been imprisoned and tortured in Germany and managed to escape. In another poem, written in the spring of 1935, verses on death and destruction contrast bizarrely with images of England's composed indifference to a world in turmoil:

Yet they stir
At this moment
The tennis players on the green lawn
Clothed in white, blessed and godlike.
Young girls, pictures of joy,
Ride on beautifully shaped mares.
England is full of flowers
At this moment. –

October–December

Bertolt Brecht and Stefan Zweig spend the autumn in London

On 4 October the London premiere of *Jew Süss* is held at the Tivoli on the Strand, one of the largest Gaumont British cinemas in the country. There are many distinguished guests, including Prince George and Queen Marie of Romania; the minister of transport, Leslie Hore-Belisha; Viscount Lee of Fareham; Lion Feuchtwanger; Aldous Huxley; Conrad Veidt; and the film's director, Lothar Mendes.

On 9 October, an article in the *Manchester Guardian* reports that the celebrated German opera singer Lotte Lehmann, who is married to an Austrian Jew and lives in Vienna, announced that she would 'never sing again in Germany'. Three days later, another famous German musician, the mezzo-soprano Elena Gerhardt, leaves her country for good and settles in London.

On 18 October, Walter Gropius and his wife Ise arrive at Victoria Station with 'little money and few possessions'. They are met by Jack Pritchard and Maxwell Fry.

On the afternoon of Tuesday 30 October, James G. McDonald meets with the archbishop of Canterbury to discuss the matter of the responsibility of the Church in the refugee crisis. Their talk is interrupted by the sudden arrival of Lady Cynthia Asquith, whom McDonald finds particularly rude: 'When told what the subject of the meeting was to be, she said, "Oh, yes, Germany; that was the reason. Tell me about it, but I'm not going to stay for the meeting. I am tired, and I can't bear speeches."'

A week later, on 7 November, McDonald attends a charity lunch at the Savoy in aid of German-Jewish women and children. One of the speakers is Lady Astor. Her views on the situation annoy the high commissioner almost as much as Cynthia Asquith's remarks during the meeting at Lambeth Palace:

Lady Astor confided to me that she had not prepared the least thing for her speech – that she was going to say that she had come much better prepared in heart than in mind; but did I not, after all, believe that there must be something in the Jews themselves which had brought them persecution throughout all the ages: was it not, therefore, in the final analysis their responsibility? To this thesis I took violent exception.

On 16 November, in a BBC broadcast about the threat posed by Nazi Germany, Winston Churchill denounces the country's domestic policy, which brought back 'the most brutish methods of ancient barbarism, namely the possibility of compelling the submission of races by terrorizing and torturing their civil population'.

On 10 December Frank Pick, outgoing president of the Design and Industries Association, recommends Walter Gropius to W. C. Eaton at the Board of Education. It is clear from Pick's letter that the great German architect is relatively unknown in Britain: 'He was one of the leaders in the reform movement in Germany, and he started half a school half an industrial institution at Dessau, called the Bauhaus … Just what use we can make of him at the moment I am not quite clear.'

On 13 December Tilly Losch performs with the British dancer Anton Dolin at the eighteenth-century costume ball held at the Austrian Embassy. It is a grand affair. According to *The Times*, 'at midnight Tilly Losch and Anton Dolin danced for the guests, who numbered over 300'.

In a letter dated 18 December, the modernist architect Godfrey Samuel explains the problems facing his exiled colleagues: 'German architects … cannot easily set up except as principals or partners in a firm … The theory is that only those who can prove personal achievement are justified in taking jobs from English architects.'

On 23 December, a brief article in *The Sunday Times* reports the suicide of a 'homesick German', probably a Jewish refugee, who had moved to London the previous year: 'Erich Kohn, a 27-year-old dental surgeon … was found dead in bed from gas poisoning at an address in Fellows Road, Hampstead.'

Chapter 5
The London life of two literary exiles

In the shadow of 'some Titan city'

In the autumn of 1934 both Bertolt Brecht and Stefan Zweig were living in London. Brecht arrived from Denmark, where he now resided, on 3 October and stayed until 20 December. Zweig, who had settled in England the previous year, returned on 9 September after spending several weeks on the Continent. He remained in London until the end of November, before travelling to the south of France and then embarking on a lecture tour of the United States. They were both escaping the clutches of Nazi Germany: Brecht as a notorious anti-Fascist, Zweig as a famous Jewish author who refused to endure the threats of violence and intimidation that had followed Hitler's seizure of power.

Neither of them had strong ties to England and neither spoke the language well, yet the stories of their English venture differ in almost every other aspect of their stay. Even their London homes were as dissimilar as their personalities and appearance. Brecht, who was thirty-six years old at the time, was visiting to promote his work in the hope of striking a deal. He rented a room in a shabby boarding house on the eastern edge of Bloomsbury, associated with left-wing friends from the German-speaking exile community, disdained the predominantly bourgeois nature of London's cultural scene and – a recurring complaint among émigrés – was appalled by the dreariness of his living conditions. The fifty-two-year-old Zweig, on the other hand, occupied a small but very respectable apartment at an exclusive address, lived off his considerable income as one of the world's bestselling authors and remained largely unpolitical.

A reflection on their experiences during those months offers a snapshot of 1930s London as a place marked by a singular mix of social extremes. At that time of year, a foreign exile would have perceived the city's contradictions more strikingly in the seasonal gloom. London was both beautiful and grim. In the autumn, its cosmopolitan opulence was paraded at film premieres and in luxury hotels, while the fashion columns announced the new season's latest trends (in October 1934, dressmakers were favouring 'lamé silks and velvets ... new moiré lamés as well as fancy woollens and fancy crêpes for coats'). But the days were sunless and short, often foggy, and the pavements felt damp under foot. There was also a general undercurrent of unease, for the spectre of unemployment, an expanding foreign presence on London's streets and disturbing news from central Europe loomed large on the horizon. In the classified columns, advertisements in which 'German Lady Secretary-Companions, Governesses, or Austrian Cooks and Maids' sought employment with English families were becoming the norm, and reports on the influx of foreigners took on an increasingly political tinge. Growing numbers of German-Jewish students hoped to find refuge abroad after the Nazi purges. On 26 October, *The Times* reported that 1,700 students had been 'forced to give up their studies and leave Germany'. At the beginning of the month, the Labour MP for Jarrow, Ellen Wilkinson, urged the home secretary not to close 'England to political refugees from fascism' and warned against 'discriminating unfairly as to the type of people he allowed in, since some of the most notorious Nazis from Germany ... were let in without question'. Meanwhile, German Social-Democratic politicians were refused admission, and many women and children faced countless bureaucratic obstacles only to be turned away in the end.

In London, poverty and urban squalor coexisted with the latest fashion trends and technological advancements in displays of bourgeois affluence. By 1934, cars, bicycles and double-decker buses were the main forms of transport, while horse-drawn carriages were disappearing from the city's streets. At the end of October that year, a traffic census revealed an ever-increasing number of motor vehicles on the roads. The danger they presented was counterbalanced by the introduction of new pedestrian crossings marked by orange-coloured globes at the top of striped poles, which had been named 'Belisha beacons' after the then minister of transport, Leslie Hore-Belisha. Thanks to this new feature, 'the number of deaths on the roads ... decreased in the third quarter of the year'. In a photograph published in *The Times* on 30 October, the corner of a Bloomsbury street shows three sets of the brand new safety globes watching over a peaceful scene of urban normality: a car approaching slowly in the distance, a woman crossing the road with a dog on a leash, men in dark coats and hats going about their business on the nearly empty pavements. Even such a simple picture of ordinary life evoked a world of genteel respectability and a sense of the British coolness that so often baffled foreign visitors.

In those same years, the author of a book on London associated the month of October with the Londoners' indifference to foreigners: 'the stranger is never the guest in London, which is the unfriendliest city in the world to him. If he comes alone and has no metropolitan friends, God help him, for no Londoner will.' London was a place steeped in its own traditions and mainly interested in events that happened within its boundaries, such as sporting occasions and all 'things that are Londinian, processions, accidents, weddings and the like'. Autumn was also the season in which the arrival of the cold weather exposed the city's features in the most arresting ways. And the frosty demeanour of a place that was rooted in the past yet also strikingly modern stood out against the 'tricks of atmosphere playing upon gasometers, factory chimneys, warehouses, power houses, junctions, tunnel stations, forlorn churches and other buildings that, when the year begins to take the veil, are turned to phantasmagoria, shapes and shades of some Titan city, reared in a distant burnt-out star'.

Most émigré writers, stranded in this impenetrable metropolitan world, deprived of their readership, anxious about political developments and often separated from their families, were both fascinated by London's insularity and discouraged by its unwelcoming mien. Authors whose livelihood, like that of actors, relied on their mother tongue were suddenly unemployed. In the early years of the Nazi takeover London counted around 5,000 German-speakers, a number that could not justify commercially sustainable publishing in their language. The precariousness of life in an alien city was not conducive to integration, and only a handful of writers made the leap into a rewarding career in English.

Stefan Zweig likes London

By the time he settled in London, Stefan Zweig was too old to commit wholeheartedly to a new beginning. The feeling that art alone can make sense of a world plunged into chaos animates all of his later work, most particularly his memoirs, *The World of Yesterday* (1942), in which he traced his own intellectual development back to Austria at the turn of the century as a place and time that had perished forever. Yet Zweig's experience of England was a positive one. His position within the London German-speaking community was unlike that of any of his friends and colleagues, since he had settled there voluntarily, insisted on a strictly apolitical stance and refused to consider himself a refugee. Moreover, he was wealthy and internationally acclaimed, probably the world's most famous person writing in German and certainly the most translated.

In 1939, tired of the frenzied tenor of London life and in search of a new stability, Zweig settled in Bath with his second wife, Lotte Altmann, shortly before the outbreak of the war that would drive the couple to New York and finally to Brazil, where they committed suicide in 1942. But in the days of his arrival in October 1933 he welcomed everything London had to offer. The city had not been an obvious destination for him, because he was a francophile, a lover of Paris, and because his only two visits to England almost thirty years earlier had been unsatisfactory experiences. As he wrote in 1906: 'I am living here in London somewhat unwillingly, because I love the sun and feel overcast skies like a ring of lead around the heart. And there are few people here who are close to me: too many cool and cautious, too few cordial.'

After the rise of the Third Reich, none of this seemed to matter anymore. The world was changing and Zweig was restless, professionally and emotionally. He felt trapped and needed to escape. In Austria, the presence of the Nazis just over the border (from his home he could see Hitler's residence at Berchtesgaden across the Alps on a clear day) was becoming uncomfortable, and the busy social life that he and his first wife, Friderike, had been leading for years in their luxurious residence on the hills above Salzburg had become too distracting. Yet Zweig did not want to become an exile: 'I need counterweight like music, people, and it is Rome or London that attracts me most, only not to drift into some corner of émigrés.' In then end, he chose England, a haven from the political noise and a place where he could work undisturbed. This time, he welcomed the British reserve and the comfort of anonymity as antidotes against the trappings of fame.

During his first two years in London Zweig divided most of his time between his apartment in Portland Place and the British Museum library. The former, decorated by Friderike with some of the furniture from their Salzburg home, was small but comfortable, while the latter provided him with abundant research material and a quiet place to study. Although he portrayed himself as reclusive in his letters, in London Zweig led an active social life and was clearly a member of the German and Austrian émigré community, albeit a privileged one. He frequented other Austrians, such as Robert Neumann, was an enthusiastic cinema and theatregoer, was often joined by acquaintances and fellow émigrés at his favourite café across the road from the London Palladium, and liked to dine in one of the Lyons' Corner Houses or at an Italian restaurant in the Euston Road called Casa Prada. He also received regular visits from British friends, such as the publishers Newman and Desmond Flower, and the critic and translator Joseph Leftwich.

Zweig was happier than he had been for a long time. He was not yet fully at home in London, but a sudden police search of his Salzburg home in February 1934 strengthened his decision to leave Austria and marked his definitive break with the past. He was still relatively free of the sense of loss and oppression that would mar the final years of his life. Moreover, his decision to settle in London coincided with a new beginning, as he fell in love with his secretary, the twenty-five-year-old Lotte Altmann.

'My excellent secretary'

Zweig's early letters to Lotte, written from Austria and Switzerland in the summer of 1934, are filled with longing for London and for his 'excellent secretary'. The young woman, a Jewish refugee with delicate health and a gentle demeanour, comforted Zweig at a time when he was suspended between the loss of old certainties – his house, his marriage, his homeland – and the instability of life in a foreign country.

Zweig was a troubled man, whose fears were averted by work and by the presence of loyal women at his side. Both Friderike and Lotte supported him through their devotion, which he usually repaid with a temperamental combination of despotism and kindness. Zweig had suffered a serious depressive episode in his mid thirties, and he remained secretive and moody all his life. Ironically, his popular success and the facility with which he expressed himself in his writings were associated with deep-seated insecurities and a tendency to melancholia. Only reading, work and seclusion helped to relieve these symptoms. Foreign travel was another means of escape, although constant activity usually resulted in more tension and in a paralysing inability to concentrate. Extreme restlessness and a more pervasive sense of despair affected Zweig during his later exile years in New York and led to his suicide. Yet eight years earlier, in England, he was still able to conquer his darkest moods. His encounter with Lotte, who enabled him to work and admired him unconditionally, coincided with the relief provided by the relative anonymity of his London existence. As opposed to his frenzied life in Salzburg, where his privacy was disturbed by steady streams of visitors and by family tensions, London and Lotte came to represent peace, safety and an industrious lifestyle.

It is difficult, but not impossible, to gauge the reasons for the attraction that drew Zweig towards a modest, inexperienced young refugee. 'I am not an easy person, and I am usually soon tired of people, but with you I felt such candour from the beginning that I felt safe', he wrote to his secretary only three months into their acquaintance. Lotte's modesty; her youth; her physical and emotional vulnerability; but also her strength; her attachment to her family; and, not least, her honest acceptance of her Jewish identity spoke to Zweig's own need for a new kind of safety and for the tranquillity that he deemed beneficial for his survival as a man and a writer.

Lotte Altmann was very different from Zweig's first wife, not only because of the twenty-six-year age difference between the two women. Friderike came from an affluent Jewish background but had converted to Catholicism in her youth. She had a university education, was a journalist and a published writer. She first met Stefan when she was thirty years old and had two children from a previous marriage. By the time he travelled to London in 1933, they had been married thirteen years and had lived together for over two decades. Zweig had been unhappy for a while; the political tensions of the early 1930s coincided with a deeper inner turmoil. On his fiftieth birthday, he had admitted to being tired of 'the difficulties at home' and fearful of 'being ill, growing old or growing bitter'. His escape to London in the autumn of 1933 and his infatuation with Lotte soon thereafter were a consequence of such disquiet. As for Friderike, her attachment to their comfortable life in Salzburg, her social ambitions and domestic concerns, prevented her from embracing the secluded existence in a foreign country chosen by her husband.

The daughter of a Jewish ironmonger from Silesia and the great-granddaughter of a famous rabbi, Lotte Altmann had enrolled to study French, English and economics at Frankfurt University and planned to become a librarian. In the spring of 1933 she was dismissed from the university without qualifications because she was Jewish. In May of that year, her older brother Manfred and his family relocated to London, where he practised as a doctor in Golders Green. Lotte followed him a month later, determined to improve her chances of finding a job by taking an English course and by learning to type. She also registered with the Association of Jewish Refugees at Woburn House. Although Friderike Zweig claimed to have recruited her husband's new secretary through Woburn House, it is more likely that Zweig met Lotte through an Austrian friend and one of Manfred Altmann's patients in London, the journalist Peter Smolka, or possibly through the founder of the Jewish Refugees Committee, Otto Schiff. What is certain is that Zweig was impressed with his new employee and that he was keen to employ her on a regular basis.

Almost every photograph of Lotte shows a dark-haired, earnest girl with a kind expression and thoughtful eyes, which look to the viewer with a mixture of honesty and gentleness. Only one photograph, taken by Zweig during their brief sojourn in Folkestone in September 1934, reveals Lotte in a more carefree pose, outdoors, wearing a light-coloured outfit and smiling to the camera while holding her hair back with one hand and carrying a folder of papers in the other.

Having suffered from asthma since childhood, Lotte had a delicate constitution. She was also reserved, hardworking and deeply devoted to her famous employer. But there was more to her personality, and Friderike's description of Lotte as silent and passive – 'a very serious, not to say melancholy girl, who looked the very embodiment of the fate that had befallen her and so many fellow sufferers' – is one-sided. Lotte's own correspondence unveils a far more nuanced, intelligent person, with 'a voice that is strong and distinct', independent-minded, capable of humour and decisiveness.

Zweig's first letter to Lotte Altmann is dated 1 May 1934. It was sent to her Frankfurt address, where she was staying with her family to be near her sick father, who died on the same day. Zweig's note is full of empathy; he was concerned for the young woman's wellbeing and downplayed the importance of his own needs compared to her private tragedy. They barely knew each other and at this early stage of their acquaintance – Lotte had begun working for him sometime between March and April – Zweig was still signing his letters from himself and his wife. He often swayed between concern that Lotte might be overburdened by his demands ('I really think not to have thanked you enough for all the kindness you have shown me') and the urgent need to keep working as

Figure 38 Stefan Zweig and Lotte Altmann.

efficiently as possible ('I beg you dearly, in the name of all the help that you have devoted to our mutual project. Do not turn your back on me now').

Their familiarity grew, and by the autumn Stefan Zweig and Lotte Altmann were almost certainly lovers. Their romantic relationship may have begun during their trip to Scotland in July, when Zweig collected research material for his biography of Mary Stuart. He spent the following month abroad. In his letters to Lotte, Zweig mused sentimentally over the days working together on his book. Lotte, London and Mary Stuart form a recurring theme around this time, with Zweig coyly expressing his concern about spoiling his secretary's clean typescripts with his corrections – a detail that could indicate a subconscious fear that his feelings might compromise such a modest young woman. His letters were also becoming personal and his attachment more palpable. On 5 August, he worried that she might be disregarding her own happiness. At the beginning of September, a few days before their reunion in Folkestone and subsequent return to London, he confessed that it was 'terrible <u>how</u> necessary' she was to him. If work was Zweig's strategy for maintaining sanity at a difficult time, Lotte had become the only person capable of ensuring his safety by providing him with the tools to write in peace. When he was away, he missed her organizational skills and the working rhythm they had established in the spring. His memories of that time suggest a desire for calm and an idealization of London as an oasis of peace.

Since Stefan's and Lotte's correspondence ceased when they were together, it does not cover the period between their meeting in Folkstone in September 1934 and their temporary separation in January 1935. Even Zweig's usually lively exchange of letters with friends and colleagues dwindled during those months. He was getting on with his work in London and finishing his biography of Mary, Queen of Scots, the historical personage who, in his mind, became closely connected with Lotte and his own exile.

Love for a 'city with its shutters down'

Zweig's London was a puzzling place and not always hospitable, but he loved it and was almost enraptured by its singularity. As he wrote from Switzerland in the summer of 1934:

> Here in Klosters all is calm and bright … from a strictly professional point of view, I found London not at all welcoming or cheerful at first, but rather reserved, a city with its shutters down. Yet the more I settled and got used to it, the more I discovered and grew to love the colours and shapes of this city, its particular atmosphere. I even became fond of its peculiarities, grateful for its oddities. And now, under this radiant blue sky, I miss London's murky light and would much rather be in Portland Place than near these beautiful mountains.

Soon after writing this, Zweig acted on his feelings and settled back in Portland Place, where he remained until the beginning of December. He had been thinking about living in England permanently for months. A landing card dated 26 February 1934 reveals that 'Dr. Stefan Zweig, Occupation Writer M.A., Nationality Austrian' had travelled first class. On the same form, the section entitled 'Other information' simply reads: 'at British Museum, Literature, 3 mths'. And a document from the Home Office Aliens Department marked 'Memorandum of Enquiry' shows that Zweig applied for a permanent residence permit on 18 May. Four days later, he sent a letter to Edward Hallett Carr, a journalist, historian and first secretary at the Foreign Office at the time, expressing his gratitude for Carr's offer to help him with his application. Zweig was careful to mention only professional reasons for wanting to live in England and avoided any references to political matters:

You know that for my historical works I want a great library and no one in the world could serve me better than the British Museum Library, where I can find for future and present work all what I could ever want. You will understand better than somebody else, dear Mr. Carr, that this is a very precious circumstance. To stay in London is therefore very important to me and to have a second home for my work.

In the final line of the typewritten text, Zweig added the word 'second' by hand, possibly so as not to draw attention to the fact that he had turned his back on Austria and was now wholly dependent on British hospitality. This detail and the clumsiness of his written English are enough to betray the difficulties he was facing at the time. According to a Home Office document dated 28 May 1934, he called to apply 'for cancellation of conditions' (the three months' limit to his stay) and 'stated to be a well known author with a bank balance of £4,500'. A few days later, the application was forwarded to MI5 where, at the end of June, it was concluded that they had 'nothing recorded against this man'.

On the same form, a small note in pencil, which reads 'again 30/9/1934', shows that Zweig made another attempt to obtain permanent residence after the summer. In the weeks following his return from the Continent, his desire to resume a regular work routine at the British Museum and with Lotte at Portland Place must have been thwarted by the need to deal with the bureaucratic procedures that would allow them to remain in England indefinitely. After Zweig's request in May, Carr had already interceded on his behalf by putting his case to C. B. McAlpine, a principal in the Home Office Aliens Department, but four months later the matter was still unresolved. This put Zweig in a difficult position, because he wanted his case to be finalized before his lecture tour.

Throughout October 1934, both Stefan and his secretary spent much time dealing with the bureaucracy for an extension of Lotte's residence permit. Whereas he turned to his friends in high places, she relied on the help of the Jewish Refugees Committee. The extent to which Zweig disliked the exposure that came with such matters is evident from an exchange of letters with his friend Antonina Vallentin, a Polish-born journalist and biographer, and Harry Crookshank, then undersecretary of state for the Home Department. On 16 October Zweig wrote to Crookshank enclosing a letter of recommendation from Vallentin and appealing for the undersecretary's help. Zweig did not explain the matter, but he was probably acting on Lotte's behalf. Four days later the politician, albeit 'so very much engaged with Parliamentary business', invited Zweig to call on him at the Home Office the following Tuesday, 23 October, at 4.30 p.m., when he hoped to be able to see him 'if at all possible'. The exchange seems to have put Zweig under considerable strain. Asking for help, being treated condescendingly by powerful people, feeling an outsider, filling in forms and engaging in impersonal correspondence instead of working – all this must have been very difficult for such a proud and sensitive man. It is also possible that Zweig refused Crookshank's offer in order to conceal his immigrant status.

On Sunday 21 October 1934, in his hesitant English and following the rules of German punctuation, Zweig wrote a letter of reply in violet ink:

> Dear Sir, it was <u>extremely</u> kind of you to give me the opportunity to see you in a moment where you are so occupied. But I will not abuse of such kindness, as the information, I hoped to get from you, regards neither myself nor is it of so important kind that I would dare to worry you when you are engaged in your far more important parlamentary [*sic*] work.
>
> Please believe me that I am <u>very</u> grateful to your proposition and that, if I won't wish to call upon you Thuesday [*sic*] it is <u>only</u> for respect of your work. But I hope that at another time a good occasion will happen, to meet you and to thank you for your kindness.

The occasion to meet in future did not present itself. Zweig and Lotte had to wait at least four more years before they could call England their home, by which time they had decided to leave Europe for good. Several months after his missed encounter with Harry Crookshank, Zweig's future was as uncertain as ever.

As for Lotte, a request for 'a further twelve months' permission to stay' was made to the undersecretary of state by an investigating officer at the Jewish Refugees Committee. The letter is dated 23 October, the same day on which Crookshank had proposed to meet Zweig. But the request was ignored, and on 26 November the same person at Woburn House appealed again to the Home Office referring to Lotte Altmann's previous application. Four days later, a Home Office document indicated that the extension was granted, albeit only until Lotte's departure to France on 4 December.

Despite these complications, in October 1934 Zweig had settled back into the routine that he had so often missed during the summer and moved into another rented apartment at 11 Portland Place. The building no longer stands, but the street still retains much of its original grandeur. A wide and beautifully proportioned thoroughfare, Portland Place was developed for the duke of Portland at the end of the eighteenth century and contains some of London's most elegant neo-classical buildings. From its inception, Portland Place had a history of illustrious residents and was traditionally home to peers, judges and ambassadors. In 1865 the Langham Hotel, then one of London's largest buildings and the most modern establishment of its kind, opened its doors at the southern end of the street. Around the turn of the twentieth century, tall blocks of flats took their place next to the grander and more expensive houses, but the address remained exclusive.

In 1934, the newly appointed director of the National Gallery, Kenneth Clark, moved into number 30, and the purpose-built headquarters of the Royal Institute of

British Architects were established at number 66. The BBC had taken up residence at Broadcasting House, opposite the Langham, in 1932. In those same years, advertisements appeared regularly in *The Times* publicizing accommodation at Portland Place as suitable for 'Professional and Residential purposes', with the 'best position in the West End and every convenience and amenity'. Zweig's building boasted some distinguished residents at the time of his arrival. They were mostly renowned doctors, politicians and lawyers: Sir Berkeley Moynihan, former president of the Royal College of Surgeons, occupied flat number 2; the Conservative politician and president of the National Chamber of Trade, Sir George G. Mitcheson, was at number 6; the German solicitor and composer Herbert Oppenheimer was at number 10 and the legal scholar Sir George W. Paton at number 11. Zweig's taste for comfort and respectability must have been amply satisfied.

London was the only European capital untouched by political extremism that could offer Zweig privacy and reserve together with the advantages and sophistication of a cosmopolitan environment. It is possible that during his first year there he still felt awkward in the vast and unfamiliar city. Yet he was safe within the walls of his perfectly appointed flat, a pleasant walk away from the British Museum library, the art galleries, the theatres and concert halls. Three years later, in a brief televised interview with the BBC, he explained his main reasons for living in London:

> I find it the ideal city for three reasons. For one thing, you have here the best libraries … Then too London is becoming the capital of music. And thirdly, one may work here completely undisturbed. There is none of that tense atmosphere which is to be found in so many big cities today. In London I have discovered it is possible for an individual to fashion his life in his own way, undisturbed by the intrusion of other people.

In the autumn of 1934, Zweig was still finding his feet within a new environment, but he had already developed a set of habits, alternating visits to the British Museum reading room with work at Portland Place in the company of Lotte. She came daily from her brother's house at 174 Willesden Lane, a discreet presence on a Northern Line train, or maybe on the number 13 bus from Golders Green. Their romantic liaison was quietly progressing, and although Zweig must have been afflicted by doubts, by fears about their age difference and about Lotte's fragile health, life in London reassured him with its formality and regular rhythm.

The problem with Zweig

In 1934 Stefan Zweig was a literary celebrity at the height of his fame; that year sealed his success in England and America. Until then, he had been known mainly as an author of novellas, which were a popular genre in German but commercially less viable in the English-speaking world. With his biography of Marie Antoinette, published in English in January 1933, Zweig's reputation began to grow. A few weeks after publication, the book was praised in the *Times Literary Supplement* as a literary biography 'of a higher order'. The following month, his version of Ben Jonson's *Volpone* opened at London's Duke of York Theatre as part of 'a season of German plays, given in German with running commentary in English, by a company of Jewish players' and produced by Leopold Jessner, the legendary director of the Berlin Staatstheater during the Weimar years. Zweig's name also carried weight in charitable circles that autumn, and despite his apolitical stance he became involved in a philanthropic event on behalf of German refugees. On 1 December 1933, *The Times* reported that he had given 'a very moving address' at a lunch held by Mrs Anthony de Rothschild 'in aid of German-Jewish women and children', at which over 100 people were present.

Stefan Zweig's special status among the exiles was undisputed. That month, he had received $7,500 from the sale of the film rights to his novella *Letter from an Unknown Woman*, and the new year promised to be just as profitable. Although he refused the lucrative offer of $3,000 a week for ten weeks to write film scripts in Hollywood, another volume of his previously untranslated short stories hit the bookshops in the spring of 1934. It was entitled *Kaleidoscope* and included 'The Burning Secret', a story about the inner torments of a young boy grappling with the drama of his mother's affair, and the novella *Buchmendel*, the moving portrayal of an old Jewish book dealer whose vocation is destroyed by the events unleashed by the First World War. This time, the *TLS* reviewer criticized the author's 'fondness for sentimental situations and the threadbareness of his imaginative material', but such objections did little to diminish Zweig's popularity. His readable style and romantic vein, his insight into the human psyche and his nostalgic depiction of a lost Mitteleuropean world were the reasons for his extraordinary success.

They still are. Today Zweig is one of the few bestselling authors in German. After decades in which his works were almost forgotten in the English-speaking world, he came back into fashion. In the popular imagination, he has become the stereotype for an idealized, often sugary version of the Habsburg past.

In 2014, *The Grand Budapest Hotel*, a comedy by the American film director Wes Anderson inspired by Zweig's writings, was released into cinemas to critical and popular acclaim. A multilayered narrative with a plot full of twists and turns, the story is set between the two world wars in a fictional central European state and in a dilapidated grand hotel the colour of candy floss. The film is colourful, vibrant and refreshingly absurd. Although this surreal reimagining of the Austro-Hungarian universe is the complete antithesis of the restrained and emotionally convoluted world of Zweig's fiction, the author's name gained even greater notoriety through the association with a successful Hollywood movie.

In the same year, an Austrian restaurant opened in Marylebone, not far from Zweig's London address. It is a smart establishment. A wood-panelled and tiled interior with Thonet-style furniture and antique light fittings evokes an early twentieth-century Viennese café with thoughtful accuracy. A similar enthusiasm for the Mitteleuropean look extends to the restaurant's toilets where, in one of the cubicles, hangs a framed photograph of Stefan and Friderike Zweig. It shows the couple seated next to each other on a bench in their garden in Salzburg, probably around the time of the writer's move to England. Stefan, his beloved spaniel Kaspar at his side, is holding a cigar. He is wearing a white linen suit with

Figure 39 Stefan and Friderike Zweig in their garden in Salzburg, *c.* 1933.

short trousers, knee socks and a spotted bow tie. Friderike, with a cat on her lap, conveys a convincing picture of domestic bliss. Smiling and gazing at the camera, they betray no sign of the turmoil that was about to erupt in their lives. That this photograph ended up in the lavatories of an Austrian-themed restaurant in twenty-first-century London as the embodiment of the cheerful old Habsburg spirit is a bizarre footnote in the story of Zweig's popularity. It also reveals the degree to which the public's fascination with his books often coincides with a superficial image of the man and his world.

Zweig himself can be held partly responsible for this deceptive version of his personality. Throughout his life, he was at pains to conceal his feelings and cultivated his public image behind an impeccably groomed exterior. He played the role of the liberal gentleman, of the assimilated Jewish intellectual who identified with bourgeois values and wrote books in a polished style that is sometimes dismissed as fake and facile. A few years ago, the poet and translator Michael Hofmann called his style 'the Pepsi of Austrian writing'. Criticism of Zweig is not new. Defined the '"best hated" author of his era', he counted many illustrious detractors, including Thomas Mann, Robert Musil, Hermann Hesse and Hannah Arendt. Another contemporary, the author Franz Blei, summed up a prevalent notion about Zweig's lack of original talent in his *Great Bestiary of German Literature* (1920), a book in which he penned satirical portraits of famous writers as imaginary creatures: 'The Steffzweig is an artificial product, manufactured at a Viennese literary congress from feathers, skin, hairs etc. taken from all sorts of European animals.'

Towards the end of his life, Zweig identified strongly with the values of western humanism and presented himself as one of the last representatives of a lost 'Golden Age of Security', the period symbolized by the old Austrian monarchy and shattered by the First World War. He celebrated it in *The World of Yesterday*, the work in which he chartered the story of his own generation and its cultural achievements on the eve of change. Despite being subtitled *An Autobiography*, the book is strangely impersonal. Zweig's unwillingness to write about himself is clear from the first sentence: 'I never considered myself important enough to feel tempted to tell others the story of my life.' The sentiment is understandable and yet, in Zweig's case, it highlights a reluctance to speak candidly, to disclose real emotion. At times, his stylization of the past appears as a lack of depth adorned with descriptions that are so polished as to seem artificial.

The lives of others

In London, Zweig did not write the fictional stories set in the Austro-Hungarian Empire with which he is often associated. He chose to work on historical biographies instead. This was a popular genre with German-speaking authors in the 1930s, one through which they tried to make sense of troubling times. Like books inspired by biblical or mythological subjects, writings on historical figures offered a way of reflecting upon one's predicament from a universal perspective. Zweig refused to engage with politics, yet turned to the past in an attempt to read the present with the help of higher authorities. Reflecting on history and the life of others gave him a sense of order and alleviated his fears of facing a threat alone. While exile caused a fracture in the writer's perception of space and time by depriving him of his home and by imposing limits on the length of his stay in a foreign country, writing about history allowed him to overcome those boundaries.

Zweig's interest in the past was also at the root of his famous collection of precious manuscripts. The collection included autographs by musical and literary giants such as Mozart and Goethe, but also more recent historical documents, such as the thirteen-page manuscript of one of Hitler's speeches, which Zweig had bought secretly in 1933. He was thoroughly fascinated by these tangible examples of history in the making and often invested historical characters with personal significance in his books. This concerned subjects as disparate as his friend Romain Rolland, the French writer whose pacifism he celebrated in a biography published after the First World War, and Erasmus of Rotterdam, the Renaissance humanist with whom Zweig identified at the beginning of his own journey into exile. He saw the Dutch scholar as a spiritual guide; a model of European cosmopolitanism and political impartiality; and, above all, an intellectual authority against fanaticism.

Erasmus was published in German early in 1934 and in English the following October. London had proved an ideal place to write, but the danger of inactivity loomed and Zweig needed another project to occupy his mind after months of intense work. The idea for his next book – the one that would seal his fame in Britain once and for all – came to him at a desk in the library of the British Museum soon after arriving in London at the end of October 1933:

> I had had enough of biographies. But then, on only my third day in London, I was in the British Museum, attracted by my old passion for autograph manuscripts and looking at those on public display. They included the handwritten account of the execution of Mary Queen of Scots … As I had nothing to read in the evening, I bought a book about her. It was a paean of praise, defending her as a saint. The book was shallow and foolish. Next day my incurable curiosity led me to buy another book, which claimed almost exactly the opposite. The case was beginning to interest me. I asked for a really authoritative work on Mary. No one could recommend one, and so by diligently searching and making my own enquiries I was involuntarily drawn into making comparisons. Without really knowing it, I had begun a book about Mary Stuart that kept me in libraries for weeks on end.

It is impossible to say whether the idea for Zweig's next project after *Erasmus* really came as such a bolt from the blue a couple of days into his visit to London, or whether he had already been looking for a subject suitable for a British readership. Be that as it may, the choice for his new biography proved to be an inspired one. The book, published in English in the autumn of 1935 as *The Queen of Scots* (later translations are entitled *Mary Stuart* and *Mary Queen of Scots*), was a great popular success.

As today, reviewers at the time did not always share the public's enthusiasm for the escapist nature of Zweig's work. The critics usually admired his entertaining style and balanced approach, but disapproved of Zweig's unreliable use of historical facts, which they saw as a way to promote his own view of his protagonists' actions and character traits. The journalist who reviewed the first English edition of *The Queen of Scots* for the *Manchester Guardian* in October 1935 appraised the book as a good read rather than a significant work of scholarship, maintaining that almost everything in the final part of the story is 'so egregiously wrong, that [it] cannot be taken seriously'.

As all of Zweig's biographical writings, *Mary Stuart* is a personal interpretation of a human story rather than a rigorous reading of history. He worked on the book throughout 1934, with Lotte's patient assistance from April onwards, and provided the finishing touches to the manuscript on his return from North America in February 1935. One of Zweig's biographers argued that many of the descriptions of Mary Stuart are reminiscent of Lotte who, like Zweig's Scottish queen, was 'young, inexperienced and immature, yet cultivated and gracious'. This is possibly true; after all, he had engaged Lotte when he was writing *Mary Stuart* and their romantic relationship had begun over those very pages. The files under Lotte's arm as she smiled at her photographer in Folkestone were surely part of the manuscript, and the days of Zweig's research trip in Scotland in July marked the first time they had travelled together. It is also plausible that some of the descriptions in the book – Mary's feelings of anguish as she left France after her first husband's death, for example – reflect Lotte's distress at being exiled from Germany. And references to Lotte could be hidden in the passages in which Zweig, describing the inexperienced young queen as a victim of fanaticism, outlined her temperament as marked by a gentle, 'pliant and accommodating disposition', counterbalanced by a unique strength of character.

But on the whole *Mary Stuart* is not a tribute to Lotte Altmann, and Zweig's reading of his protagonist's personality is another veiled reflection on his own experience and a commentary on the destructive nature of power. His tale is an absorbing read, but Zweig's inflated vocabulary and his use of rhetoric for emphatic effect risk turning historical reality into cliché. In the first chapter, for instance, his description of Scotland as the 'last outpost of Europe towards the northern seas that lash its rugged coasts and as a tragic land, perpetually rent in sunder by antagonistic passions, dark and romantic as a saga' is overburdened by a reiteration of similar images.

Zweig romanticized history by emphasizing the machinations of politics and the brutality of fate. The theme of the bitterness of exile recurs throughout *Mary Stuart*, as does the sense of being alone at the mercy of uncontrollable forces. Once again, Zweig's own convictions resonate in his condemnation of politics ('one who has vowed himself to politics is no longer a free agent') and tyrannical fanaticism (John Knox, 'domineering and authoritarian', is 'the most finished example of the religious fanatic'). This is a tragic world portrayed with exaggerated pathos. Zweig's awareness of history's indifference to 'the innermost longings of individuals, often involving persons and powers, despite themselves, in her murderous game' is surely a reference to the struggles of his own time.

Boredom in the soup

In the autumn of 1934, back at Portland Place, Zweig was again becoming restless. London had begun to bore him, he was tired of Europe and increasingly alarmed by its political developments. On 4 October, he wrote a long letter to Romain Rolland, in which his words sound more genuine than those in his books, and his fears more real than those he attributed to the subjects of his biographies:

> Half of Europe is now living under a dictatorship, free speech is being suffocated … And the worst is that one is becoming used to it! That people are no longer aware of being enslaved. The human capacity to forget is so great, so terrible, people take the situation for granted without realising it, they accept it without question. In Germany the Jews have become used to their ghetto with a speed that makes one shudder, while the others write their 'Heil Hitler' so mechanically at the end of their letters that a man who wanted to make me happy by writing how much he loved my book, forgot himself and signed his letter, which was meant to express his <u>admiration</u> for <u>me</u>, with 'Heil Hitler' (I kept it as a record) … I see now that people have only <u>known</u> freedom without <u>feeling it</u>. They have internalised it so little that they now fail to notice their enslavement.

Zweig's moral and political indignation ran deeper than his publicly neutral stance would lead us to believe. Moreover, his suppressed outrage and his inability to find refuge in his work now that the book on Mary Stuart was coming to an end were dampening his enthusiasm. He began to see London – the place he had praised and pined for all summer – with different eyes:

I'm staying in London until the end of November. The country is beginning to bore me. People are too content and with too little. On the one hand, this is very good – one doesn't breathe in the hate or suffer the grouchy discontent which is making Austria uninhabitable at the moment. But on the other hand one doesn't breathe at all. The air has no ozone, nothing inspiring. People are very nice here, yet as distant from us 'foreigners' as we are from them. They don't understand, they just accept what is written and said. A fog of boredom rests over everything, you can taste it even in the soup. I am pleased that England was such a good sanatorium for my nerves, but as one suddenly tires of the white walls of a sanatorium, I can no longer breathe this dry air which lacks the spice of vitality.

These complaints echo those of Zweig's fellow exiles. After his initial enthusiasm he, too, began to resent the Londoners' indifference towards outsiders and the oddity of a city that – despite its size, energy and diversity – appeared impenetrable and ruled by rigid customs. Zweig's discontent was caused not only by anxiety over present events, but also by an innately nervous disposition. Fearful thoughts were always lurking somewhere in his mind and inactivity made the situation worse. He was easily disturbed by external factors and by his own demons, and used to alternate work and travel in order to control his dark moods. There were even rumours, circulating among his friends and colleagues, that his problems were linked to a sexual perversion. The rumours referred to Zweig's supposedly predatory nature, to his fixation with young women and exhibitionist tendencies. Zweig's alleged 'burning secret' and the mystifying combination of his popular success and his reticent personality continue to attract the curiosity of critics to this day.

It is unlikely that any of this played a part during Zweig's time in London, for he had just met Lotte, was busy with practical matters and keen to project an image of authority and respectability in a new environment. Above all, he worried, as shadows from the world he had left behind mixed with fears about an uncertain future. In Germany and Austria, his name was in the public eye because he had written the libretto for Richard Strauss's latest opera, *The Silent Woman*, and Zweig feared the Nazis' reaction to having a Jewish writer attached to Germany's most famous composer. Also, his need to be in London to carry out research was becoming irrelevant now that *Mary Stuart* was finished. On 29 November 1934 he headed south again.

A promising visit

At the beginning of November 1934 Bertolt Brecht was also bored with London. He had been there barely a month and was already dissatisfied. The city had not fulfilled his expectations. He had been persuaded to travel to England by friends who saw good opportunities for his work in the British film and publishing industries. They were the composer Hanns Eisler, with whom Brecht was collaborating on the anti-Nazi satirical play *Round Heads and Pointed Heads*; the scriptwriter Leo Lania, who had adapted Brecht's *Threepenny Opera* for the screen and was hoping to work with him on a new film project for a British production company; and the philosopher Karl Korsch, Brecht's teacher and advisor on Marxist matters. Brecht also had an agent in London, Elias Alexander, who was then negotiating with English and American publishers for an English version of *The Threepenny Novel*, a book whose dark, sardonic view of Victorian London may have interested English-speaking readers. Other people acting on Brecht's behalf were Margaret Mynatt, an Austrian-born British citizen, Communist agent and friend of Brecht's assistant and collaborator Elisabeth Hauptmann, and Fritz Kortner, whom Brecht had known since their theatrical glory days in Weimar Berlin.

In some émigré circles, London seemed the ideal place for business. For a foreign writer, the chance of being translated into English held the promise of conquering both the British and American markets (as Stefan Zweig was doing). The German-speaking actors who had found success on the London stage and in the English film studios gave hope to their compatriots. Writing to Brecht from the United States at the end of September 1934, Elisabeth Hauptmann reminded him that the British entertainment industry – and London in particular – 'still played an important role', and cited as proof 'Bergner's huge success in *Catherine* [*the Great*]'.

Throughout that year, Brecht's friends kept insisting that he should go to England. In April, Eisler announced the possibility of staging their play at a London theatre through the help of none other than Otto Katz, the notorious Soviet agent with more than twenty aliases, founder of several political magazines and editor, with Willi Münzenberg, of the book that posed one of the greatest challenges to the Nazi propaganda machine outside Germany, *The Brown Book of the Hitler Terror and the Burning of the Reichstag* (1933). Katz was a shadowy figure, but he was also charming and counted many famous people among his friends, from Marlene Dietrich to Ellen Wilkinson, from Noel Coward to Peter Lorre. Brecht and Eisler knew him well. On 17 April, Eisler informed Brecht that Katz was on his way to London with a copy of the play. At the end of the month, he wrote again describing Katz's vision of the city as a potential hub for left-wing culture ('London is enjoying a sort of prosperity and since they're expecting a Labour Government in the autumn, the left-leaning middle class is flourishing').

A rough translation of *Round Heads and Pointed Heads* was being prepared, and the play had roused the interest of Charles Laughton, the actor – Eisler explained – 'known for the film *The Private Life of Henry VIII*'. Years later in America, Laughton and Brecht became friends and collaborated on a famous

Figure 40 Bertolt Brecht (right) and Hanns Eisler, *c.* 1932.

production of *The Life of Galileo*, but in 1934 they didn't know each other and England's mainstream audience was not ready for political theatre. The optimistic predictions came to nothing. In June, however, Eisler was on his way to London to talk to an agent about the play, and was still hopeful. In July, Margaret Mynatt wrote encouragingly to Brecht about the English translations of *Round Heads and Pointed Heads* and of *The Threepenny Novel*. She also thought that *The Threepenny Opera* could be a success on the London stage.

Activities on Brecht's behalf continued through the summer. In August Mynatt gave a copy of *Round Heads and Pointed Heads* to Fritz Kortner, who foresaw good prospects for the play and suggested that Brecht spend a couple of weeks in London as soon as possible. She also added a note of caution ('your chances here are very good, provided you don't hit people over the head with politics and observe certain restrictions'), but his visit was seen as a good idea.

Hanns Eisler, albeit dissatisfied with his meagre pay and with the English film world, urged Brecht to visit, since everything there was 'already in full swing'. The following week, from his new permanent address (a flat at 147 Abbey Road in West Hampstead), Eisler asked Brecht to join him as soon as possible. His next letter, on 11 September, was less hopeful, because Elias Alexander's response on the possibility of a successful English production of *Round Heads and Pointed Heads* had been categorically negative. Kortner, too, although 'hugely enthusiastic about the play', did not think that it would do well in London. Around the same time, Margaret Mynatt's efforts to organize a production of *The Threepenny Opera* at the Gate Theatre were stalling, as the copyright agency would not release the rights to the play on account of the disagreement between Brecht and his composer, Kurt Weill. Despite these setbacks, there was still a chance to find work in film. On 21 September, Eisler and Lania wrote to Brecht about the English translation of a play by Lania, which they hoped would interest a film production company: 'The English language version is a <u>very urgent</u> matter … So do come as quickly as possible.' Less than two weeks later, Brecht set off for London. He was to stay at the house of Herbert Levy, an exiled doctor and friend of Karl Korsch. When Brecht reached the modest building in Calthorpe Street at the beginning of October, a cold wind was blowing. Apart from a faint echo of his success on the Continent, not many people in England had heard of Bertolt Brecht or his subversive plays.

'The problematical Bert Brecht'

The odd-looking young man who arrived at the door of a Bloomsbury boarding house sometime after 3 October 1934 was, in Leo Lania's words, 'in his early thirties, with a lean, ascetic face. His glasses sat awry on his thin, prominent nose; one bow was broken and mended with a string. Atop his close-cropped head he wore a leather cap. This was Bertolt Brecht, the greatest of our younger poets.' Brecht was not only a great poet, but also the most important German playwright of his generation. He wrote a clear, simple prose of unusual transparency, with a provocative tone and a political message. His aims were revolutionary, in politics as on the page. He worked unwaveringly to achieve his goals, mostly surrounded by various collaborators, friends and lovers. He had a forceful personality and a firm belief in his own talent.

Brecht's name had first appeared in the British press in 1928 after the Berlin premiere of *The Threepenny Opera*, the musical play that, as a combination of social and political satire and catchy tunes, launched a type of theatre such as had never been seen before. Yet in Britain acknowledgement of Brecht's rise to fame did not include a full recognition of his talent. Earlier that year, *The Times*'s Berlin correspondent had mentioned Brecht's play *Man Equals Man* (1926) – a comedy about human exploitation set in an imaginary British India – in a piece that lamented the Germans' 'chronic incapacity to produce drawing-room comedies'. Six months later, a reviewer of *The Threepenny Opera* recognized the utter originality of Brecht's work, but also felt that his readers would dislike it, since such a daring theatrical novelty would easily provoke the more conservative aesthetic sensibilities of the British: 'An English visitor … would wonder during the first scene what it was all about … What Herr Kurt Brecht [*sic!*] and his associates have done may be indefensible to many minds, but it is an interesting example of the more earnest efforts now being made to break new ground on the German stage.'

Brecht's inimitable brand of theatre was difficult to export. In January 1933, the author of an article about recent German plays in the *Manchester Guardian* remarked on the audiences' 'clamour for gaiety and light-hearted entertainment', and referred to 'the problematical Bert Brecht'. This did not bode well for the playwright's future in England. However, six months later his name was associated with the London stage when a ballet with songs composed by Kurt Weill, choreographed by Balanchine and with a libretto by Brecht, was performed at the Savoy Theatre.

The piece, entitled *Anna Anna* (later renamed *The Seven Deadly Sins*) and on tour from Paris with Balanchine's troupe *Les Ballets 1933*, was danced, acted and sung, and told the story of two sisters who symbolized a contrast within the same person: the split between one's natural inclinations and the need to make money. It featured two magnetic performers, Weill's wife Lotte Lenya, who had triumphed as Pirate Jenny in *The Threepenny Opera*, and the seductive Tilly Losch, the Viennese dancer who lived in London and was tempestuously married to wealthy socialite Edward James. With such an array of talent, *Anna Anna* must have provided an unforgettable experience, but its unusual content and jazzy sounds did not appeal to a British audience. The author of a review in the *Illustrated London News*, for example, mentioned the gloom and the 'intense Mittel-Europa cynicism and miming rather than dancing'.

The Mitteleuropean gloom intensified during that fatal year for Germany. Brecht, who had fled abroad with his family after the Reichstag fire, did not believe in the humanist sentiments voiced by some members of the exile community – of which Stefan Zweig was a typical representative – and his work was becoming increasingly militant. In 1934, Brecht published two works that testify to his combative stance during his first year in exile: *The Threepenny Novel* and *Songs, Poems and Choruses*, co-authored with Eisler. The latter contains some memorable political poems, such as the one entitled *Germany*, a strong indictment of the country's self-destructive fate sealed, in the poet's view, by a culture of militarism and economic exploitation ('O Germany, pale mother / How you sit defiled / Among the peoples').

In *The Threepenny Novel* Brecht also advanced a political agenda. He did retain the satirical plot of the opera, but he also presented a dark world of bankers and financiers, in which Macheath ('Mack the Knife') is a powerful businessman, crime an integral part of society, and legality and lawlessness have become undistinguishable. In 1934, the more entertaining elements of *The Threepenny Opera*, with its comic effects and jazzy songs, made way for a more ambitious ideological argument aimed at denouncing the shady dealings between the commercial bourgeoisie and the ruling classes. Brecht now advocated a revolutionary transformation of economic conditions and regarded Fascism as an extremely cruel form of capitalist exploitation. In the novel, which, like the opera, is set in Victorian London, the city itself is the embodiment of such cruelty. Here, too, as in the play, Brecht evoked an imaginary city drawn from Rudyard Kipling's colonial vision and from Edgar Wallace's American-style dockland thrillers. But in a book of several-hundred pages the setting plays a more significant role than in a text written for the stage. And so the London of *The Threepenny Novel* is 'the greatest city in the world', a slippery maze of intrigue and corruption, a strangely indeterminate metropolis, in which recognizable features (the bridges, the docks, the fog) and evocative names (Old Oak Street, Lower Blacksmith Square, Limehouse and Whitechapel) conjure up a murky atmosphere rather than a physical world.

Life in 'a wicked, hardbitten town'

In Brecht's work, metropolitan squalor and the harshness of city life stand for a society dominated by human suffering and brutal economic interests. London in the 1930s was such a hard city, and it is tempting to imagine that the playwright's lodgings matched – if not quite surpassed – the gloom of his fictional urban creations.

Parma House, a four-storey dark-brick building on Calthorpe Street – 'a continuation of the still presentable Guilford Street' on the eastern edge of Bloomsbury – stood at the end of 'a shabby terrace of small houses without a garden'. A fellow exile and former employee of the German publishing house that published Brecht's first book of poems, Grete Fischer, remembers arriving at this somewhat dispiriting place one day that autumn: 'I was standing a little doubtfully before the narrow entrance, haggling with the friendly Italian landlady. Suddenly a voice sounded out from the dark stairway: "You can easily move in, Miss Fischer, I live here too." It was Bertolt Brecht.'

The house still stands on the corner between Calthorpe Street and Phoenix Place. The latter is an industrial, undistinguished-looking road that then, as now, backed onto one of the largest mail sorting offices in the country. Parma House does not figure in the 1934 Street Directory, but the occupations of some nearby residents at the time – a masseur at number 26, a tobacconist at number 50 and a hairdresser at 50A – reveal a working-class milieu in keeping with the general character of the area. As part of an early Victorian development south of King's Cross, Calthorpe Street extends through one of the oldest London neighbourhoods. Here stood churches, almshouses, a prison, a school for poor Welsh children, a hospital and an eighteenth-century burial ground. Tucked away behind the high buildings that separate it from a busy main road, and a few steps from number 24, a small cemetery, St Andrew's Gardens, contains the remains of the pre-Romantic poet Thomas Chatterton, who committed suicide

Figure 41 24 Calthorpe Street, London, 2017.

at the age of seventeen and, more in keeping with Brecht's convictions, 'those of the paupers interred in Shoe Lane Workhouse graveyard'. Perhaps Brecht was aware of the history of the area; he was certainly interested in the conditions of the poor. Kortner remembers an occasion when the playwright visited him and his family and told them of seeing some of the London slums with a doctor friend – possibly Herbert Levy – who had also shown him evidence of 'the frightful inadequacy of the welfare and health systems'.

Brecht's situation in London was precarious. He felt lonely, was hampered by his delicate health (he had recently been in hospital for a kidney complaint, had a long-standing heart problem and frequent bouts of fever) and was keen to conclude a work deal in order to return home as soon as possible. Brecht was a pragmatist. One of his first letters to his wife, Helene Weigel, ten days after his arrival, is characteristically unsentimental and to the point: 'Dear Helli, Please send the scene of the "Round Heads" that is only typed – I hope you have received the money in the meantime ... What are the children up to? – How's the chess? – I'm feeling fine. Septum all right. – I'm staying at a pension, without meals, Korsch is living over me. The theatres are antediluvian.'

The last comment highlights the gulf between the culture of Weimar Berlin and London's conventional offerings. During the first week of Brecht's stay, London theatres showed a typical mixture of musical entertainment (such as 'the new light operetta *By Appointment*, in which Miss Maggie Teyte will play the part of Mrs. Maria Fitzherbert and Mr. Charles Mayhew will appear as George IV') and traditional versions of stage classics (a production of *King Lear* had just transferred to the West End from the Croydon Repertory Theatre). Even the staging of more recent plays, such as one by Luigi Pirandello, winner of that year's Nobel Prize for Literature, was intended to please and entertain the public. In *The Times*, the notice announcing the British premiere of Pirandello's *The Life that I Gave Him* informed prospective spectators that the production would be 'followed by a one act play entitled *Murder Trial*', and that 'in the Pirandello play Miss Nancy Price and Miss Peggy Ashcroft had emotional parts'. To Brecht, whose dramatic practice discouraged the public's identification with the characters and aimed at making audiences think critically about the events on stage, such bland, emotionally manipulative theatre was an abomination. Later that autumn, he was impressed by the Group Theatre production of T. S. Eliot's experimental, fragmentary verse play *Sweeney Agonistes*, and described the performance – at which, it seems, W. B. Yeats was also present – as 'the best thing [he had] seen for a long time and the best thing in London'. But on the whole he was dismayed by the lack of originality in English theatre.

London both intrigued and annoyed Brecht. On the one hand, its dreariness and magnitude satisfied his fascination with the modern metropolis (he found it 'better than Paris, bigger and greyer, so better'). On the other, he bemoaned the lack of comforts, the tastelessness of the food and the general diffidence of the people. His letters, though mostly brief and practical, include all the familiar complaints of other continental immigrants living in London. Just over three weeks after his arrival, Brecht described London as 'not too hospitable'. A few days later, frustrated by having to deal with bureaucracy, he was bored and wondered if his wife might want to join him ('I am fine. A little bored. People nice. A bit boring'). At the beginning of November he wrote: 'Here things are improving slowly, but on the move. I'm trying to do some stories for the cinema, it would bring some money. But I'm gradually getting fed up with London.'

Grete Fischer used to join Brecht on walks 'in the old proletarian London around Sadler's Wells' and remembers going with him to 'a cinema in King's Cross'. One day, she cooked him some porridge in the landlady's kitchen 'because he had stomach pains and was afraid'. Brecht's anxiety about his health revealed his more vulnerable side. He needed to eat well, to keep warm and to avoid physical strain. As he wrote to his young lover and collaborator, Margarete (Grete) Steffin, on 19 October, London was not a suitable place in this respect. He was spending his days running around in the hope of getting some work or waiting for things to happen, and found the effort of dealing with the underground and buses particularly difficult. A few days later, impatient to have news from Steffin, he wrote to her again: 'I'm freezing. They only have open fireplaces here. Mine's a coal fire; above me Korsch has a gas fire in his fireplace. He's freezing too. The English eat leather and grass.'

During those same weeks, Brecht was negotiating the foreign rights for *The Threepenny Novel* with his Dutch publisher in his own obstinate and businesslike way, yet at the same time he was astounded by London's uncompromising attitude towards money. He saw England as a particularly callous capitalist society: 'convincing the English to cough up some money is a tough job. It's a very old, hardened and seasoned form of capitalism. They just don't let go of their shillings.' Sometime in December, he described London to a friend as 'a wicked, hardbitten town', whose people were 'among the most vicious in Europe'. He felt that there was 'a high culture of corruption, which is all but closed to the tourist'. And he added, referring to the much-publicized wedding between the duke of Kent and Princess Marina of Greece on 29 November 1934: 'Did you read that on the occasion of a marriage in the Royal family the London unemployed gave the prince a wedding present? Can the Stavisky case [a financial scandal that had rocked French politics earlier that year] hold a candle to such corruption?'

United against the coming danger

While in England, Brecht was keenly aware of the importance of his allegiance to the Communist cause. His recent revision of *The Threepenny Novel*, his discussions on Marxism with Karl Korsch and the ongoing work with Eisler – their latest composition, the 'Saar Song', had been written in protest before the Saar plebiscite paved the way for Hitler's annexation of the region in January 1935 – enhanced Brecht's perception of his political mission. He may have been bored and disappointed in what London had to offer, but he wasn't idle. Grete Fischer recalls that once or twice he had sat in her room trying to convert her: 'He was recruiting at the time, and had good reasons to find collaborators for "the cause". The Communists seemed to be the only ones who fought actively against Hitler … Brecht had brilliant dialectical skills, was super-swift and ready to answer any objection.'

Despite Brecht's misgivings about the place, he must have appreciated the fact that London was also a hub of anti-Fascist sentiment. The atmosphere was politically charged. On 17 October, Ernst Toller, one of Germany's major exiled playwrights, signed the introduction to an English edition of his plays that, he felt, bore 'witness to human suffering, and to fine yet vain struggles to vanquish this suffering'. Toller was writing from London and, speaking in the third person, concluded his piece with praise for England, 'the land which has become a second home to him'. Toller's political beliefs (he had been a leader of the short-lived Soviet Republic of Bavaria in 1919) were less idealistic than Brecht's and tinged with pessimism. But he enjoyed an international reputation and in England he was far better known than Brecht. Moreover, Toller's active involvement, since the autumn of 1933, in the Commission of Inquiry into the Burning of the Reichstag, set up in London by Willi Münzenberg to counteract the Nazi trial into the Reichstag fire, had brought him considerable notoriety as one of the most authoritative voices within the English exile community.

In March, Toller's political memoir, *I Was a German*, had been published in English with Wickham Steed's endorsement. A few months later, it had featured in *The Times* among a list of 'Books for the Holidays'. This inclusion, together with two other new books about Germany (Douglas Reed's *The Burning of the Reichstag* and Jakob Wassermann's *My Life as German and Jew*), was a clear sign of the growing relevance of politics in British society. Other symptoms of a new awareness that year were the opening, on Charing Cross Road, of Collet's bookshop, which dealt in socialist and Communist material and, in the autumn, the founding of the Marxist literary journal *Left Review*.

The rise of British Fascism, rampant unemployment and alarming reports from Austria and Nazi Germany filled the news. Many people were aware of the need to defend democracy, and London was becoming a centre for political activism. Leo Lania, arriving back from the Continent in 1934, found that 'despite appeasement and isolationism, London had a better understanding than Paris for the events in Germany and Russia. That was the work of the English Press. The air was clearer in Fleet Street than in the Champs Elysées.' Lania referred to figures such as Churchill and Wickham Steed, arguing that 'quite a number of men in public life saw the coming danger, and that British democracy had not lost faith in itself'.

In 1934, another event that justified Lania's belief in British democracy was the campaign to free Carl von Ossietzky, the pacifist activist arrested by the Nazis after the Reichstag fire and held in a concentration camp under inhuman conditions ever since. Albeit ultimately unsuccessful, the campaign – organized in Paris – gained international momentum through the efforts of the immigrant community. One of its main promoters in London was Toller, but there were also several prominent British supporters, such as Princess Elizabeth Bibesco, Harold Laski, Julian Huxley, Lord Ponsonby, J. B. Priestley and Wickham Steed.

This kind of climate implied the constant presence of surveillance, as most exiles came to the attention of the Secret Services from the moment they landed in Britain. It is still unclear whether Brecht was spied on during his time in London. Since he was closely associated with well-known Communist sympathizers such as Eisler and Korsch (both of whom were kept under surveillance), it is likely that the authorities were aware of his movements. Yet there are no records of this, and the author of a recent study into the matter concluded that 'we do not have access to [Brecht's] MI5 file (if it indeed exists)', although 'his inability to find meaningful work in London' could be linked to the fact that he was known to the Secret Services.

Thanks to an extensive network of friends, Brecht was also connected with some of the British personalities who sympathized with the German exiles, and his presence in England was acknowledged, albeit tenuously, by the liberal press. On 7 November, the *Manchester Guardian* ran an article about Brecht's and Eisler's newly completed 'Saar Song':

> Brecht, who as a poet has a touch of François Villon, has now written a 'Song of the Saar' entitled 'The 13th January', the day of the Saar plebiscite. Eisler has set it to music … It is meant to be a marching song, and suggests long, winding columns of grimy Saar miners on the march … The Saar Nazis have a rousing anthem in the Horst Wessel Lied; their opponents will now have an impressive song that will give the status quo a powerful, contagious, emotional contact.

Brecht and Eisler were by no means isolated in their endeavour to use the power of music for political ends and their work, for example, came to the attention of the British composer Alan Bush. A Communist who had studied in Berlin, Bush was committed to the ideals of the British Labour Movement. He was the conductor of the London Labour Union and a friend of the German composer and music scholar Ernst Hermann Meyer, a Communist refugee who had settled in England in 1933 and had quickly managed to find work as a BBC broadcaster and baroque music expert. According to Meyer, who had contacted Bush about the possibility of staging one of Brecht's and Eisler's plays, Bush also 'wrote songs of freedom, songs of struggle against fascism, songs of solidarity'. As Brecht and Eisler were meeting regularly in London to work on their political compositions, Bush was busy organizing 'The Pageant of Labour', a large theatrical pageant that traced the development of the Trades Unions and for which he wrote original music. This impressive political spectacle, which boasted nearly 1,500 performers and which Bush conducted, assisted by Michael Tippett, premiered at the Crystal Palace on 15 October 1934.

Although Britain lacked the type of permissive metropolitan community to which German political artists had been accustomed, London did offer the possibility of effective cooperation in the fight against social injustice. Brecht's activities during his stay at Calthorpe Street marked a small yet significant moment in the history of that fight. Sometime between November and December 1934, he wrote to a friend who had criticized the 'Saar Song' that the work had been 'published in all the anti-fascist papers, even in England' and that it was 'more important than half a dozen plays'.

A meeting of opposites

One fellow émigré in London who would have disagreed with Brecht's idea of the superior importance of a political song was Stefan Zweig. The two men were antipodes of each other. Zweig was polite, generous, eager to please and generally insecure about his talent. With his moustache neatly trimmed, his hair neatly combed and still dark despite his advancing age, he was always well dressed. He could be impatient with those closest to him and troubled by secret fears, but outwardly he was at pains to maintain the assured demeanour of a cultured gentleman of affluent means.

Brecht, on the other hand, was controlling and self-assured. He liked to surround himself with friends and lovers and had a seductive, magnetic charm that drew many people towards him. He behaved inconsistently and was full of contradictions. He could be gentle and brutal at the same time, dependent on others yet uniquely original, idealistic yet disenchanted. His appearance also challenged the conventional view of a successful poet and intellectual. In this respect, too, Brecht was provocatively incoherent: he liked to assume a macho working-class persona – he was fascinated by boxing and fast cars and smoked cheap cigars – yet suffered from delicate health and was physically unprepossessing. Usually unkempt, unshaven and unwashed, he wore wire-frame glasses and liked crumpled clothes that, even when handmade from expensive fabric, made him look like a proletarian and advertised his anti-bourgeois stance.

Whereas Zweig endeavoured to hide his émigré status behind fame and privilege, Brecht flaunted his non-conformist bad-boy persona. In London his attitude, so in keeping with the rebellious spirit of Weimar Berlin, was bound to be misunderstood. One Tuesday that autumn, Brecht experienced first-hand the inflexible nature of the British class system. Having arranged to meet Princess Elizabeth Bibesco at the Savoy, he was stopped at the door of the hotel and refused entrance. His attempt to procure business and possibly financial support from his aristocratic yet socialist-minded acquaintance failed because of his scruffy appearance:

> A man of ministerial rank was standing in the entrance of the lobby; he began to question me in one of the languages that are regarded as English in these parts. Unfortunately, he did not recognize me as a man of lofty intellectual stature, a true socialist, etc., but let my exterior mislead him into regarding me as a dangerous individual, or anyway one who would poison the atmosphere of the Savoy. I felt certain that if I had mentioned your name to him, he would instantly have called the police and my intentions towards you would have been exposed. I tried to get into that Tower of Babel by yet another entrance. But there I was buffeted by such a stream of lofty, richly adorned persons who have obviously made their way over dead bodies, that I gave up hope. The feeling was just too strong in me that I was attempting something forbidden. It was clear to me that without the help of at least fifty heavily armed dockers I could not hope to extract you from that building. I left in dismay, for I would very much have liked to talk to you.

Brecht brushed the incident wittily aside, striking a confident pose. Perhaps he assumed a similarly caustic, defiant attitude when he met Stefan Zweig, through a mutual acquaintance, in Eisler's Abbey Road flat, sometime before the end of November.

It is difficult to imagine Brecht and Zweig facing each other, and strange to think that such a meeting really took place. Did Zweig's dignified, accommodating demeanour clash against Brecht's boldness? Or did Brecht behave politely on this occasion, trying to ingratiate himself with his famous colleague, displaying the gentleness of which he was capable, while inwardly dismissing Zweig as the embodiment of the same corrupt bourgeois elite that made its 'way over dead bodies' and frequented luxury hotels?

There are no records of Brecht's reaction to an encounter that appears to have been awkward for all concerned, but Eisler's disdain towards Zweig as a representative of bourgeois privilege was unambiguous. In an account published several decades after the event, Eisler recalled how Brecht and Zweig had come together for the first and possibly only time:

> On one occasion someone brought Stefan Zweig to the house. He's a very elegant man, you know, Stefan Zweig – this famous industrialist, this business-man publisher … I can't grant him more than a cold-blooded stock-exchange

humanism or stock-exchange pacifism. An unpleasant man – anyway, there he was. This extremely elegant man had a superb apartment on Portland Place … so there they were: Stefan Zweig, some writer who had brought Zweig, and Brecht, all in my room. And Brecht, who always thought along the lines: 'Ah, there's a rich man … there might be a possibility of some funding for the theatre.' He had never read a word Zweig had written, but Zweig knew Brecht's name from the Weimar Republic days when he was very famous. So, there was a certain friendly interest, although it is likely … well, they were worlds apart. 'You know what, Zweig', Brecht said, 'Eisler ought to play something for you. We have just finished a play.' I asked: 'What shall I play?', and Brecht said: 'Play Mr. Zweig *Song of the Invigorating Effect of Money*.' So I played it for him. I just knew things would turn out badly. To play for a man famous for his wealth (inherited wealth) – the man who financed the 'Insel' publishing house, financed his whole career – that song! When you hear the text of it … Zweig listened to it with a stony face. It was one in the eye for him but he said nothing – a man from polite society. Then I played him the song 'Water Wheel' and by then he'd had enough. He said it would all be very interesting, quite simply 'interesting'.

After Eisler played their 'little song about the Saar', Zweig took his revenge for the insult of being confronted with a song about money:

'Well', Brecht said to Zweig, 'that was just a trifle, you know, a by-product to help the cause', to which came the reply: 'Don't call it a trifle, Mr Brecht; it might be your best!'. This is how it goes between writers – one stab in the back after another … So the two men were equal on points and went out to lunch.

About the miserliness of this lunch – I didn't go with them; the two writers wanted to be by themselves – I have only this to say. When I asked Brecht how much Zweig had paid for the lunch, he said: 'Two and six' (two shillings and sixpence). So he must have led, no, invited, Brecht to one of those awful mediocre London restaurants, this man who usually likes to dine at the Savoy, and paid for a wretched meal. And that was the one and only meeting between Brecht and Zweig.

Eisler's insistence on Zweig's wealth was a political point, and the idea that the famous author had bought his own success because he could pay for it disregards the evidence of Zweig's immense popular appeal. But Eisler was probably accurate about the awkwardness of the situation. One could almost picture Brecht's delight at the prospect of good business, and his enjoyment in performing his own poems in front of an illustrious colleague, even though he had no knowledge of or interest in his work. Zweig, on the other hand, must have felt ill at ease in the company of two men who regarded him with a sceptical eye and provoked him by playing music that he disliked.

The songs with which Brecht and Eisler entertained their guest challenged Zweig's sense of reserve and his aversion to the use of art as a political tool. In *The Round Heads and the Pointed Heads*, the 'Song on the Invigorating Effect of Money' is performed by a judge who praises the transformative power of cash in a world ruled by cynical calculation and corruption ('Generous meals, stylish clothes / And the man is now another man'). 'The Ballad of the Water Wheel' is also aimed at an age-old system of power. Sung by a waitress and prostitute in the play, it depicts an order of things according to which the rich are subjected to reversals of fortune, while the poor – unable to progress – are forever condemned to turn the wheel that drives those changes. Both pieces strive for transparency through a simple rhythm, regular metre and recitative passages. Their authors rejected high aesthetic ambitions in order to drive home a clear message.

Perhaps for Zweig, after such a disconcerting episode, the thought of going out to lunch, albeit in the company of the shabby young Brecht, came as a relief. What did the two talk about during their meal in a cheap restaurant? It seems unlikely that literary matters were considered, since they had no common interests. It is possible that Brecht made a last, unsuccessful attempt at convincing Zweig to part with some of his money, and maybe they discussed mutual acquaintances or exchanged stories of their life in exile. Perhaps they both parted doubting that they would meet again. After all, the most revealing aspect of the whole episode is that neither Brecht nor Zweig left a written record of this meeting. Their encounter failed to become a significant memory because the distance that separated them – despite a common language and a common destiny of exile – was too great, and their exchanges too incomplete to become meaningful.

Comrade Korsch

Parma House did not have much to offer. It didn't provide meals and the rooms were a barely adequate refuge from the London weather, but at least it gave Brecht the comfort of some friendly faces: the Italian landlady, who greeted her guests with a smile and occasionally let them use her kitchen; Grete Fischer, who was good company and reminded Brecht of Berlin; and, above all, his friend and teacher Karl Korsch.

Apart from the hope of a publishing deal and the likelihood of lucrative business with British film studios, it was Korsch's presence in London that had enticed Brecht away from the relative safety of his Danish exile into the inhospitable prospect of autumn in Bloomsbury. Often referred to as 'the professor' in

Figure 42 Karl Korsch.

Brecht's letters, Korsch had been his mentor in economic and political matters since they had first met in Berlin in 1928.

Twelve years Brecht's senior, Karl Korsch was a Marxist philosopher and a dissident Communist. He was a cultured, well-read man and a rigorous thinker, but he also had a rich life experience. After studying law, economics and philosophy, he worked in London for the professor of law – and Stephen Spender's grandfather – Sir Ernest Shuster, joined the Fabian Society and, back in Germany, served in the First World War despite being a pacifist. In 1920 he joined the German Communist Party (Kommunistische Partei Deutschlands, KPD) and three years later was elected minister for justice in the short-lived social democratic-Communist government of Thuringia, before moving to Berlin as a member of the Reichstag. Critical of the party's dependence on the Soviet Union, Korsch was expelled from the KPD in 1926, but he continued to lecture. According to his wife, Korsch 'also went deeply into the problems of what today would be called the Third World and studied the development of the various colonial countries because he thought that the liberation of the colonies was perhaps imminent and could change world politics completely'.

It was around this time that Brecht and Korsch met in Berlin and a friendship developed. They began to work together, meeting in cafés and organizing regular gatherings with other Communists. In the autumn of 1933, forced into exile, Korsch joined Brecht in Denmark and then moved to London. He still had connections in the world of English academia and with a younger generation of left-wing writers such as Stephen Spender and Christopher Isherwood. He joined a socialist discussion group and – though regarded suspiciously by members of the British Communist Party, who denounced him to the Home Office – was commissioned to write a textbook on Karl Marx by the London School of Economics. He remained in London until 1935.

Hedda Korsch's account of her husband's life and personality may not be wholly reliable, for 'the professor' also had a shady side. It is certain, for example, that his expulsion from England in 1935 came as a result of the authorities' distrust towards him after his involvement in a possible murder case that shook London and the exile community. The previous year, probably around the time of Brecht's residence at Parma House, Korsch appears to have been romantically involved with the Communist activist Dora Fabian. This was the woman whose mysterious death, with her friend Mathilde Wurm, in a flat at 12 Great Ormond Street in April 1935 became 'a cause célèbre, with public interest fanned by accompanying revelations of an unhappy love affair of Dora Fabian's with … Karl Korsch'. The episode, tantalizingly complex and unresolved to this day, damaged Korsch's reputation, since he was accused by the Home Office not only of having 'played a sinister role in the suicides' of the two women, but also of being a Nazi agent. None of these extraordinary revelations transpires from Brecht's correspondence with 'the professor', and their relationship was sustained by mutual admiration.

Brecht learnt a great deal from Korsch, regarded him as a close ally and trusted his judgement. He was consistently courteous towards the older man and his letters to him are devoid of the ironic, argumentative posture he so often reserved for others. They both believed in the transformative power of political thought against the rigid conception of Communism as advocated by party orthodoxy. The professor's influence strengthened the playwright's sense of the importance of Marxism more as a force for social change than as an ideology. As Brecht wrote to Korsch in January 1934, 'my sole hope lies … in a strictly concrete study of our situation … Good old dialectics, as I see it, are far from obsolete.' Eight months later, and exactly a week after Brecht's arrival in London, Korsch wrote a short essay entitled 'Why I Am a Marxist', in which he also advocated the importance of discussing the 'practical necessities of the struggle' and Marxism's potential for an 'active transformation' of society.

Korsch's views on Marxian theory – on its transformative power and on the need to apply it to the class struggle in the real world – influenced Brecht's reworking of the story about the gangster Macheath and the beggar boss Peachum in *The Threepenny Novel*. The novel's emphasis on economic processes (Macheath's capitalist strategies) and its imperialist setting (London at the time of the Boer War) reflected Korsch's interest in the links between capitalism and colonial exploitation. Korsch was also the source of more specific facts about England. In March 1934, writing from a Gower Street address, he sent his friend details about the different costs of illegal abortion, which Brecht needed for the plot about Polly Peachum's pregnancy in the novel, as well as explanations about English legal procedures and London's judicial system.

Korsch was a reassuring presence at Parma House. Brecht's knowledge of English was still inadequate (according to Fritz Kortner, he spoke 'a few words of a Chinese-sounding English in a childlike, almost delicate manner'), and in London he faced several difficult tasks, such as hunting for new deals and grappling with practical problems, from the lack of good food to a confusing transport system. At least Korsch's proximity satisfied Brecht's need for intellectual exchange with like-minded friends who accepted his unconventional manners. The fact that Korsch was a person with a sense of stability, natural authority and a propensity to adapt to austere living conditions must have helped. According to Hedda Korsch, her husband was extremely methodical in his habits, with a taste 'for complete order and clarity' from an early age – so much so that as a school boy, he used to work in a shed in his garden that was 'like a monk's cell, with no rug on the floor, just a table and a few hard chairs … All his pencils lay absolutely straight along the desk.' Korsch's room at Parma House may have been just another version of the monk-like shed of his youth. And it is possible to imagine that Brecht found comfort in his friend's orderliness and disregard for material possessions.

Yet Korsch could not possibly satisfy Brecht's emotional needs. Despite his matter-of-fact attitude and multiple infidelities, the poet's romantic streak and his habit of creating an erotic bond with the women he worked with were irrepressible. In London, the lack of collaborators and the city's aloofness intensified his longing for his distant lover, Grete Steffin, to whom Brecht wrote, teasing her for her jealousy: 'You ask whether I've come here alone. Of course not, I've taken 3–4 girls with me, dear Muck. You can be reassured … there's nothing here … I'm living with the professor, but he's no substitute for you.'

My general, my soldier

Brecht had met Steffin, a young actress, political activist and clerical worker, three years earlier. Born in Berlin into a working-class family, she had contracted tuberculosis in her early twenties. Steffin was blonde, with blue eyes and regular features; most photographs show her with a broad,

Figure 43 Margarete Steffin, c. 1936.

gentle smile. After her death in June 1941 in Moscow, a few days after Brecht left for America, a friend remembered that her 'big, loyal eyes were always smiling and fun' and that 'she bore the stamp of death on her face with a sunny calm'. Despite the way he exploited her talent and devotion for his own ends, Brecht loved her deeply.

If Korsch was his political mentor, Steffin was his 'little teacher from the working class'. To Brecht, teaching and learning were vital processes. He regarded teaching not only as acceptance of another person's authority, but as development and enrichment through inquisitive dialogue. Brecht often stylized himself in the image of either pupil or teacher, because he believed that the acquisition and communication of ideas were necessary to any human and artistic endeavour. He wanted theatre to be didactic. His plays raised questions and spoke to the audience in order to provoke reflection and instigate change. His poetry, too – for example his poems to Steffin, who used to reply with her own verse – reveals a similar need for a productive exchange of thoughts and feelings. The same could be said of Brecht's correspondence, especially during his time in exile. As an immigrant, deprived of an audience and a home, Brecht needed his army of friends and assistants more than ever, because the distance from his collaborators intensified the desire to keep the communication going.

On the one hand there was the political imperative of the fight against Fascism, and on the other a more personal need to listen and to be heard.

As for Steffin, her illness – which reflected his own physical vulnerability – her talent and resilience drew Brecht towards this remarkable woman. Both the poems and letters to his 'little wife', as he used to call her, show that despite his tendency to dominate and exploit, Brecht could be tender and protective. The private dialogue between them often revolved around his wish to look after her and to be looked after. As in the relationship between teacher and pupil, the two roles could be interchangeable and the fluidity kept the dialogue alive.

Brecht's letters to Steffin – who in the autumn of 1934 was in a sanatorium in the Soviet Union – were succinct and pragmatic, but more affectionate than the ones he addressed to his wife. Although emphatic displays of affection were not in his nature, his devotion to her was apparent. Brecht worried about her health and reported about his own. And he often declared his love in his typically understated style ('It turns out that unfortunately I have grown very used to you'), asking her to write more frequently so as to reduce the distance between them ('You should write to me often, without waiting for my letters, the distance is too great'). In exile, letters acted as a bridge to a safer, familiar world. For this reason, Brecht's missives to Steffin are full of questions, as if keeping a conversation going could shorten the geographical gulf that separated them ('Are you keeping warm? Is the coat good? The shoes? ... Do you have your own room? Does anybody speak German? ... Are the doctors good? Do they also operate there? Do they treat patients for money? Have you received my sonnets?').

Steffin's health was often on his mind. At the same time, Brecht's desire to protect her became a reflection of his own displacement, and in his wanderings through London he looked at his surroundings with the eyes of someone who needs to communicate his experience in order to understand his predicament. On one occasion, he even imagined Grete with him in London. The letter is dated 13 November 1934, but the episode is likely to have happened the previous evening, probably on one of those typical autumnal days made heavy by 'fogs and chills and stolid rains'. Walking down Tottenham Court Road, Brecht noticed a fruit-seller with a cart full of oranges. Forgetting his plight for a moment, he thought of buying some fruit for Grete, as if she had been waiting for him in his room. His mind was trying to lessen the distance between them and defy the misery of exile.

'Buying Oranges'

For all its apparent banality, that chance encounter on Tottenham Court Road inspired one of Brecht's finest poems from this period and an arresting snapshot of 1930s London as seen through the prism of exile. The poem, entitled 'Buying

Oranges', is a sonnet for Grete Steffin based on the episode Brecht described in his letter. It is also the first of the three *English Sonnets* he wrote for her while in London. The poems were probably meant as an addition to the other sonnets he had composed for Grete over the years and, like his letters to her, they were numbered.

Traditionally, the sonnet form – with its fourteen lines of iambic verse and dialectical structure of contrasting images and emotions – was well suited to the kind of lively personal dialogue such as the one that animated Brecht's relationship with Steffin. The contrast between spontaneity and the restraint imposed by the sonnet creates tension and produces a text that is rounded and impulsive, plain and complex at the same time. Like all great poets, Brecht was a master in the art of infusing a simple message with universal meaning, and his poems are pervaded by a sense of vividness and emotional authenticity. 'Buying Oranges' is a case in point.

The story is simple, yet the sonnet leaves the reader with the impression of having witnessed something out of the ordinary. On a foggy day in a London street, the poet chanced upon an orange-seller and, struck by the sight of the fruit, searched his pockets for money to buy some for his lover, until he realized that she was not in the same city and that the purchase would be in vain. The poem contains almost the full gamut of human experience: love, exile, money, natural beauty, the city's bleakness. With only a handful of words, Brecht evoked London's grimy allure. By simply mentioning the fruit, he created a sort of enchantment, and through the final disillusionment he expressed – almost without saying it – all the bitterness of exile:

Buying Oranges
In yellow fog along Southampton Street
Suddenly a fruit barrow, and an old hag
Beneath a lamp, fingering a paper bag.
I stood surprised and dumb like one who sees
What he's been after, right before his eyes.

Oranges! Always oranges as of old!
I blew into my hands against the cold
And searched my pockets for a coin to buy.

But while I clutched the pennies in my hand
Looked at the price and saw it written down
With grubby crayon on some newspaper
I saw that I was softly whistling, and
At once the bitter truth was all too clear:
That you are not here with me in this town.

An everyday occurrence turns into a poetic tableau, and something personal and trivial becomes universally significant. Brecht's London is the unreal city of his imagination, a mixture of Victorian suggestions (the fog, the fruit barrow, the old hag) and modern sensibility (the business of buying). But he also portrays the place as he saw it in the autumn of 1934, when he was just another German exile looking for work, missing his loved ones yet fascinated by the great metropolis. As ever in Brecht's writing, feelings and experience, theory and practice are linked, so that a love sonnet is also a lesson about investing basic gestures with deeper meanings. In this case, the impulse of reaching into his pocket to find money in order to pay for the fruit indicates the need to look after the woman he loves. And since he is unable to do so because she is not there, the poem itself becomes his 'love-gift, luminous as the oranges, standing in for them'.

Significantly punctuated by two exclamation marks and mentioned in the title, the oranges are the heart of the sonnet. They are a thing of beauty balanced among urban squalor (the yellow fog, the newspaper with the grubby sign), commercial interests (the pennies, the price, the act of buying) and human emotion (the realization of the lover's absence). Brecht's oranges are real and symbolic: healthy food to keep his sick girlfriend alive, but also a mythical fruit, golden spheres that resemble the sun.

The flowing rhythm of the poem's iambic pentameter – surely the reason for turning Tottenham Court Road, where the episode took place, into Southampton Street – exemplifies the vitality of the romantic and intellectual exchange between Brecht and Steffin. But it also attests to Brecht's gift as a poet. Although he did not produce many during his brief and ultimately futile stay at Calthorpe Street, his poems from this time are among the most powerful representations of London in the history of exile literature in German. 'Buying Oranges' is one example; another example is a sequence of three poems inspired by the Caledonian Market.

'The frightful god' of the Caledonian Market

A famous proletarian institution, the Caledonian Market became established at the beginning of the twentieth century on a huge expanse of land in Islington – north of the city and not far from Brecht's lodgings – in one of the dreariest parts of London at the time. Today the area has changed beyond recognition. The only landmark from the days when thousands of traders in second-hand goods sold their wares is a tall Victorian clock tower. Once the centrepiece of London's Metropolitan Cattle Market, next to which the Caledonian Market developed as

Figure 44 Bric-a-brac for sale at the Caledonian Market, 1932.

the trade for livestock began to diminish, the tower still stands on its old spot. Now it is surrounded by sports fields and modern blocks of flats, and appears redundant, strangely remote.

Brecht must have visited the market on one his walks through north London's working-class districts. He had almost certainly already heard of it, for the place was legendary, both in Britain and abroad. A notorious domain of the poor, in the early decades of the twentieth century the 'Cally' – also known as 'the Stones' because of the cobble-stones impoverished traders slept on, and over which the goods were spread – began to attract a more refined class of people. In the words of Jerry White, historian of modern London:

It was apparently during the First World War that browsing among the stalls became fashionable and 'Mayfair began to visit Caledonian Market in its Rolls Royces'. During the 1920s and 1930s the 'Pedlars' Market' grew enormously. Tuesdays as well as Fridays were given over to the trade and by 1932 3,400 stalls were setting up there over the two days.

In English fiction, the Caledonian Market appears in two of H. G. Wells's novels, and Virginia Woolf, who was a regular visitor, mentions it in *Mrs*

Dalloway, as Clarissa Dalloway used to frequent the market in her youth. Among the foreign tourists fascinated by this extraordinary place was the German writer and satirist Kurt Tucholsky. In one of his travel sketches, entitled *The Market of Silence* (1931), Tucholsky gave a striking description of the things for sale on the market, which he found so big that it would have taken hours to walk through it, but eerily quiet compared to the lively markets of southern Europe:

> There is: silverware, silver-plated ware, galvanized silver, stamped silver. Granddad's chairs, chairs with chamber pots in them, normal chairs. New dentures. Barely used dentures. Replacement wheels for children's prams. Old boots and a picture of General Kitchener. Many more old boots. Upholstery filling. Horrible wooden knick-knacks. A real young boy standing inside an enormous gold frame: it is not clear which of them is for sale. Delft porcelain dogs. Chamber pots. Nearly a square mile of books. Shoelaces as well as sweets and lemonade.

Not surprisingly, this visual and social phenomenon attracted several photographers, especially those interested in the surreal elements of modern urban life and in the oddities of the British class system, such as Bill Brandt, or those keen to provide evidence of social inequalities, such as Edith Tudor-Hart – both immortalized the market. A year before Brecht's arrival in England, a journalist writing in *The Listener* called London 'this great Caledonian Market of a city'. The market's immensity, its unparalleled offer of every conceivable object, made it a kind of city-within-the-city, a metaphor for London's vastness, commercial power and colonial identity.

In the autumn of 1934, Brecht wrote three poems about the Caledonian Market. Unlike the orange-seller in the previous poem, a text inspired by an actual event, the market does not figure in Brecht's correspondence. Perhaps he went there with Grete Fischer on one of their local walks, or with the doctor who had taken him to see the slums, or maybe he visited it with Eisler, co-author of their proletarian songs (Korsch, whom Brecht regarded as 'only a guest of the proletarians', was the least likely companion for such a pursuit). It is also possible that Brecht ventured there unaccompanied, on a solitary stroll that took him from the Gray's Inn Road, the main road north at the end of Calthorpe Street, past King's Cross Station and up the railway landscape of the York Road (today's York Way), where the market sprawled eastwards towards the Caledonian Road.

However Brecht experienced it, that gigantic selling machine stirred his imagination.

The Caledonian Market

I

Under Troy lie seven cities.
Someone dug the whole lot up again.
Are seven cities buried under London?
Is this were they sell the bottommost remains?

By the stall with the phosphorescent fish
Underneath old socks you see a hat.
Yer won't get a new one under seven bob, tosh
And this one's just a florin and not too bad at that.

II

The frightful god sat eternally, the soles of his feet pointing outwards
Then one day his nose broke, a toe came off, and his menacing arm
But the bronze body was too heavy, just the hand went travelling downwards
From the thief's to the Caledonian Market, through many living hands.

III

'Oh, East is East and West is West!'
Their hireling minstrels cried.
But I observed with interest
Bridges across the great divide
And huge guns trundling East I've seen
And cheerful troops keeping them clean.
Meanwhile, from East to West, back rolled
Tea soaked in blood, war wounded, gold.

And the Widow at Windsor, all dressed in black
Grins, takes the money, stuffs it in her pocket
And gives the wounded a pat on the back.
And sends them down the Caledonian Market.
Their walk may have lost its spring, but they try
To hobble around the stalls and buy
A second-hand wooden leg instead
To match their equally wooden head.

Often printed as one long fragment, the poem is composed of three parts. The
first section evokes London as a modern Troy – the ancient city believed to have
been built on top of seven older layers – and the market as the site where 'the
bottommost remains' are being sold. Like others before him, Brecht was struck
by the bizarre randomness of the merchandise on offer ('phosphorescent fish',

'old socks'), but – seeing the world as shaped by the rules of commerce – he also remarked on the price of things ('seven bob', 'a florin'). The second section, too, reveals a fascination with the market's bizarre offerings. This time it is a bronze statue of some sort, a 'frightful god', a figure of menace and a piece of stolen goods that passed 'through many living hands'. The final, unfinished section is the most political of the three, and an ironic homage to Rudyard Kipling's imperialist poems, as both stanzas begin with quotations from Kipling's *Barrack-Room Ballads* ('The Ballad of East and West' (1889) and 'The Widow at Windsor' (1890)).

Brecht had long been familiar with Kipling's poetry, which was one of his main inspirations for the social and colonial background to *The Threepenny Opera*. The German author, however, was at the other end of the political spectrum and, ironically, turned to Kipling's imperial verse to protest against the hypocrisy of a nation that exploited the poor for its own good. Yet although he opposed Kipling's admiration for the British Empire, the Communist Brecht was captivated by the Englishman's vivid portrayal of the colonial world and by the simple speech of his working-class characters. In the final section of 'The Caledonian Market', Brecht uses Kipling's own words, his galloping rhythm and prophetic tone ('Oh, East is East and West is West!'), and his famous image of Queen Victoria ('the Widow at Windsor') as an ambiguous symbol of motherliness and indifference, in order to denounce the greed of those in power and the stupidity of their victims. The victims were the people trying their luck at the market, a great pit at the bottom of the crumbling imperial edifice. Typically, Brecht does not celebrate the heroism of the soldiers, the 'cheerful troops' who keep the guns clean. Nor does he empathize with the poor, whose stupidity he derides by comparing their head with the wooden leg they have come to buy.

In his criticism of the capitalist system, Brecht refers to two major achievements in the history of western colonialism during the second half of the nineteenth century: Schliemann's archaeological expedition to Asia Minor and the British imperial rule in India. In so doing, the poet shows contemporary London as the embodiment of the cultural forces and political interests responsible for crushing the lives of the disadvantaged. Brecht's portrayal of 1930s London conveys the sense of an empire on the eve of extinction. In the first half of his final poem, the contrast between power ('huge guns') and misery ('Tea soaked in blood') leads to a satirical take on the empire's deceptive benevolence – the queen who stuffs money in her pocket while patting the wounded soldiers on the back – and on the Caledonian Market as the grotesque embodiment of such a state of affairs.

This is not a poem about exile. Compared with 'Buying Oranges' – a love sonnet and a meditation on solitude – 'The Caledonian Market', with its political message and visionary quality, reveals Brecht's fascination with London's past. In his dialectical view of the world, history was not just a backdrop, but rather the scene of an ever-changing, dynamic relationship between people and their surroundings. This flow between past and present and Brecht's ability to hide literary allusions and sophisticated technical skills behind a veil of directness ensured that, despite spending just over two uneventful months in London, he captured its essence far more memorably than other exiles at the time.

While Brecht was drawn to areas such as Clerkenwell, Bloomsbury and Holborn, around which 'London was at its most metropolitan', Stefan Zweig frequented the 'gilded interiors' of the luxury hotels and felt safe under the big dome of the round reading room in the British Museum. In England, Zweig sought anonymity, and his only concession to British culture was a biography of Mary Stuart. He lived in the past (his English friend Desmond Flower thought that 'he lived in a dream'), and in his letters London features mainly as a place he pined for from afar.

On 29 November, the day after his fifty-third birthday, Zweig travelled to the south of France. He was ready for a change of scene, unsettled in his private life and anxious about being exposed to racial hostility because of the imminent premiere in Nazi Germany of Strauss's opera *The Silent Woman*, for which Zweig had written the libretto. Brecht, as pragmatic as ever, was looking forward to going home, and at the beginning of December, 'because of Christmas', he was thinking of booking a ticket for his passage back to Denmark in good time. Although Zweig lived in London for four more years and Brecht returned once in 1936, neither settled there in the end. The autumn of 1934 was for both of them a brief episode at the beginning of a difficult path to come.

Epilogue

Bertolt Brecht's and Stefan Zweig's departure from London at the end of 1934 provides an arbitrary closure to a year of exile stories. Many more could be told. The focus on a limited number of émigrés who worked, with varying degrees of success, throughout their time in England is bound to obscure the lives of those who were less famous or less fortunate. I am thinking of Loo Hardy's generous spirit, for example, and of the faceless refugees who chose to put an end to their lives in a London hotel room.

The city was less welcoming to strangers than it is nowadays, but Britons in the 1930s were more attuned to German culture than they are now. The influence of the Mitteleuropean musical tradition – from symphonies to operetta – was profound, and holidays in German-speaking countries as well as the employment of German governesses were common amongst the English upper and middle classes. The exiles' presence partly reinforced these ties. Some of their contributions have proved more lasting than others – the Glyndebourne Festival and the Warburg Institute are well-established British institutions, and the photographic style pioneered by the émigrés entered the mainstream a long time ago. Other aspects have been largely forgotten (for instance the work of the actors, whose talent was too firmly rooted in the Germanic tradition to make a lasting difference in England), but this does not make them less relevant.

The exiles from Nazi Germany should be remembered for their rich cultural legacy and for the universal nature of their experience. This is particularly true today, when arguments about freedom of movement and national identity are constantly in the news. And the way in which contemporary Britain is struggling with internal conflicts in its attitude towards Europe and immigration evokes memories of the 1930s. (An example comes to mind: back in 1934, James Hilton's famous fictional character Mr Chips feared a chaotic present and lived in the past, whereas J. B. Priestley, referring to the refugee question in his *English Journey*, urged his country to overcome nationalism and to open its doors.)

More recently, in 2002, the historian Daniel Snowman concluded his extensive survey on the cultural impact of the Hitler émigrés by reminding us of the differences between the prewar years and the multicultural country Britain had become at the turn of the twenty-first century. Snowman did express cautious concern about Britain's isolationist tendencies, but on the whole his conclusions were optimistic. As I write, while the United Kingdom and a large section of the Western world are witnessing a resurgence of nationalism and xenophobia, the outlook is sadly different. For this reason, too, the lessons of the people who populate this book are deeply relevant, and the memory of their time in London is a reminder of the city's capacity to absorb foreign influences and to inspire.

Sources

Throughout this book, I have drawn on published, archival and online material and on personal communication. Translations from German, unless otherwise stated, are my own. Bibliographical details about quotations in the individual chapters are indicated below.

Preface

'Food mansions', Paul Cohen-Portheim, *The Spirit of London* (London, 2011), 88.

Introduction

A monster called Man

'The light … breaking', *The Times*, 1 January 1934, 12.
'Official: Germany …', ibid.
'Sinister side', *Manchester Guardian*, 1 January 1934, 8.
'Gloomy view of civilization', Richard Overy, *The Morbid Age: Britain and the Crisis of Civilization, 1919–1939* (London, 2009), 34.
'By the mid-1930s predicting', ibid., 315.
'There is no convincing …', *Manchester Guardian*, 5 January 1934, 8.
'None of their business', Stefan Manz and Panikos Panayi (eds.), *Refugees and Cultural Transfer to Britain* (London and New York, 2013), 72.
'Winter in the West Indies …', *The Times*, 4 January 1934, 2.
'The world's finest furs', ibid., 1 January 1934, 7.
'An improved car with no lack of power …', ibid., 2 January 1934, 8.
'During 1933 the deaths …', ibid., 1 January 1934, 8.
'Promise of greater …', ibid.
'I do not know …', *Illustrated London News*, 6 January 1934, 4.
'In spite of statements …', *The Times*, 4 October 1933, 14.
'Lighthouses and lightships', Albert Einstein, 'Speech in Royal Albert Hall, 3 October 1933', in David E. Rowe and Robert Schulmann (eds.), *Einstein on Politics: His Private Thoughts and Stand on Nationalism, Zionism, War, Peace, and the Bomb* (Princeton, 2007), 279. See also https://www.youtube.com/watch?v=xPS-EliCOzU (accessed 15 April 2019).

January–March

The Austrian actress Elisabeth Bergner becomes a star of the London stage and a close friend of J. M. Barrie

'Unlikely long to withstand …', *The Times*, 23 January 1934, 8.

'A good interest in the furtherance of Communism …', The National Archives, Kew, Edith Tudor-Hart, file KV2/1012.

'Fresh from a series …', Charmian Brinson, Richard Dove, Marian Malet and Jennifer Taylor (eds.), *'England? Aber wo liegt es?' Deutsche und österreichische Emigranten in Großbritannien 1933–1945* (London, 1996), 101.

'A cleaner, healthier atmosphere …', Hans Wilhelm Thost, *Als Nationalsozialist in England* (Munich, 1939), 285.

'To advise them on the interior …', Volker M. Welter, *Ernst L. Freud, Architect: The Case of the Modern Bourgeois Home* (New York and Oxford, 2012), 122.

Chapter 1 Limelight and fading shadows: Elisabeth Bergner and J. M. Barrie

A portrait of J. M. Barrie

'What happened was …', Barrie to Robin Dundas, 15 November 1922, in Andrew Birkin, *J. M. Barrie and the Lost Boys* (New Haven, CT, 2003), 295.

'Sir James Barrie was warmly …', *The Times*, 28 August 1933, 13.

'One severe bronchial attack …', Cynthia Asquith, *Portrait of Barrie* (London, 1954), 185.

'How do I like the picture? …', Barrie to Lady Hilton Young, 28 January 1934, in James Matthew Barrie, *Letters*, ed. Viola Meynell (London, 1942), 55.

Enter Bergner

'Here, I thought …', Charles B. Cochran, *Cock-a-Doodle-Do* (London, 1941), 3.

'The fall of the curtain …', ibid., 4.

'Echoes of her success …', ibid., 5.

'H. G. Wells wrote …', ibid., 7.

'People applaud in the streets …', *John Gielgud, Letters*, ed. Richard Mangan (London, 2005), 407.

'A German genius', Prompter, 'Bergner Shatters Two Illusions: A German Genius Comes to London', *Western Independent* (Plymouth), 7 January 1934.

'In the madness scene …', Alexander Granach, *Da geht ein Mensch: Roman eines Lebens* (Munich, 1984), 406.

'The whole of Berlin …', Margaret Heymann, *Elisabeth Bergner: Mehr als eine Schauspielerin* (Berlin, 2008), 7.

'One could see from a change …', ibid., 22f.

'Dear Jewish child', ibid., 33.

'Elisabeth Bergner has not personal …', Prompter.
'All the actors …', Elisabeth Bergner, *Bewundert und viel gescholten … Elisabeth Bergners unordentliche Erinnerungen* (Munich, 1978), 103.

A foreign star in London

'The applicant married …', The National Archives, Kew, Paul and Elisabeth Czinner, file HO405/7511.
'My father, my brother …', Brigitte Mayr and Michael Omasta, 'Das Cabinet des Dr. Czinner: Tribut an einen Regisseur aus Vienna', in *Paul Czinner: Der Mann hinter Elisabeth Bergner* (Vienna, 2013), 6.
'Complete command …', Klaus Völker, *Elisabeth Bergner: Das Leben einer Schauspielerin* (Berlin, 1990), 302.
'The manager knew …', Charles Graves, *The Price of Pleasure* (London, 1935), 365.
'A very petit bourgeois …', Bergner, 116.
'Known as Freedy …', Graves, 364.
'May the Almighty …', Freedman to Elisabeth Bergner, undated. Akademie der Künste, Berlin (henceforth AdK), Elisabeth-Bergner-Archiv, Bergner 620.
'My most beloved …', ibid.
'Es spielt aus ihr überall', Völker, 7, 117.
'As tough as …', Shaw to H. K. Ayliff, 18 April 1938, in George Bernard Shaw, *Theatrics*, ed. Dan H. Laurence (Toronto, Buffalo and London, 1995), 205.

Behind the Bergner myth

'The diminutive mercurial …', Perdita Schaffner, introduction to John Helforth [H. D.], *Nights* (New York, 1986), xiv.
'I could smack …', Bryher to H. D., 8 October 1929, in Susan Stanford Friedman (ed.), *Analyzing Freud: Letters of H. D., Bryher and Their Circle* (New York, 2002), 83.
'A certain shop', Barbara Guest, *Herself Defined: The Poet H. D. and Her World* (New York, 1984), 210.
'I am sure the photos …', Stanford Friedman, 105f.
'I do feel with E. B.', ibid., 310.
'Melted into London …', ibid., 317.
'I went to see …', ibid., 316.
'Elizabeth … is at point …', ibid., 132.
'A dismal flop …', Bryher to H. D., 1 June 1933, in ibid., 338.
'Spent two days …', ibid., 331.
'Such a scene …', ibid., 396.
'Her tighten …', Bryher, 'Manchester', *Life and Letters Today*, 13 (1935), 91.
'Ernest … could see …', ibid., 102.
'Chestnut-red-lion-hair …', John Helforth [H. D.], *Nights,* ed. Perdita Schaffner (New York, 1986), 75f.
'She liked [Ernest] …', Bryher, 'Manchester', *Life and Letters Today*, 14 (1935), 97.

One night in January

'Dark glasses …', Peter Scott, *The Eye of the Wind: An Autobiography* (London, 1961), 189.
'Found her curled up …', ibid.

'How could you! …', ibid.
'Barrie was full …', ibid., 187
'I told you …', ibid., 188.
'Neither immersed …', Asquith, 201.
'He knew as little …', Bergner, 132–4.
'Barrie stood up …', ibid., 133f.
'Devilish of one …', James M. Barrie, *The Plays of J. M. Barrie* (London, 1942), 1245.
'In terrific eruption …', Asquith, 202.
'Sir James Barrie is …', *The Times*, 18 June 1934, 14.

'Goodbye, David'

'To my loved …', Janet Dunbar, *J. M. Barrie: The Man behind the Image* (Boston, MA, 1970), 391.
'The David in …', *Observer*, 22 November 1936, 19.
'Are you going to …', Bergner, 144.
'Which is the wheel …', James Matthew Barrie, *The Little White Bird* (London, 1902), 134, 137f., 127, 142.

A friendship in trying times

'If only you could help …', Albert Ehrenstein to Bergner, 28 January 1934, AdK, Elisabeth-Bergner-Archiv, Bergner 916.
'Gnawed by …', Albert Ehrenstein to Bergner, 10 February 1934, ibid.
'I am so worried …', Charles Cochran to Bergner, 13 February 1934, ibid.
'I am sorry that …', Bergner to Albert Ehrenstein, 9 March 1934, ibid.
'The production …', *The Times*, 7 March 1934, 12.
'Make good use …', Charles Cochran to Bergner, 24 March 1934, AdK, Elisabeth-Bergner-Archiv, Bergner 582.
'Miss Bergner and other …', *The Times*, 13 April 1934, 12.
'It is part of her …', ibid., 8 May 1934, 14.
'I was very …', Bergner to Albert Ehrenstein, 19 June 1934, AdK, Elisabeth-Bergner-Archiv, Bergner 916.
What the little devil …, G. B. Shaw to H. K. Ayliff, 18 April 1938, in Shaw, *Theatrics*, 205.
'A most affectionate …', George Bernard Shaw, 'Barrie: The Man with Hell in His Soul' (1937), in *Shaw and Other Playwrights*, ed. John Anthony Bertolini, Vol. XIII (University Park, (1993), 151.
'You make me cry …', Heymann, 57.

April

Stefan Lorant settles in London. Wolf Suschitzky, Edith Tudor-Hart and Bill Brandt take photographs of the city and its inhabitants

'Make films', The National Archives, Kew, Richard Tauber, file T365/1-6.

'News from Germany ...', Robert Bernays, *The Diaries and Letters of Robert Bernays, 1932–1939: An Insider's Account of the House of Commons*, ed. Nick Smart (Lewiston, Queenston and Lampeter, 1996), 129.
'Herr Hitler ...', *The Times*, 21 April 1934, 9.
'The old-established club ...', James J. Barnes and Patience P. Barnes, *Nazis in Pre-War London 1930–1939: The Fate and Role of German Party Members and British Sympathizers* (Brighton, 2005), 38.
'In the discussion ...', *Advocate for the Doomed: The Diaries and Papers of James G. McDonald 1932–1935* ed. Richard Breitman, Barbara McDonald Stewart and Severin Hochberg (Bloomington, IN, 2007), 374.
'Accompanied by ...', *The Times*, 28 April 1934, 10.

Chapter 2 A living art: the work and world of refugee photographers

A talented family

'I left because ...', interview with Daria Santini, 13 October 2014.
'My father ...', ibid.
'They published ...', ibid.
'Just after ...', ibid.
'I mainly learnt ...', interview with Grant Scott, 11 January 2012: see ibook at www.unitednationsofphotography.com, 2 (accessed 19 April 2019).
'I couldn't get ...', interview with Daria Santini, 13 October 2014.
'Yes, I always ...', ibid.
'The Corner Houses ...', www.wolfsuschitzkyphotos.com/photo_3204311.html (accessed 10 April 2015).
'Not really ...', interview with Daria Santini, 13 October 2014.
'I met him ...', ibid.
'I was the first ...', http://www.thejc.com/arts/arts-interviews/83905/wolf-suschitzky-man-who-invented-wildlife-photography (accessed 15 April 2019).
'There are some ...', http://www.webofstories.com/play/wolfgang.suschitzky/23 (accessed 15 April 2019).

'The Eye of Conscience'

'To be on friendly ...', Charmian Brinson and Richard Dove, *A Matter of Intelligence: MI5 and the Surveillance of Anti-Nazi Refugees 1933–1950* (Manchester and New York, 2014), 81.
'Ceased to be ...', Robert Radford, *Art for a Purpose: The Artists' International Association, 1933–1953* (Winchester, 1987), 80.

Conspirators

'Efforts ...', The National Archives, Kew, Edith Tudor-Hart, file KV2/1012.
'Margarete Charlotte ...', ibid.
'Dr. Hart's sister ...', ibid.

'A casual …', Duncan Forbes, 'Politics, Photography and Exile in the Life of Edith Tudor-
     Hart (1908–1973)', in *Arts in Exile in Britain 1933–1945*, ed. Shulamith Behr and
     Marian Malet (Amsterdam, 2005), 65.
'Attractive, tall …', Peter Stephan Jungk, *Die Dunkelkammern der Edith Tudor-Hart:
     Geschichte eines Lebens* (Frankfurt am Main, 2015), 96.
'Edith wanted …', ibid., 187.
'Possibly a talent …', ibid., 72.

A new medium

'When I went to …', interview with Daria Santini, 13 October 2014.
'The prime minister …', Michael Hallett, *Stefan Lorant: Godfather of Photojournalism*
     (Lanham, MD, Toronto and Oxford, 2006), 33 (the author writes, erroneously, that
     Lorant travelled to England with Chancellor Brüning in 1929).
'I love England …', Stefan Lorant, *I Was Hitler's Prisoner* (1935), trans. James Cleugh
     (Harmondsworth, 1939), 222.
'The arrested man …', Hallett, 39.
'By reason of official …', Lorant, 87.

A most productive week

'Always, even when …', Emma Laird [Alison Blair], *Of Former Love* (Boston, MA,
     1951) 74.
'Half a dozen …', Hallett, 49.
'Every thinking …', *The Times*, 7 April 1934, 12.
'Sprung up …', Laird, 36.
'The hair, grey …', ibid., 16f.
'The centre of a creative …', Burcu Dogramaci, 'Der Kreis um Stefan Lorant: Von der
     Münchner illustrierten Presse zur *Picture Post*', in *Netzwerke des Exils: Künstlerische
     Verflechtungen, Austausch und Patronage nach 1933*, ed. Burcu Dogramaci and
     Karin Wimmer (Berlin, 2011), 183.
'*I Was Hitler's Prisoner*', *Manchester Guardian*, 28 April 1935, 5.
'John Dunbar …', Hallett, 50.
'As the extent of our …', Tom Hopkinson, *Of This Our Time: A Journalist's Story
     1905–1950* (London and Melbourne, 1982), 147.
'The expert knowledge …', Hallett, 51.

Loo Hardy and the boarding house on Cleveland Square

'O second room …', Robert Neumann, *By the Waters of Babylon*, trans. Anthony Dent
     (London, New York and Melbourne, 1944), 142.
'Thirty shillings …', Lilli Palmer, *Change Lobsters – and Dance: An Autobiography*
     (London, 1976), 84.
'The city seemed …', ibid.
'Lo Hardy in particular …', ibid., 86.
'At the inquest …', *The Times*, 27 April 1938, 5.

Thinking in pictures

'Real face ...', Felix H. Man, *Man with Camera: Photographs from Seven Decades*
  (London, 1983), 57.
'An entirely new ...', Felix H. Man, *Sixty Years of Photography*, exhibition catalogue
  (London, 1983), 18.
'You are exactly ...', Man, *Man with Camera*, 121.

A different gaze

'Made delightful ...', *The Times*, 2 April 1934, 7.
'A very good artist', interview with Daria Santini, 13 October 2014.
'A great deal', Paul Delany, *Bill Brandt: A Life* (London, 2004), 63.
'There is a force ...', Odette Keun, *I Discover the English* (London, 1934), 79.
'The secret of London ...', Cohen-Portheim, 105.
'Nervous tension ...', Zweig to Anton Kippenberg, 31 March 1934, in Richard Dove,
  Journey of No Return: Five German-Speaking Literary Exiles in Britain, 1933–1945
  (London, 2000), 46.
'About an hour ...', Delany, 91.

May–June

The Warburg Institute opens its doors

'It was the first time ...', David Elliott, 'Gropius in England: A Documentation
  1934–1937', in *A Different World: Emigré Architects in Britain 1928–1958*
  ed. Charlotte Benton (London, 1995), 107.
'In the full glare ...', Brinson, *England?*, 103.
'Rare entertainment ...', *The Times*, 29 May 1934, 12.
'The head of the ...', Richard von Stradiot to Walter Engelberg, 27 June 1934, The
  National Archives, Kew, Hans Wilhelm Thost, file KV2/953
'A drizzle ...', *The Times*, 28 June 1934, 6.
'German plans ...', ibid., 8.
'The First Lord ...', ibid., 29 June 1934, 8
'Bergner is all ...', John Evans (ed.), *Journeying Boy: The Diaries of the Young Benjamin
  Britten 1928–1938* (London, 2009), 307.
'An announcement ...', McDonald, 413.

Chapter 3 London gains a library

In June, between then and now

'Commitment to a Europe ...', http://warburg.sas.ac.uk/about/directors-statement-
  brexit (accessed 9 July 2016).

The Warburg Institute opens its doors

'The library is now ...', Saxl to Richard Livingstone, 4 May 1934, Warburg
    Institute Archive, General Correspondence (henceforth WIA, GC), Professor
    R. W. Livingstone, 1934.
'Handsome volume ...', E. Harrison, 'England's Debt to Greece and Rome', *Classical
    Review*, 48, no. 2 (May 1934), 83.
'It was vaguely ...', Gertrud Bing, 'Fritz Saxl: A Biographical Memoir', in D. J. Gordon
    (Ed.), *Fritz Saxl (1890–1948): A Volume of Memorial Essays from His Friends in
    England*, (London, 1957), 25.
'How could the six ...', Fritz Saxl, '*The History of the Warburg Library (1886–1944)*', in
    Ernst Gombrich, *Aby Warburg: An Intellectual Biography* (London, 1970), 337.
'We are prepared ...', Sir Louis Vaughan to Lord Lee of Fareham, 8 January 1934, WIA,
    GC, Lord Lee of Fareham, 1934.
'Small outstanding ...', Lord Lee of Fareham to Sir Louis Vaughan, 9 January 1934,
    ibid.
'Thanks to the disinterested ...', Gertrud Bing, *The Warburg Institute Report, February
    1934*, WIA, I a 2.1.1.
'We have now ...', Sir Louis Vaughan to Lord Lee of Fareham, 8 January 1934, WIA,
    GC, Lord Lee of Fareham, 1934.
'Naturally ...', Fritz Saxl to Eric M. Warburg, 7 May 1934, WIA, GC, Eric M.
    Warburg, 1934
'We have spent ...', Saxl to Felix Warburg, 1 June 1934, ibid., Felix Warburg 1933–4.

Not a beautiful flowery meadow

'First came into touch ...', Gombrich, *Aby Warburg*, 28.
'At last a book ...', ibid., 72.
'God dwells ...', ibid., 13.
'A number of works ...', Aby Warburg, 'Sandro Botticelli's *Birth of Venus* and *Spring*', in
    *The Renewal of Pagan Antiquity: Contributions to the Cultural History of the European
    Renaissance*, ed. Kurt W. Forster, trans. David Britt (Los Angeles, 1999), 125.
'Unfortunately so-called ...', Gombrich, *Aby Warburg*, 39–40.

A centre for scholars of various descriptions

'After a brief ...', Gombrich, *Aby Warburg*, 22.
'Was sizeable ...', ibid., 325.
'Made his discoveries ...', Ron Chernow, *The Warburgs: A Family Saga* (London,
    1993), 120.
'The sensitive wife ...', ibid.
'A new method ...', ibid., 121.
'In a favorite refrain ...', ibid., 117.
'The two preoccupations ...', Gombrich, *Aby Warburg*, 215.
'Edison's copper ...', ibid., 225.
'Would have said ...', ibid., 224.
'On two fronts ...', Bing, *Fritz Saxl*, 11.
'The books were ...', Gombrich, *Aby Warburg*, 332.

'Warburg ... spoke ...', ibid., 334.
'There was no lecture ...', ibid., 327.
'Something Incomprehensible ...', see H. Hipp, 'Strebende und tragende Kräfte: Die
    Fassade der K. B. W.', in *Porträt aus Büchern: Bibliothek Warburg und Warburg
    Institute. Hamburg–1933–London*, ed. Michael Diers (Hamburg, 1993), 47.

Mnemosyne

'Agreed that it was ...', Gordon, 17.
'Nun-like care', Kenneth Clark, *Another Part of the Wood* (London, 1974), 190.
'Dr. Steinmann ...', ibid.

A scholarly pantheon

'The philosophical problems ...', Fritz Saxl, 'Ernst Cassirer', in *The Philosophy of Ernst
    Cassirer*, ed. Paul Arthur Schilpp (La Salle, IL, 1949), 48.
'From animal reactions ...', Ernst Cassirer, *An Essay on Man: An Introduction to a
    Philosophy of Human Culture* (New Haven, CT, 1972), 27.
'Simple lived-experience ...', Ernst Cassirer, 'The Problem of the Symbol and Its Place
    in the System of Philosophy', in *The Warburg Years: Essays on Language, Art, Myth,
    and Technology*, trans. with an introduction by Steve G. Lofts with Antonio Calcagno
    (New Haven, CT, 2013), 258–9.
'Every summer ...', Sigrid Bauschinger, *Die Cassirers: Unternehmer, Kunsthändler,
    Philosophen. Biographie einer Familie* (Munich, 2015), 157.
'Most seduced ...', Dorothea McEwan, *Fritz Saxl: Eine Biographie. Aby Warburgs
    Bibliothekar und erster Direktor des Londoner Warburg Institute* (Vienna, 2012), 110.
'Branch of the ...', Erwin Panofsky, *Studies in Iconology: Humanistic Themes in the Art
    of the Renaissance* (New York, 1939), 3.
'Primary or natural ...', ibid., 5–7.
'Labyrinthine paradise', Carol Doyon, 'Hommage à Raymond Klibansky/Tribute to
    Raymond Klibansky', *RACAR: Revue d'art canadienne/Canadian Art Revue*, 27
    (2000), 136.
'It was a library ...', interview with Raymond Klibansky in *Aby Warburg: Archive of
    Memory* (2003), https://vimeo.com/62673080 (accessed 17 April 2019).
'Kept fit ...', Mario Bunge, *Between Two Worlds: Memoirs of a Philosopher-Scientist*
    (Cham, 2016), 179.
'The drama of civilization', Edgar Wind, introduction to *A Bibliography on the Survival of
    the Classics*, Vol. I: *The Publications of 1931: The Text of the German Edition with
    an English Introduction*, ed. Hans Meier, Richard Newald and Edgar Wind (London,
    1934), VI.
'The crown prince ...', Franz Engel, 'Though This Be Madness: Edgar Wind and the
    Warburg Tradition', in *Bildakt at the Warburg Institute*, ed. Sabine Marienberg and
    Jürgen Trabant (Berlin and Boston, MA, 2014), 90.
'Tendency ...', ibid., 101.
'A magician with words', Elizabeth Sears, 'Edgar Wind on Michelangelo', in Edgar Wind,
    The Religious Symbols of Michelangelo: The Sistine Ceiling (Oxford, 2000), XVIII.
'The sense of form ...', John Pope-Hennessy, *Learning to Look* (London, 1991), 126.
'An unnerving ...', ibid., 127.

Man is at the centre and history is alive

'The observation tower …', Dorothea McEwan, 'Mapping the Trade Routes of the Mind: The Warburg Institute', in *Intellectual Migration and Cultural Transformation: Refugees from National Socialism in the English-Speaking World*, ed. Edward Timms and Jon Hughes (Vienna and New York, 2003), 39–40.

'In the centre …', Erwin Panofsky, 'Introduction: The History of Art as a Humanistic Discipline' (1940), in *Meaning in the Visual Arts* (Harmondsworth, 1983 [1944]), 24.

'The individual mind …', Fritz Saxl, *Hans Holbein and the Reformation* (1925), in *Lectures*, Vol. I (London, 1957), 285.

'A force stirring …', Raymond Klibansky, 'The Philosophic Character of History', in *Philosophy and History: Essays Presented to Ernst Cassirer*, ed. Raymond Klibansky and Herbert James Paton (Oxford, 1936), 324–5.

'Sgr. Sassetti …', Bing to Klibansky, 26 July 1933, WIA, GC, Klibansky, 1933–4.

'What about the Vento's …', Klibansky to Bing, 12 October 1933, ibid.

'With the profound …', Bing to Paul Ruben, 22 February 1934, in Björn Biester, *Der innere Beruf zur Wissenschaft: Paul Ruben (1866–1943). Studien zur deutsch-jüdischen Wissenschaftsgeschichte* (Berlin, 2001), 229.

'1 – Do nothing rash …', Eric M. Warburg to Saxl, 16 June 1933, WIA, GC, Eric M. Warburg, 1933–4.

'Race and religion …', Ernst H. Gombrich, *A Lifelong Interest: Conversations on Art and Science with Didier Eribon* (London, 1993), 28.

Bad times for a German library

'Loss of incalculably …', Emily J. Levine, *Dreamland of Humanists: Warburg, Cassirer, Panofsky, and the Hamburg School* (Chicago and London, 2013), 224.

'As for the Warburg …', Erwin Panofsky, *Korrespondenz 1910 bis 1936*, ed. Dieter Wuttke (Wiesbaden, 2001), 578.

'Some very beautiful …', Wind to Saxl, 16 May 1933, in Bernard Buschendorf, *Auf dem Weg nach England: Edgar Wind und die Emigration der Bibliothek Warburg*, in Diers, *Porträt aus Büchern*, 100.

'Things are too good …', ibid., 104.

'Much fresher …', ibid., 108.

'We find that it would be …', Bing to Eric M. Warburg, 28 September 1933, WIA, GC, Eric M. Warburg, 1933–4.

'Majority ownership …' George Messersmith to Eric M. Warburg, 10 May 1933, ibid.

'Owing to the present …', The National Archives, Kew, Warburg Institute, file HO213/1661 (Lord Lee of Fareham's letter to the undersecretary of state, Home Office, 10 November 1933; and MI5 file cover, 21 November 1933).

'We have nothing …', The National Archives, Kew, Warburg Institute, file HO213/1661.

Hermia afloat

'1. Library staff should …', WIA, Warburg Family Box; also in McEwan, *Fritz Saxl*, 147.

'Travelling adventures …', *Manchester Guardian*, 13 December 1944, 4.

'The final scene …', Eric M. Warburg, 'The Transfer of the Warburg Institute to England in 1933', in *The Warburg Institute Annual Report 1952–1953*, http://warburg-archive.sas.ac.uk/home/aboutthewarburginstitute/history/migration/(accessed 26 March 2019).

'Hermia afloat', McEwan, *Fritz Saxl*, 148. On the steamboat's actual name see the note at the end of Eric M. Warburg's account of the move on the Warburg Institute's website.

'The future of the Library …', Saxl to S. Fürth, 12 December 1933, in McEwan, *Fritz Saxl*, 149.

'More traffic …', *The Times*, 23 December 1933, 7.

'Paddington …', ibid.

'For the beautiful card …', Kenneth Clark to Saxl, 6 January 1934, WIA, GC, Kenneth Clark, 1933–4.

'Smoothly …', Saxl to Eric M. Warburg, 26 December 1933, in McEwan, *Fritz Saxl*, 150.

'An incalculable gain to English scholarship'

'Hall, reading room …', Bing to Saxl, 30 December 1933, in McEwan, *Fritz Saxl*, 151–2.

'I would ask …', McEwan, *Fritz Saxl*, 152.

'She'd rather eat …', Bing to Paul Ruben, 28 September 1934; Biester, 231.

'An incalculable gain …', Kenneth Clark to Saxl, 6 January 1934, WIA, GC, Kenneth Clark, 1933–4.

'Am quite worried …', Klibansky to Saxl, 22 January 1934, WIA, GC, Raymond Klibansky, 1933–4.

'Indispensable for keeping …', Saxl to Eric M. Warburg, 30 January 1934, WIA, GC, Eric M. Warburg, 1933–4.

'You can find me …', Cassirer to Saxl, 29 January 1934, WIA, GC, Ernst Cassirer, 1933–4.

'In all its splendor', Bing to Eric M. Warburg, 12 February 1934, WIA, GC, Eric M. Warburg, 1933–4.

'Thanks to the …', *The Warburg Institute Report, February 1934*, WIA, I a 2.1.1.

'As we are now …', ibid.

'A matter of fact people', Panofsky to Walter Friedländer, 5 January 1934, in Panofsky, *Korrespondenz*, 695.

'He had learnt to …', Saxl to Walter Friedländer, 22 January 1934, in McEwan, *Fritz Saxl*, 156.

'Distanced themselves …', Susie Harries, *Nikolaus Pevsner: The Life* (London, 2011), 138.

'A centre for a study …', Saxl to W. G. Constable, 16 March 1934, WIA, GC, W. G. Constable, 1934.

'The advent of the trained …', Roger Fry, 'The Artist as Critic', *Burlington Magazine*, 64 (1934), 80.

The faces of humane scholarship

'For Saxl the situation …', Bing, 23–4.

'More than once …', ibid., 45.

'Such a laughing face', ibid., 37.

'The almost magical spell …', 'Fritz Saxl, 8 January 1890–22 March 1948', *Journal of the Warburg and Courtauld Institutes*, 10 (1947).

'His grandfather used to …', Gordon, XIII.

'A vagrant …', Bing, 46.

'She had a great skill …', Ernst Gombrich and the Warburg Institute (eds.), *Gertrud Bing 1892–1964* (London, 1965), 2.

'If Saxl alarmed …', ibid., 17.

'I never thought …', ibid., 21.

The unimaginable becomes real

'At Bedford College ...', Klibansky to Saxl, 13 February 1934, WIA, GC, Klibansky, 1933–4.

'All still very messy ...', Saxl to Eric M. Warburg, 16 March 1934, WIA, GC, Eric M. Warburg, 1933–4.

'One can ...', Bing to Paul Ruben, 18 April 1934; Biester, 231.

'I should have liked ...', Kenneth Clark to Bing, 9 May 1934, WIA, GC, Kenneth Clark, 1933–4.

'I am optimistic ...', Saxl to Eric M. Warburg, 7 May 1934, WIA, GC, Eric M. Warburg, 1933–4.

'A notable addition ...', *Aberdeen Press and Journal*, 2 June 1934, 6.

'A library of a kind ...', *Observer*, 10 June 1934, 9.

'Because of a previous ...', Sir Stephen Gaselee to Saxl, 22 June 1934, WIA, GC, Stephen Gaselee.

'Certainly do much ...', Bing to C. S. Gibson, 27 June 1934, WIA, GC, Professor C. S. Gibson, 1934.

'As we do not ...', Saxl to R. W. Livingstone, 15 June 1934, WIA, GC, R. W. Livingstone, 1934.

'About seventy guests ...', Saxl to Eric M. Warburg, 2 July 1934, WIA, GC, Eric M. Warburg, 1933–4; and Saxl to Felix Warburg, 3 July 1934, WIA, GC, Felix Warburg, 1933–4.

'Harmonious reception ...', Cassirer to Saxl, 9 July 1934, WIA, GC, Ernst Cassirer, 1933–4.

'Semi-archeological matter', Saxl to Roger Hinks, 1 July 1934, WIA, GC, London, British Museum, Dept of Greek and Roman Antiquities, Roger Hinks, Esq.

'The afterlife ...', Bing to Eric M. Warburg, 25 September 1934, WIA, GC, Eric M. Warburg, 1933–4.

'Offer foreign scholars ...', Klibanski to Saxl, 15 September 1934, WIA, GC, Raymond Klibansky, 1933–4.

'Re-opened after ...', Saxl to R. W. Livingstone, 26 September 1934, WIA, GC, Professor R. W. Livingstone, 1934.

'A certain overestimation ...', Max Warburg to Bing, 21 July 1934, WIA, GC, Max Warburg, 1934–6.

'The Warburg Institute is ...', Nicholas Mann, 'Two-Way Traffic: The Warburg Institute as a Microcosm of Cultural Exchange between Britain and Europe', in *The British Contribution to the Europe of the Twenty-First Century*, ed. Basil S. Markesinis (Oxford, 2002), 99.

'The nation's best ...', ibid., 94.

July–September

The Austrian director Berthold Viertel and the actors Conrad Veidt and Fritz Kortner work on some popular English films

'In a studio flat ...', Andrea Hammel, 'Jack Pritchard, Refugees from Nazism and Isokon Design', in *Exile and Patronage: Cross-Cultural Negotiations beyond the Third Reich* ed. Andrew Chandler, Katarzyna Stoklosa and Jutta Vinzent (Berlin, 2006), 26.

'The Coroner ...', *The Times*, 7 July 1934, 4.

'To present a petition …', ibid., 16 July 1934, 17.

'Mobilizing of public …', *The Times*, 16 August 1934, 6.

'Residing at Berkeley …', British Film Institute National Archive, London, ITM-16510, Mischa Spoliansky, 1934–41.

'I am looking forward to …', Walter Gropius to Maxwell Fry, 18 September 1934; Benton, 110.

'It was one of the very few …', Andrew Barrow, *Gossip: A History of High Society, 1920–1970* (New York, 1978), 73.

Chapter 4 'Spell your name': German-speaking exiles in British film studios

Three kings

'Tobacco, buttered toast …', Peter Parker, *Isherwood* (London, 2004), 271.

'The finest position …', *The Times*, 1 January 1929, 23.

'The loss of …', Kortner to Else [Schreiber Shdanoff], 2 June 1934, AdK, Berlin, Fritz-Kortner-Archiv, Kortner 695.

'Unfortunately I am …', Veidt to Mr Madden, 10 February 1934, British Film Institute National Archive, London, ITM-6677.

'Went into exile like …', Berthold Viertel, *Dichtungen und Dokumente. Gedichte. Prosa. Autobiographische Fragmente* (Munich, 1956), 322.

'He was such an …', Michael Powell, *A Life in Movies: An Autobiography* (London, 1986), 272.

'There is a swimming-pool …', *1920s Hollywood Movie Star Home Movies*, www.youtube.com/watch?v=QPS4BzW4rNg (accessed 17 April 2019).

'The respectability …', Christopher Isherwood, *Christopher and His Kind* (London, 2012), 34.

'100 per cent German …', Robert Peck, '*Atlantic*: The First *Titanic* Blockbuster', in *The Titanic in Myth and Memory: Representations in Visual and Literary Culture*, ed. Tim Bergfelder and Sarah Street (London, 2004), 114.

'Language clown', Fritz Kortner, *Aller Tage Abend* (Munich, 1970), 247.

'Yes, I refused …', ibid., 248.

The way to England

'K. should not come', Kortner, *Aller Tage*, 272.

'Months later …', ibid., 273.

'Women fight …', John T. Soister, *Conrad Veidt on Screen: A Comprehensive Illustrated Filmography* (Jefferson, NC, and London, 2002), 319.

'Fifteen years of …', Jerry C. Allen, *Conrad Veidt: From Caligari to Casablanca* (Pacific Grove, CA, 1987), 119.

'With a quite magnificent …', *The Times*, 21 November 1932, 10.

'Father in the flesh', Soister, 20.

'One hundred per cent Aryan', Victor Saville and Roy Moseley, *Evergreen: Victor Saville in His Own Words* (Carbondale and Edwardsville, 2000), 71.

'Veidt is a dominant …', Sue Harper, '"Thinking Forward and Up": The British Films of
    Conrad Veidt', in *The Unknown 1930s: An Alternative History of the British Cinema
    1929–1939*, ed. Jeffrey Richards (London and New York, 1998), 127.

A London summer

'Over most of the British …', *The Times*, 11 July 1934, 16.
'An ancient man …', anon., 'The Picture Postcard', *Life and Letters*, 10, no. 55 (July
    1934), 496.
'They forget themselves …', Malcolm Muggeridge, 'Tongues of Men and of Angels', *Life
    and Letters*, 10, no. 56 (August 1934), 562.
'Lenin's Corner …', ibid., 565–6.
'There are references …', G. B., 'War and Peace', *Life and Letters*, 10, no. 56 (August
    1934), 618.
'It is just possible …', *Manchester Guardian*, 28 June 1934, 10.
'The size of large …', Evelyn Waugh, *A Handful of Dust* (London, 2000), 191.

Little Friend: creative teamwork

'After finishing …', Viertel to Michael Balcon, 11 July 1934, British Film Institute National
    Archive, London, MEB-1115.
'Viertel thought of himself …', Isherwood, *Christopher*, 158.
'For hours, Viertel …', ibid., 161–2.
'Bergmann had told …', Christopher Isherwood, *Prater Violet* (London, 2012), 11.
'Bread and butter …', James K. Lyon, *Bertolt Brecht in America* (Princeton NJ, 1980), 59.
'Six foreign designers …', Laurie N. Ede, *British Film Design: A History* (London and New
    York, 2010), 29.
'The phlegmatic tempo …', Salka Viertel, *The Kindness of Strangers* (New York, Chicago
    and San Francisco, 1969), 196.
'The face of …', Isherwood, *Prater Violet*, 14.

Shylock as a pantomime villain

'Invasion of the American …', *New York Times*, 22 September 1934, 12.
'Central and outstanding …', David Puttnam, preface, in *Michael Balcon: The Pursuit of
    British Cinema*, ed. Geoff Brown and Laurence Kardish (New York, 1984), 7 (see also,
    in the same volume, Laurence Kardish, 'Michael Balcon and the Idea of a National
    Cinema', 43–73).
'On modern German lines', Laurie N. Ede, 'Lost in Siberia: Ernö Metzner in Britain', in
    Destination London: German-Speaking Emigrés and British Cinema 1925–1950, ed.
    Tim Bergfelder and Christian Cargnelli (Oxford and New York, 2012), 116.
'The Eastern settings …', *The Times*, 20 August 1934, 8.
'Heartily operatic …', ibid.
'A child's pantomime', *Manchester Guardian*, 16 August 1934, 7.
'Germany's losses …', *Observer*, 11 February 1934, 21.
'Come alive', Kortner, *Aller Tage*, 51.

'The director was …', Alfred Kerr, *Mit Schleuder und Harfe: Theaterkritiken aus drei Jahrzehnten* (Munich, 1985), 167.
'*The Merchant of Venice* …', Kortner, *Aller Tage*, 243.

Hidden politics

'Always wanting …', *The Times*, 6 February 1924, 8.
'Anaemia of expression …', Kortner, *Aller Tage*, 274–5.
'The grip to the throat …', Kortner to Else [Schreiber Shdanoff], 2 June 1934, AdK, Fritz-Kortner-Archiv, Kortner 695.
'I was now drawn …', Kortner, *Aller Tage*, 275–6.
'My last big scene …', Kortner to Else [Schreiber Shdanoff], 21 June 1934, AdK, Fritz-Kortner-Archiv, Kortner 696.
'Still battling …', Kortner to Else [Schreiber Shdanoff], 31 [*sic*] September 1934, AdK, Fritz-Kortner-Archiv, Kortner 697.
'Fritz Kortner dropped in …', PEM [a.k.a. Paul E. Marcus], *Stage and Film*, in Association of Jewish Refugees in Great Britain, 56.
'Cruel and cunning …', Walter C. Mycroft, *The Time of My Life: The Memoirs of a British Film Producer*, ed. Vincent Porter (Lanham, MD, 2006), 184.
'A small German …', Eisler, letter from London, August 1934, in Albrecht Betz, *Hanns Eisler: Political Musician*, trans. Bill Hopkins (Cambridge, 1982), 141.
'Politically respectful …', Eisler to Brecht, 22 August 1934, in Hanns Eisler, *Briefe 1907–1943*, ed. Jürgen Schebera and Maren Köster (Wiesbaden, Leipzig and Paris, 2010), 89.
'An Editor …', Charles Drazin, *Alexander Korda: Britain's Movie Mogul* (London and New York, 2002), 109.
'Decline in German …', *The Times*, 15 August 1934, 9.

The making of *Jew Süss*

'Veidt refused …', *Focus on Film*, 19–31 (1974), 36.
'Everybody is reading …', *The Sunday Times*, 28 August 1927, 6.
'In 1730, Württemberg …', Arthur Richard Rawlinson and Dorothy Farnum, *'Jew Süss': Scenario. From the Novel by Lion Feuchtwanger* (London, 1935), 1.
'A very distinguished-looking …', ibid., 4.
'Large brown eyes …', Lion Feuchtwanger, *Jew Süss*, trans. Willa Muir and Edwin Muir (London, 1986), 73.
'I'm going to show them …', Rawlinson, 6.
'One and Eternal …', ibid., 173.
'A plea for sympathy …', *Observer*, 7 October 1934, 18.
'Emeric …', Powell, 305.

A genuine living being: Conrad Veidt's *Jew Süss*

'Jew Suss [*sic*] …', *Film Weekly*, 29 December 1933, 11.
'I don't want …', ibid.
'Veidt, as the Jew …', *Picture Show*, 6 January 1934.

'Tireless German sincerity …', *The Listener*, 27 December 1934, 1079.
'Two memories …', Isherwood, *Christopher*, 172–3.

After 1934

'I feel so much connected …', Viertel to Michael Balcon, 14 July 1934, British Film
    Institute National Archive, London, ITM-1115.
'Main task …', ibid.
'Mr. Veidt in the Role of Uncle', *Daily Herald*, 11 September 1934, 3.
'Was non-committal …', Fritz Kortner, *Letzten Endes: Fragmente*, ed. Johanna Kortner
    (Munich, 1971), 167.
'Seemed a stranger …', Salka Viertel, 201.
'Physically he was …', John Lehmann, *The Whispering Gallery: Autobiography I*
    (London, 1955), 305.
'Yet they stir …', Berthold Viertel, *Dass ich in dieser Sprache schreibe: Gesammelte
    Gedichte*, ed. Günther Fetzer (Munich and Vienna, 1981), 73.

October–December

Bertolt Brecht and Stefan Zweig spend the autumn in London

'Never sing …', *Manchester Guardian*, 9 October 1934, 11.
'Little money …', David Burke, *The Lawn Road Flats: Spies, Writers and Artists*
    (Woodbridge, 2014), 51–2.
'When told …', McDonald, 534.
'Lady Astor …', ibid., 544.
'The most brutish …', Martin Gilbert, *Winston S. Churchill*, Vol. V: *The Prophet of Truth:
    1922–1939* (Boston, MA, 1977), 566.
'He was one of the leaders …', Frank Pick to W. C. Eaton, 10 December 1934, The
    National Archives, Kew, Walter Gropius, file ED 46/13.
'At midnight Tilly Losch …', *The Times*, 14 December 1934, 21.
'German architects …', Godfrey Samuel to Doris Herz, 18 December 1934, Benton, 49
'Homesick German …', *The Sunday Times*, 23 December 1934, 13.

Chapter 5 The London life of two literary exiles

In the shadow of 'some Titan city'

'Lamé silks …', *The Times*, 18 October 1934, 9.
'German Lady …', *The Times*, 4 October 1934, 3.
'Forced to give up …', *The Times*, 26 October 1934, 10.

'England to political …', *The Times*, 4 October 1934, 7.
'The number of deaths …', ibid., 9.
'The stranger is never …', Harold John Massingham, *London Scene* (London, 1933),
    117.
'Tricks of atmosphere …', ibid., 122.

Stefan Zweig likes London

'I am living here …', Donald Prater, *European of Yesterday: A Biography of Stefan Zweig*
    (Oxford, 1972), 32.
'I need counterweight …', ibid., 213–14.

'My excellent secretary'

'Excellent secretary', Zweig to Lotte Altmann, 20 August 1934, in Oliver Matuscheck
    (ed.), *Stefan Zweig: 'Ich wünschte, dass ich Ihnen ein wenig fehlte.' Briefe an Lotte
    Zweig 1934–1940* (Frankfurt am Main, 2013), 49.
'I am not an easy person …', Zweig to Lotte Altmann, 5 August 1934, ibid., 37.
'The difficulties …', Prater, 198.
'A very serious …', Oliver Matuschek, *Three Lives: A Biography of Stefan Zweig*, trans.
    Allan Blunden (London, 2011), 27.
'A voice that is …', Darién J. Davis and Oliver Marshall (eds.), *Stefan and Lotte Zweig's
    South-American Letters: New York, Argentina and Brazil 1940–1942* (New York, 2010), 2.
'I really think …', Zweig to Lotte Altmann, 5 August 1934, in Matuscheck, *Stefan Zweig*, 37.
'I beg you dearly …', Zweig to Lotte Altmann, 4 September 1934, ibid., 55.
'Terrible how necessary', ibid.

Love for a 'city with its shutters down'

'Here in Klosters …', Zweig to Lotte Altmann, 14 August 1934, in Matuscheck, *Stefan
    Zweig*, 46.
'Dr. Stefan Zweig …', Zweig's arrival card, 26 February 1934, The National Archives,
    Kew, Stefan Zweig, file HO382/4.
'You know that …', Zweig to E. H. Carr, 22 May 1934, ibid.
'For cancellation …', Home Office minutes, 28 May 1934, ibid.
'Nothing recorded …', ibid.
'So very much engaged …', Harry Crookshank to Zweig, 20 October 1934, ibid.
'Dear Sir …', Zweig to Harry Crookshank, 21 October 1934, ibid.
'A further twelve months' …', letter from the Jewish Refugees Committee to the
    undersecretary of state, Aliens Department, Home Office, 23 October 1934, ibid.
'Professional and Residential …', *The Times*, 19 January 1933, 23.
'I find it the ideal city …', Matuschek, *Three Lives*, 304.

The problem with Zweig

'Of a higher order', *Times Literary Supplement*, 2 February 1933, 69.

'A season of German plays …', *The Times*, 28 September 1933, 8.

'A very moving …', *The Times*, 1 December 1933, 17.

'Fondness for sentimental …', *Times Literary Supplement*, 12 July 1934, 491.

'The Pepsi …', Michael Hofmann, 'Vermicular Dither', *London Review of Books*, 28 January 2010, 9.

'"Best hated" author …', Vivian Liska, 'A Spectral Mirror Image: Stefan Zweig and His Critics', in *Stefan Zweig Reconsidered: New Perspectives on His Literary and Autobiographical Writings*, ed. Mark H. Gelber (Tübingen, 2007), 203.

'The Steffzweig …', Franz Blei, *Das große Bestiarium der deutschen Literatur* (Berlin, 2016), 56.

'Golden Age of Security', Stefan Zweig, *The World of Yesterday: An Autobiography*, trans. Anthea Bell (London, 2009), 23.

'I never considered …', ibid., 17.

The lives of others

'I had had enough …', Zweig, *The World of Yesterday*, 406.

'So egregiously wrong …', *Manchester Guardian*, 28 October 1935, 5.

'Young, inexperienced …', Davis, 7. The biographer in question is the Brazilian journalist Alberto Dines.

'Pliant and accommodating …', Stefan Zweig, *Mary Stuart*, trans. Eden Paul and Cedar Paul (London, 2010), 78.

'Last outpost …', ibid., 18.

'One who has vowed …', ibid., 35.

'Domineering …', ibid., 73.

'The most finished …', ibid., 75.

'The innermost longings …', ibid., 108.

Boredom in the soup

'Half of Europe …', Zweig to Romain Rolland, 4 Ocotber 1934, in Romain Rolland and Stefan Zweig, *Briefwechsel 1910–1940*, Vol. II (Berlin, 1987), 580–1.

'I'm staying in London …', ibid., 582–3.

'Burning secret'; the expression refers to the title of one of Zweig's best-known novellas, but is also the title of a recent study about his life: Ulrich Weinzierl, *Stefan Zweigs brennendes Geheimnis* (Vienna, 2015).

A promising visit

'Still played …', Elisabeth Hauptmann to Brecht, 28 September 1934, in Hermann Haarmann (ed.), *Briefe an Bertolt Brecht im Exil (1933–1949)*, Vol. I: *1933–1936*, (Berlin, 2014), 273.

'London is enjoying …', Eisler to Brecht, 30 April 1934, ibid., 185.

'Known for the film …', Eisler to Brecht, 14 May 1934, ibid., 198.

'Your chances here …', Margaret Mynatt to Brecht, 16 August 1934, ibid., 247.

'Already in full swing', Eisler to Brecht, 22 August 1934, Eisler, 90.

'Hugely enthusiastic …', Eisler to Brecht, 11 September 1934, ibid., 92.
'The English language …', Eisler and Lania to Brecht, 21 September 1934, ibid., 93–4.

'The problematical Bert Brecht'

'In his early thirties …', Leo Lania, *Today We are Brothers: The Biography of a Generation*, trans. Ralph Marlowe (London, 1942), 235.
'Chronic incapacity …', *The Times*, 29 March 1928, 14.
'An English visitor …', ibid., 25 September 1928, 12.
'Clamour for gaiety …', *Manchester Guardian*, 8 January 1933, 10.
'Intense …', *Illustrated London News*, 8 July 1933, 80.
'O Germany …', *Germany* (trans. John Willett), in Bertolt Brecht, *Poems*, ed. John Willett and Ralph Mannheim (London, 1976), 218–19.
'The greatest city …', Bertolt Brecht, *Threepenny Novel*, trans. Desmond Ivo Vesey (Harmondsworth, 1961), 8.

Life in 'a wicked, hardbitten town'

'A continuation …', Grete Fischer, *Dienstboten: Brecht und andere Zeitgenossen in Prag, Berlin, London* (Olten and Freiburg im Breisgau, 1966), 251.
'I was standing …', ibid.
'Those of the paupers …', Walter Hindes Godfrey and William McB. Marcham (eds.), 'The Calthorpe Estate', in *Survey of London*, Vol. XXIV: *The Parish of St Pancras*, Part IV: *King's Cross Neighbourhood* (London, 1952), 60.
'The frightful inadequacy …', Kortner, *Aller Tage*, 278–9.
'Dear Helli …', Bertolt Brecht, *Letters*, ed. John Willett, trans. Ralph Mannheim (London, 1990), 186.
'The new light …', *The Times*, 4 October 1934, 10.
'Followed by …', ibid.
'The best thing …', Steven Parker, *Bertolt Brecht: A Literary Life* (London, 2014), 337.
'Better than Paris …', Brecht to Margarete Steffin, 19 October 1934, in Bertolt Brecht, *Briefe I. Briefe 1913–1936*, ed. Werner Hecht (Frankfurt am Main 1998), 449.
'Not too hospitable', Brecht to Weigel, 29 October 1934, in Bertolt Brecht and Helene Weigel, *'ich lerne: gläser + tassen spülen': Briefe 1923–1956*, ed. Erdmut Wizisla (Frankfurt am Main, 2012), 115.
'I am fine …', Brecht to Weigel, October–November 1934, ibid., 117.
'Here things are improving …', Brecht to Weigel, 7 November 1934, in Brecht, *Letters*, 187.
'In the old proletarian …', Fischer, 251.
'Because he had …', ibid.
'I'm freezing …', Brecht to Steffin, 2 November 1934, in Parker, *Bertolt Brecht*, 337.
'Convincing the English …', Brecht to Steffin, 19 November 1934, in Brecht, *Briefe I*, 459.
'A wicked, hardbitten …', Brecht to Margot von Brentano, December 1934, in Brecht, *Letters*, 189

United against the coming danger

'He was recruiting …', Fischer, 251.
'Witness to human suffering …', Ernst Toller, *Seven Plays* (London, 1935), IX–X.
'Despite appeasement …', Lania, 279.
'We do not have access …', James Smith, 'Brecht, the Berliner Ensemble, and the
    British Government', *New Theatre Quarterly*, 22 (2006), 310.
'Brecht, who as a poet …', *Manchester Guardian*, 7 November 1934, 8.
'Wrote songs of freedom …', Ernst Hermann Meyer, 'Alan Bush in the Thirties', in
    Alan Bush: An 80th Birthday Symposium, ed. Ronald Stevenson (Kidderminster,
    1981), 74.
'Published in all …', Brecht to Bernhard Reich, November–December 1934, in Brecht,
    Letters, 190.

A meeting of opposites

'A man of ministerial …', Brecht to Princess Elisabeth Bibesco, late 1934, in Brecht,
    Letters, 188.
'On one occasion …', Sabine Berendse and Paul Clements (eds.), *Brecht, Music and
    Culture: Hanns Eisler in Conversation with Hans Bunge* (London, 2014), 88–9.
'Generous meals …', Bertolt Brecht, *Song on the Invigorating Effect of Money*, in *Werke:
    Große kommentierte Berliner und Frankfurter Ausgabe*, Vol. IV (Frankfurt am Main,
    1988), 212.

Comrade Korsch

'Also went deeply …', Hedda Korsch, 'Memories of Karl Korsch', in *Lives on the Left: A
    Group Portrait*, ed. Francis Mulhern (London and New York, 2011), 24.
'A cause célèbre …', Brinson, *A Matter of Intelligence*, 32.
'Played a sinister role …', Home Office report, ibid., 35.
'My sole hope …', Brecht to Korsch, 25 January 1934, in Brecht, *Letters*, 167.
'Practical necessities …', Karl Korsch, *Why I Am a Marxist*, www.marxists.org/archive/
    Korsch/1934/why-marxist.htm (accessed 26 March 2019).
'A few words …', Kortner, *Aller Tage*, 278.
'For complete order …', Hedda Korsch, 15.
'You ask whether …', Brecht to Steffin, 15 October 1934, in Brecht, *Briefe I*, 448.

My general, my soldier

'Big, loyal eyes …', Parker, *Bertolt Brecht*, 420.
'Little teacher …', from Brecht's poem 'Casualty List', in Brecht, *Werke*, Vol. XV, 43.
'Little wife', Parker, *Bertolt Brecht*, 308.
'It turns out …', Brecht to Steffin, 15 October 1934, in Brecht, *Briefe I*, 448.
'You should write …', Brecht to Steffin, 19 October 1934, ibid., 450.
'Are you keeping warm?..'., Brecht to Steffin, 21 October 1934, ibid.
'Fogs and chills …', Massingham, 145.

'Buying Oranges'

'In yellow fog …', Brecht, *Poems*, 231 (trans. Edith Roseveare).

'Love-gift …', David Constantine, 'Brecht's Sonnets', in *Empedocles' Shoe: Essays on Brecht's Poetry*, ed. Tom Kuhn and Karen J. Leeder (London, 2002), 172.

'The frightful god' of the Caledonian Market

'It was apparently …', Jerry White, *London in the Twentieth Century: A City and Its People* (London, 2016), 251.

'There is …', Kurt Tucholsky, 'Der Markt des Schweigens', in *Gesammelte Werke*, Vol III: *1929–1932* (Hamburg, 1961), 892.

'This great Caledonian …', anonymous review of Massingham's *London Scene, The Listener*, 6 September 1933, 367.

'Only a guest …', Werner Hecht, *Brecht-Chronik 1898–1956* (Frankfurt am Main, 1997), 418.

'Under Troy …', Brecht, *Poems*, 232–3 (trans. John Willett).

'London was at its most …', Massingham, 172.

'Gilded interiors', ibid., 181.

'He lived in a dream', Norman Flower, 'Stefan Zweig', in *Just as It Happened* (London, 1950), 180.

'Because of Christmas', Brecht to Weigel, early/mid-December 1934, in Brecht, *Briefe I*, 466.

Bibliography

Archives

Akademie der Künste, Berlin
British Film Institute National Archive, London
The National Archives, Kew
Warburg Institute Archive, London

Books and other sources

Allen, Jerry C., *Conrad Veidt: From Caligari to Casablanca* (Pacific Grove, CA, 1987).

Anon., 'Fritz Saxl, January 8th, 1890–March 22nd, 1948', *Journal of the Warburg and Courtauld Institutes*, 10 (1947), [n.p.].

Anon., 'The Picture Postcard', *Life and Letters*, 10, no. 55 (July 1934), 494–6.

Asquith, Cynthia, *Portrait of Barrie* (London, 1954).

Association of Jewish Refugees in Great Britain, *Britain's New Citizens: The Story of the Refugees from Germany and Austria, 1941–1951* (London, 1951).

B., G., 'War and Peace', *Life and Letters*, 10, no. 56 (August 1934), 618–19.

Balcon, Michael, *Michael Balcon Presents … A Lifetime of Films* (London, 1969).

Barnes, James J. and Patience P. Barnes, *Nazis in Pre-War London 1930–1939: The Fate and Role of German Party Members and British Sympathizers* (Brighton, 2005).

Barrie, James Matthew, *Letters*, ed. Viola Meynell (London, 1942).

Barrie, James Matthew, *The Little White Bird* (London, 1902).

Barrie, James Matthew, *The Plays of J. M. Barrie* (London, 1942).

Barrow, Andrew, *Gossip: A History of High Society, 1920–1970* (New York, 1978).

Bauschinger, Sigrid, *Die Cassirers: Unternehmer, Kunsthändler, Philosophen. Biographie einer Familie* (Munich, 2015).

Benton, Charlotte, *A Different World: Emigré Architects in Britain 1928–1958* (London, 1995).

Berendse, Sabine and Paul Clements (eds.), *Brecht, Music and Culture: Hanns Eisler in Conversation with Hans Bunge* (London, 2014).

Bergfelder, Tim and Christian Cargnelli (eds.), *Destination London: German-Speaking Emigrés and British Cinema 1925–1950* (Oxford and New York, 2012).

Bergner, Elisabeth, *Bewundert und viel gescholten … Elisabeth Bergners unordentliche Erinnerungen* (Munich, 1978).

Bernays, Robert, *The Diaries and Letters of Robert Bernays, 1932–1939: An Insider's Account of the House of Commons*, ed. Nick Smart (Lewiston, Queenston and Lampeter, 1996).

Betz, Albrecht, *Hanns Eisler: Political Musician*, trans. Bill Hopkins (Cambridge, 1982).

Biester, Björn, *Der innere Beruf zur Wissenschaft: Paul Ruben (1866–1943). Studien zur deutsch-jüdischen Wissenschaftsgeschichte* (Berlin, 2001).

Bing, Gertrud, 'Fritz Saxl: A Biographical Memoir', in *Fritz Saxl (1890–1948): A Volume of Memorial Essays from His Friends in England*, ed. D. J. Gordon (London, 1957), 1–46.

Birkin, Andrew, *J. M. Barrie and the Lost Boys* (New Haven, CT, 2003).

Blei, Franz, *Das große Bestiarium der deutschen Literatur* (Berlin, 2016).

Boyd, Julia, *Travellers in the Third Reich: The Rise of Fascism through the Eyes of Everyday People* (London, 2018).

Brecht, Bertolt, *Briefe: I. Briefe 1913–1936*, ed. Werner Hecht (Frankfurt am Main, 1998).

Brecht, Bertolt, *Journals 1934–1955*, ed. John Willett, trans. Hugh Rorrison (London, 1993).

Brecht, Bertolt, *Letters*, ed. John Willett, trans. Ralph Mannheim (London, 1990).

Brecht, Bertolt, *Poems*, ed. John Willett and Ralph Mannheim (London, 1976).

Brecht, Bertolt, *Threepenny Novel*, trans. Desmond Ivo Vesey (Harmondsworth, 1961).

Brecht, Bertolt, *Werke: Große kommentierte Berliner und Frankfurter Ausgabe*, ed. Werner Hecht, Jan Knopf, Werner Mittenzwei and Klaus-Detlev Müller (Berlin/Weimar and Frankfurt am Main, 1988–2000).

Brecht, Bertolt and Helene Weigel, *'ich lerne: gläser + tassen spülen': Briefe 1923–1956*, ed. Erdmut Wizisla (Frankfurt am Main, 2012).

Brinson, Charmian and Richard Dove, *A Matter of Intelligence: MI5 and the Surveillance of Anti-Nazi Refugees 1933–1950* (Manchester and New York, 2014).

Brinson, Charmian, Richard Dove, Marian Malet and Jennifer Taylor (eds.), *'England? Aber wo liegt es?' Deutsche und österreichische Emigranten in Großbritannien 1933–1945* (London, 1996).

Brown, Geoff and Laurence Kardish (eds.), *Michael Balcon: The Pursuit of British Cinema* (New York, 1984).

Brunnhuber, Nicole, *The Faces of Janus: English-Language Fiction by German-Speaking Exiles in Great Britain 1933–1945* (Bern, 2005).

Bryher, *Manchester, Life and Letters Today*, 13 (1935), 89–112; 14 (1935), 74–98.

Bunge, Mario, *Between Two Worlds: Memoirs of a Philosopher-Scientist* (Cham, 2016).

Burke, David, *The Lawn Road Flats: Spies, Writers and Artists* (Woodbridge, 2014).

Cassirer, Ernst, *An Essay on Man: An Introduction to a Philosophy of Human Culture* (New Haven, CT, 1972).

Cassirer, Ernst, 'The Problem of the Symbol and Its Place in the System of Philosophy', in *The Warburg Years: Essays on Language, Art, Myth, and Technology*, trans. with an introduction by Steve G. Lofts with Antonio Calcagno (New Haven, CT, 2013), 254–71.

Chernow, Ron, *The Warburgs: A Family Saga* (London, 1993).

Clark, Kenneth, *Another Part of the Wood* (London, 1974).

Cochran, Charles B., *Cock-a-Doodle-Do* (London, 1941).

Cohen-Portheim, Paul, *The Spirit of London* (London, 2011 [1935]).

Constantine, David, 'Brecht's Sonnets', in *Empedocles' Shoe: Essays on Brecht's Poetry*, ed. Tom Kuhn and Karen J. Leeder (London, 2002), 155–73.

Davis, Darién J. and Oliver Marshall (eds.), *Stefan and Lotte Zweig's South-American Letters. New York, Argentina and Brazil 1940–1942* (New York, 2010).

Delany, Paul, *Bill Brandt. A Life* (London, 2004).

Diers, Michael (ed.), *Porträt aus Büchern: Bibliothek Warburg und Warburg Institute. Hamburg–1933–London* (Hamburg, 1993).

Dogramaci, Burcu, 'Der Kreis um Stefan Lorant: Von der *Münchner illustrierten Presse* zur *Picture Post*', in *Netzwerke des Exils: Künstlerische Verflechtungen, Austausch und Patronage nach 1933*, ed. B. Dogramaci and Karin Wimmer (Berlin, 2011), 163–83.

Dove, Richard, *Journey of No Return: Five German-Speaking Literary Exiles in Britain, 1933–1945* (London, 2000).

Doyon, Carol, 'Hommage à Raymond Klibansky/Tribute to Raymond Klibansky', *RACAR: Revue d'art canadienne/Canadian Art Revue*, 27 (2000), 135–6.

Drazin, Charles, *Alexander Korda: Britain's Movie Mogul* (London and New York, 2002).

Dunbar, Janet, *J. M. Barrie: The Man behind the Image* (Boston, MA, 1970).

Ede, Laurie N., *British Film Design: A History* (London and New York, 2010).

Ede, Laurie N., *Lost in Siberia: Ernö Metzner in Britain*, in Tim Bergfelder and Christian Cargnelli (eds.), *Destination London: German-Speaking Emigrés and British Cinema 1925–1950* (Oxford and New York, 2012), 111–22.

Eisler, Hanns, *Briefe 1907–1943*, ed. Jürgen Schebera and Maren Köster (Wiesbaden, Leipzig and Paris, 2010).

Elliott, David, 'Gropius in England: A Documentation 1934–1937', in *A Different World: Emigré Architects in Britain 1928–1958*, ed. Charlotte Benton (London, 1995), 107–23.

Engel, Franz, 'Though This Be Madness: Edgar Wind and the Warburg Tradition', in *Bildakt at the Warburg Institute*, ed. Sabine Marienberg and Jürgen Trabant (Berlin and Boston, MA, 2014), 87–115.

Evans, John (ed.), *Journeying Boy: The Diaries of the Young Benjamin Britten 1928–1938* (London, 2009).

Feuchtwanger, Lion, *Jew Süss*, trans. Willa Muir and Edwin Muir (London, 1986).

Fischer, Grete, *Dienstboten: Brecht und andere Zeitgenossen in Prag, Berlin, London* (Olten and Freiburg im Breisgau, 1966).

Flower, Norman, 'Stefan Zweig', in *Just as It Happened* (London, 1950), 176–80.

Forbes, Duncan (ed.), *Edith Tudor-Hart: In the Shadow of Tyranny* (Ostfildern, 2013).

Forbes, Duncan, 'Politics, Photography and Exile in the Life of Edith Tudor-Hart (1908–1973)', in *Arts in Exile in Britain 1933–1945*, ed. Shulamith Behr and Marian Malet (Amsterdam: Rodopi, 2005), 45–87.

Fry, Roger, 'The Artist as Critic', *Burlington Magazine*, 64 (1934), 78–80.

Gielgud, John, *Gielgud's Letters*, ed. Richard Mangan (London, 2005).

Gilbert, Martin, *Winston S. Churchill*, Vol. V: *The Prophet of Truth: 1922–1939* (Boston, MA, 1977).

Godfrey, Walter Hindes and William McB. Marcham (eds.), 'The Calthorpe Estate', in *Survey of London*, Vol. XXIV: *The Parish of St Pancras*, Part IV: *King's Cross Neighbourhood* (London, 1952), 56–69.

Gombrich, Ernst H., *Aby Warburg: An Intellectual Biography. With a Memory on the History of the Library by F. Saxl* (London, 1970).

Gombrich, Ernst H., *A Lifelong Interest: Conversations on Art and Science with Didier Eribon* (London, 1993).

Gombrich, Ernst H. and the Warburg Institute (eds.), *Gertrud Bing 1892–1964* (London, 1965).

Gordon, D. J. (ed.), *Fritz Saxl (1890–1948): A Volume of Memorial Essays from His Friends in England* (London, 1957).

Granach, Alexander, *Da geht ein Mensch: Roman eines Lebens* (München, 1984).

Graves, Charles, *The Price of Pleasure* (London, 1935).

Guest, Barbara, *Herself Defined: The Poet H. D. and Her World* (New York, 1984).

Haarmann, Hermann (ed.), *Briefe an Bertolt Brecht im Exil (1933–1949)*, Vol. I: *1933–1936* (Berlin, 2014).

Hallett, Michael, *Stefan Lorant: Godfather of Photojournalism* (Lanham, MD, Toronto and Oxford, 2006).

Hammel, Andrea, 'Jack Pritchard, Refugees from Nazism and Isokon Design', in *Exile and Patronage: Cross-Cultural Negotiations beyond the Third Reich*, ed. Andrew Chandler, Katarzyna Stoklosa and Jutta Vinzent (Berlin, 2006), 23–32.

Harper, Sue, '"Thinking Forward and Up": The British Films of Conrad Veidt', in *The Unknown 1930s: An Alternative History of the British Cinema 1929–1939*, ed. Jeffrey Richards (London and New York, 1998), 121–37.

Harries, Susie, *Nikolaus Pevsner: The Life* (London, 2011).

Harrison, E. 'England's Debt to Greece and Rome', *Classical Review*, 48, no. 2 (May 1934), 83–4.

Hecht, Werner, *Brecht-Chronik 1898–1956* (Frankfurt am Main, 1997).

Helforth, John [H. D.], *Nights*, ed. Perdita Schaffner (New York, 1986).

Heymann, Margaret, *Elisabeth Bergner: Mehr als eine Schauspielerin* (Berlin, 2008).

Hipp, H., 'Strebende und tragende Kräfte: Die Fassade der K. B. W.', in *Porträt aus Büchern: Bibliothek Warburg und Warburg Institute. Hamburg–1933–London*, ed. Michael Diers (Hamburg, 1993), 43–70.

Hofmann, Michael, 'Vermicular Dither', *London Review of Books*, 28 January 2010, 9–12.

Hopkinson, Tom, *Of This Our Time: A Journalist's Story 1905–1950* (London and Melbourne, 1982).

Isherwood, Christopher, *Christopher and His Kind* (London, 2012).

Isherwood, Christopher, *Prater Violet* (London, 2012).

Jungk, Peter Stephan, *Die Dunkelkammern der Edith Tudor-Hart: Geschichte eines Lebens* (Frankfurt am Main, 2015).

Kerr, Alfred, *Mit Schleuder und Harfe: Theaterkritiken aus drei Jahrzehnten* (Munich, 1985).

Keun, Odette, *I Discover the English* (London, 1934).

Klibansky, Raymond and Herbert James Paton (eds.), *Philosophy and History: Essays Presented to Ernst Cassirer* (Oxford, 1936).

Korsch, Hedda, 'Memories of Karl Korsch,' in *Lives on the Left: A Group Portrait*, ed. Francis Mulhern (London and New York, 2011), 15–26.

Korsch, Karl, *Why I Am a Marxist*, https://www.marxists.org/archive/korsch/1934/why-marxist.htm (accessed 26 March 2019).

Kortner, Fritz, *Aller Tage Abend* (Munich, 1970).

Kortner, Fritz, *Letzten Endes: Fragmente*, ed. Johanna Kortner (Munich, 1971).

Laird, Emma [Alison Blair], *Of Former Love* (Boston, MA, 1951).

Lania, Leo, *Today We are Brothers: The Biography of a Generation*, trans. Ralph Marlowe (London, 1942).

Lehmann, John, *The Whispering Gallery: Autobiography I* (London, 1955).

Levine, Emily J., *Dreamland of Humanists: Warburg, Cassirer, Panofsky, and the Hamburg School* (Chicago and London, 2013).

Liska, Vivian, 'A Spectral Mirror Image: Stefan Zweig and His Critics', in *Stefan Zweig Reconsidered: New Perspectives on His Literary and Autobiographical Writings*, ed. Mark H. Gelber (Tübingen, 2007), 203–17.

London, Louise, *Whitehall and the Jews 1933–1948: British Immigration Policy and the Holocaust* (Cambridge, 2000)

Lorant, Stefan, *I Was Hitler's Prisoner* (1935), trans. James Cleugh (Harmondsworth, 1939).

Lyon, James K., *Bertolt Brecht in America* (Princeton, NJ, 1980).

Man, Felix H., *Man with Camera: Photographs from Seven Decades* (London, 1983).

Man, Felix H., *Sixty Years of Photography*, exhibition catalogue (London, 1983).

Mann, Nicholas, 'Two-Way Traffic: The Warburg Institute as a Microcosm of Cultural Exchange between Britain and Europe', in *The British Contribution to the Europe of the Twenty-First Century*, ed. Basil S. Markesinis (Oxford, 2002), 93–104.

Manz, Stefan and Panikos Panayi (eds.), *Refugees and Cultural Transfer to Britain* (London and New York, 2013).

M[arcus], P[aul] E., *Stage and Film*, in Association of Jewish Refugees in Great Britain, *Britain's New Citizens: The Story of the Refugees from Germany and Austria, 1941–1951* (London, 1951), 55–7.

Massingham, Harold John, *London Scene* (London, 1933).

Matuschek, Oliver (ed.), *Stefan Zweig: 'Ich wünschte, dass ich Ihnen ein wenig fehlte.' Briefe an Lotte Zweig 1934–1940* (Frankfurt am Main, 2013).

Matuschek, Oliver, *Three Lives: A Biography of Stefan Zweig*, trans. Allan Blunden (London, 2011).

Mayr, Brigitte and Michael Omasta, 'Das Cabinet des Dr. Czinner: Tribut an einen Regisseur aus Wien', in *Paul Czinner: Der Mann hinter Elisabeth Bergner* (Vienna, 2013), 3–8.

Mayr, Brigitte and Michael Omasta, 'A Lucky Man. Wolf Suschitzky: Photographer and Cameraman', in *German-Speaking Exiles in the Performing Arts in Britain after 1933*, ed. Charmian Brinson and Richard Dove (Amsterdam, 2013), 253–76.

McDonald, James G., *Advocate for the Doomed: The Diaries and Papers of James G. McDonald 1932–1935*, ed. Richard Breitman, Barbara McDonald Stewart and Severin Hochberg (Bloomington, IN, 2007)

McEwan, Dorothea, *Fritz Saxl: Eine Biographie. Aby Warburgs Bibliothekar und erster Direktor des Londoner Warburg Institute* (Vienna, 2012).

McEwan, Dorothea, *Mapping the Trade Routes of the Mind: The Warburg Institute* in *Intellectual Migration and Cultural Transformation. Refugees from National Socialism in the English-Speaking World*, ed. Edward Timms and Jon Hughes (Vienna and New York, 2003), 37–50.

Meier, Hans, Richard Newald and Edgar Wind (eds.), *A Bibliography on the Survival of the Classics*, Vol. I: *The Publications of 1931: The Text of the German Edition with an English Introduction* (London, 1934).

Meyer, Ernst Hermann, 'Alan Bush in the Thirties', in *Alan Bush: An 80th Birthday Symposium*, ed. Ronald Stevenson (Kidderminster, 1981), 74–5.

Muggeridge, Malcolm, 'Tongues of Men and of Angels', *Life and Letters*, 10, no. 56 (August 1934), 562–7.

Mycroft, Walter C., *The Time of My Life: The Memoirs of a British Film Producer*, ed. Vincent Porter (Lanham, MD, 2006).

Neumann, Robert, *By the Waters of Babylon*, trans. Anthony Dent (London, New York and Melbourne, 1944).

Overy, Richard, *The Morbid Age: Britain and the Crisis of Civilization, 1919–1939* (London, 2009).

Palmer, Lilli, *Change Lobsters – and Dance: An Autobiography* (London, 1976).

Panofsky, Erwin, *Korrespondenz 1910 bis 1936*, ed. Dieter Wuttke (Wiesbaden, 2001).

Panofsky, Erwin, *Meaning in the Visual Arts* (Harmondsworth, 1983 [1944]).

Panofsky, Erwin, *Studies in Iconology: Humanistic Themes in the Art of the Renaissance* (New York, 1939).

Parker, Peter, *Isherwood* (London, 2004).

Parker, Steven, *Bertolt Brecht: A Literary Life* (London, 2014).

Peck, Robert, '*Atlantic*: The First *Titanic* Blockbuster', in *The Titanic in Myth and Memory: Representations in Visual and Literary Culture*, ed. Tim Bergfelder and Sarah Street (London, 2004), 111–20.

Pope-Hennessy, John, *Learning to Look* (London, 1991).

Powell, Michael, *A Life in Movies: An Autobiography* (London, 1986).

Prater, Donald, *European of Yesterday: A Biography of Stefan Zweig* (Oxford, 1972).

'Prompter', 'Bergner Shatters Two Illusions: A German Genius Comes to London', *Western Independent*, 7 January 1934.

Radford, Robert, *Art for a Purpose: The Artists' International Association, 1933–1953* (Winchester, 1987).

Rawlinson, Arthur Richard and Dorothy Farnum, '*Jew Süss*': Scenario. From the Novel by Lion Feuchtwanger* (London, 1935).

Richards, Jeffrey (ed.), *The Unknown 1930s: An Alternative History of the British Cinema 1929–1939* (London and New York, 1998).

Rolland, Romain and Stefan Zweig, *Briefwechsel 1910–1940*, Vol. II (Berlin, 1987).

Rowe, David E. and Robert Schulmann (eds.), *Einstein on Politics: His Private Thoughts and Stand on Nationalism, Zionism, War, Peace, and the Bomb* (Princeton, NJ, 2007).

Saville, Victor and Roy Moseley, *Evergreen: Victor Saville in His Own Words* (Carbondale and Edwardsville, 2000).

Saxl, Fritz, 'Ernst Cassirer', in *The Philosophy of Ernst Cassirer*, ed. Paul Arthur Schilpp (La Salle, IL, 1949), 47–51.

Saxl, Fritz, 'The History of the Warburg Library (1886–1944)', in *Aby Warburg: An Intellectual Biography*, ed. Ernst Gombrich (London, 1970), 325–38.

Saxl, Fritz, *Lectures*, 2 vols. (London, 1957).

Scott, Peter, *The Eye of the Wind: An Autobiography* (London, 1961).

Sears, Elizabeth, 'Edgar Wind on Michelangelo', in *The Religious Symbols of Michelangelo: The Sistine Ceiling*, ed. Edgar Wind (Oxford, 2000), XVII–XL.

Sears, Elisabeth, 'The Warburg Institute, 1933–1944: A Precarious Experiment in International Collaboration', *Art Libraries Journal*, 38 (2013), 7–15.

Shaw, George Bernard, '"Barrie: The Man with Hell in His Soul" (1937)', in *Shaw and Other Playwrights*, ed. John Anthony Bertolini, Vol. XIII (University Park, 1993), 151–3.

Shaw, George Bernard, *Theatrics*, ed. Dan H. Laurence (Toronto, Buffalo and London, 1995).

Smith, James, 'Brecht, the Berliner Ensemble, and the British Government', *New Theatre Quarterly*, 22 (2006), 307–23.

Snowman, Daniel, *The Hitler Emigrés: The Cultural Impact on Britain of Refugees from Nazism* (London, 2002).

Soister, John T., *Conrad Veidt on Screen: A Comprehensive Illustrated Filmography* (Jefferson, NC and London, 2002).

Stanford Friedman, Susan (ed.), *Analyzing Freud: Letters of H. D., Bryher and Their Circle* (New York, 2002).

Tegel, Susan, '*Jew Süss': Life, Legend, Fiction, Film* (London, 2011).
Thost, Hans Wilhelm, *Als Nationalsozialist in England* (Munich, 1939).
Toller, Ernst, *Seven Plays* (London, 1935).
Tucholsky, Kurt, 'Der Markt des Schweigens', in *Gesammelte Werke*, Vol III: *1929–1932* (Hamburg, 1961), 892–4.
Viertel, Berthold, *Dass ich in dieser Sprache schreibe: Gesammelte Gedichte*, ed. Günther Fetzer (Munich and Vienna, 1981).
Viertel, Berthold, *Dichtungen und Dokumente. Gedichte. Prosa. Autobiographische Fragmente* (Munich, 1956).
Viertel, Salka, *The Kindness of Strangers* (New York, Chicago and San Francisco, 1969).
Völker, Klaus, *Elisabeth Bergner: Das Leben einer Schauspielerin* (Berlin, 1990).
Warburg, Aby, 'Sandro Botticelli's *Birth of Venus* and *Spring*', in *The Renewal of Pagan Antiquity: Contributions to the Cultural History of the European Renaissance*, ed. Kurt W. Forster, trans. David Britt (Los Angeles, 1999), 89–156.
Warburg, Eric M., 'The Transfer of the Warburg Institute to England in 1933', in *The Warburg Institute Annual Report 1952–1953*, https://warburg.sas.ac.uk/about-us/history-warburg-institute/transfer-institute/ (accessed 26 March 2019).
Waugh, Evelyn, *A Handful of Dust* (London, 2000).
Weinzierl, Ulrich, *Stefan Zweigs brennendes Geheimnis* (Vienna, 2015).
Welter, Volker M., *Ernst L. Freud, Architect: The Case of the Modern Bourgeois Home* (New York and Oxford, 2012).
White, Jerry, *London in the Twentieth Century: A City and Its People* (London, 2016).
Zweig, Stefan, *Mary Stuart*, trans. Eden Paul and Cedar Paul (London, 2010).
Zweig, Stefan, *The World of Yesterday: An Autobiography*, trans. Anthea Bell (London, 2009).

Index

Note: Photographs and images are indicated by page numbers in italics. Except where otherwise indicated, literary/creative works are listed under the name of the author/artist/creator.